FOREWORD BY **DR. MARK HITCHCOCK**

LOOK UP!

Awaiting the Rapture and Our Final Redemption

BESTSELLING AUTHOR

JIMMY EVANS

For more information, address Endtimes.com
PO Box 59888
Dallas, Texas 75229
1-800-380-6330
xomarriage.com

Tipping Point Press

ISBN: 978-1-950113-90-3 (Paperback)
ISBN: 978-1-950113-91-0 (eBook)
ISBN: 978-1-950113-92-7 (Audiobook)

So when all these things begin to happen,
stand and **look up**, for your salvation is near!

—Luke 21:28 NLT, bold added

Dedication

To our assistant, Shelly Millheim, who has faithfully served my wife, Karen, and me and our ministry for the past eleven years. She is leaving us to move with her family to Hawaii. We pray God's continued blessings upon her and her family in their exciting new adventure.

Contents

Foreword

Rapture ... what emotions do you feel when you hear or read that word? Recently, I recorded a video for endtimes.com about an article written by A. J. Willingham and posted online by CNN titled "For some Christians, 'rapture anxiety' can take a lifetime to heal" (27 September 2022). At first, I thought it was a little odd for CNN to even address a subject like that, but then I saw a number of Christians discussing it. I needed to respond to it because there were a few things I needed to correct.

Willingham correctly states that many of us grew up in churches where the Rapture was discussed. We knew it could happen at any time. Those who trusted in Christ would immediately ascend to be with Jesus, while others would be left behind to suffer. Faithful Christians differ in their opinions about the details of this event, but they take it seriously. They know believers should welcome it. On the other hand, unbelievers should fear it, at least fear it enough to repent and turn to Jesus Christ in faith. As believers, we should pray and prepare for it to happen at any moment.

Willingham then discusses "Rapture Anxiety," which she says is "recognized by some faith experts and mental health professionals as a type of religious trauma" that leads to anxiety, depression, paranoia, and even obsessive-compulsive disorder. She cites a former church member who describes the Rapture as a "scary campfire story," along with other researchers who say it should be treated like a "poetic metaphor."

Of course, I refuted this article in the video I recorded. Discounting teaching of the Rapture is a huge mistake. I don't, however, ignore that some people, including believers, have taken teaching on the Rapture as something to be feared rather than anticipated with hope.

It is for this reason that *Look Up!: Awaiting the Rapture and Our Final Redemption* has arrived just in time! Most Christian readers have encountered books about the Rapture at some point in their lives, but most of those books discuss people who will be left behind. I don't know of any book specifically dedicated to those who will be taken to be with the Lord. This book is needed, and now is exactly the right time for it. Christians need to know and be able to communicate that the Rapture is reason for great hope. Jesus said, "Do not let your heart be troubled." Paul said talking about the Rapture was a way for believers to comfort one another and described it as a "blessed hope."

Jimmy Evans is a careful Bible teacher and, although he is humble and won't admit it, he's really a scholar. He has studied God's Word as though his life depends on it, because he knows it gave him life. It will give you life too. Jimmy has taken teaching about the Rapture to a different level. His focus isn't on fear, although he doesn't avoid discussing topics such as hell and the Tribulation. In *Look Up!,* Jimmy is really writing a letter of hope and assurance for the believer, straight from the heart of a caring pastor.

In this book, readers will discover the great story of God's redemption, and how the Rapture will deliver and restore every person who puts their trust in Christ. There's no place for anxiety, and Jimmy Evans teaches from the Bible the reason for our hope and excitement when we talk about the Rapture. It's an incentive to live a godly life of service to the Lord. It's a powerful, important truth for us to proclaim until Jesus returns.

Our common interest in Bible prophecy drew us together. I am honored to work alongside him to tell others all the great things God has planned for our future. I have learned to love and trust Pastor Jimmy's heart. He believes the Bible is really Good News, and so is every promise and prophecy in it. This book comes from that spirit of hope, and it will give you comfort and assurance if you have given your life to the Lord.

Dr. Mark Hitchcock
Author,
Senior Pastor, Faith Bible Church

Acknowledgements

To my precious wife, Karen—Thank you for always encouraging and supporting me. You always make me better.

To my son, Brent—Thank you for your leadership and direction. Your desire for excellence makes me proud and encourages me every day.

To the publishing team at XO Marriage, Daniel Van and Karina Lopez—Thank you for your diligent work and staying with me to bring this book to completion.

To John Andersen—Thank you for walking with me through every step of this process. I know it gives you as much joy as it does me to deliver this book to the world.

To God be the glory, now and forever.

Introduction

I titled this book *Look Up!* for a reason. I have taught many lessons and preached many sermons and series about the end times because I believe we are living at the end of those times, meaning the times before the Rapture. The signs are incredible and undeniable, and I want people to know what is happening in the world in the context of what God is doing for His people. However, I want to take you a step further, beyond what is happening right now. I want you to know what will happen when all of this is over. I want you to know what God has planned for you.

But as it is written:

"Eye has not seen, nor ear heard,
Nor have entered into the heart of man
The things which God has prepared for those who love Him"
(1 Corinthians 2:9 NKJV).

Your future is better and brighter than you know or even imagine. The best day of your life is coming, and I believe it's coming very soon. So look up!

LOOK UP!

Your future is better and brighter than you know or even imagine.

Here is what Jesus said concerning the end times:

And there will be signs in the sun, in the moon, and in the stars; and on the earth distress of nations, with perplexity, the sea and the waves roaring; men's hearts failing them from fear and the expectation of those things which are coming on the earth, for the powers of the heavens will be shaken. Then they will see the Son of Man coming in a cloud with power and great glory. Now when these things begin to happen, **look up** and lift up your heads, because **your redemption draws near** (Luke 21:25–28 NKJV, bold mine).

Can you see what Jesus is saying in this passage? He is telling His followers that when they see the beginning of the end, they should really pay attention and keep their focus on heaven because the end is very near—close enough to touch it. The word *fear* in verse 26 comes from the Greek word *phobos* (from where we get our word *phobia*) and is also translated "terror." Jesus was saying that in the end times, people's hearts will actually begin giving out because of terror. He prophesied worldwide terrorism. We have been seeing the signs Jesus spoke about at a rapid rate, which I describe in my book, *Tipping Point*, so time is short.

Please understand that when I say we have just a brief period before the end, I am not telling you to panic. No, I am urging you to stay alert, get dressed, and prepare for the Bridegroom! Look at how Jesus described this time in the parable of the 10 virgins:

Then the kingdom of heaven shall be likened to ten virgins who took their lamps and went out to meet the bridegroom. Now five of them were wise, and five *were* foolish. Those who *were* foolish took their lamps and took no oil with them, but the wise took oil in their vessels with their lamps. But while the bridegroom was delayed, they all slumbered and slept.

And at midnight a cry was *heard:* "Behold, the bridegroom is coming; go out to meet him!" Then all those virgins arose and trimmed their lamps. And the foolish said to the wise, "Give us *some* of your oil, for our lamps are going out." But the wise answered, saying, "*No,* lest there should not be enough for us and you; but go rather to those who sell, and buy for yourselves." And while they went to buy, the bridegroom came, and those who were ready went in with him to the wedding; and the door was shut.

Afterward the other virgins came also, saying, "Lord, Lord, open to us!" But he answered and said, "Assuredly, I say to you, I do not know you."

Watch therefore, for you know neither the day nor the hour in which the Son of Man is coming (Matthew 25:1–13 NKJV).

Why should you get up spiritually and prepare for the Lord's return? Yes, there should be some appropriate fear and concern if you are not ready, but that is not the main point for believers. Jesus told His followers why they should be watchful and ready: "Your redemption is near" (Luke 21:28 CSB). That is not dreadful news; that is great news! Do you realize that Jesus is bringing about your *total redemption?* If you are a Christian, the first thing He did is redeem your personal relationship with God the Father. If you are not yet a believer, you can believe this: redemption is available to you. But I don't want your mind to stop there. God has so much more for your future. If you can understand this truth, then you will realize what a big deal it really is.

Total Redemption

God is so good. He formed you in your mother's womb and brought you into the world. Then He called you to be His child, and *He redeemed you*. Still, God did not stop. Through His Holy Spirit, He is sanctifying and conforming you into the likeness of Christ, and *He is redeeming you*. But on the day when Jesus returns for the Church, *God will fully redeem you*. He will fix and restore everything about you— body, soul, and spirit. His redemption works in you, past, present, and future.

There are several Greek terms for "redeem" and "redemption." For example, the apostle John talks about how the people of God from every nation will one day sing praises to Jesus for giving His blood as a sacrifice to redeem them:

And they sang a new song, saying:

"You are worthy to take the scroll,
And to open its seals;
For You were slain,
And **have redeemed** us to God by Your blood
Out of every tribe and tongue and people and nation"
(Revelation 5:9 NKJV, bold mine).

In this case, the Greek word translated "redeemed" is *agorazo,* which means 'to buy or acquire, such as in purchasing property.' The people are singing that Jesus' blood bought those of us who are believers in the same way you might buy a house or something from a store.

A second Greek word translated "redeem" or "redemption" is *exagorazo.* This word is found, for example, in Paul's letter to the Galatians.

> Christ **has redeemed** us from the curse of the law, having become a curse for us (for it is written, "Cursed *is* everyone who hangs on a tree") (Galatians 3:13 NKJV, bold, mine).

> ———

> But when the fullness of the time had come, God sent forth His Son, born of a woman, born under the law, **to redeem** those who were under the law, that we might receive the adoption as sons (Galatians 4:4–5 NKJV, bold mine).

This word translated "redeemed" and "redeem" in these two verses means 'to buy back something or deliver someone.' Paul is saying that we belong to God, but someone else (the devil) bought or stole us. Jesus had to repurchase us by His life and death on the cross. For example, imagine you lost your spouse's wedding ring through gambling or a bad business deal. This term means you would then buy it back at a high price and return it to your spouse (after you did some serious repenting and explaining). It also is a term used to describe buying a slave only to set them free after the purchase.

A third relevant Greek New Testament word is *peripoieo*, which means 'to purchase something for yourself.' Luke uses a form of this word in the book of Acts:

> Therefore take heed to yourselves and to all the flock, among which the Holy Spirit has made you overseers, to shepherd the church of God which He **purchased** with His own blood (Acts 20:28 NKJV, bold mine).

Luke is saying that God has bought the Church as His own *exclusive personal possession*. In Ephesians, Paul ties this word together with a form of *lutroo* (the next word I will discuss) in the very same sentence:

> In Him you also *trusted*, after you heard the word of truth, the gospel of your salvation; in whom also, having believed, you were sealed with the Holy Spirit of promise, who is the guarantee of our inheritance until the **redemption** [*lutroo*] of the **purchased possession** [*peripoieo*], to the praise of His glory (Ephesians 1:13–14 NKJV, bold mine).

Paul is saying God has purchased us so we can forever exclusively belong to Him.

Finally, a form of *lutroo* is used in the passage in Luke I shared earlier:

> Now when these things begin to happen, look up and lift up your heads, because **your redemption draws near** (Luke 21:28 NKJV, bold mine).

The word translated here as "redemption" means 'to free some-one by paying a ransom, to rescue, and to set free.' You might use this word to describe a hostage who has been rescued either by paying a ransom or through a commando raid. Paul uses this term in his closing message to Titus:

> Looking for the blessed hope and glorious appearing of our great God and Savior Jesus Christ, who gave Himself for us, that He might **redeem** us from every lawless deed and purify for Himself *His* own special people, zealous for good works (Titus 2:13–14 NKJV, bold mine).

In these verses Paul is telling Titus that Jesus' sacrifice rescued us from sinful works or deeds. Peter also uses this term in his first letter:

> Knowing that you were not **redeemed** with corruptible things, *like* silver or gold, from your aimless conduct *received* by tradition from your fathers, but with the precious blood of Christ, as of a lamb without blemish and without spot (1 Peter 1:18–19 NKJV, bold mine).

Peter is saying that not only did Jesus pay the ransom, but also the price was high and precious.

So which one of these types of redemption is Jesus bringing to us through His return? *All of them!* Here is the whole story: God purchased us, but Satan took us hostage and made us slaves. Then through a "commando raid," by coming into the world, Jesus paid the price, defeated the enemy, and set us free. The price was high and precious, and it cost Him His own life. Through that price He is restoring everything the enemy had stolen. So when Jesus tells His followers their redemption is "near," He means He is getting ready to free us from all bondage and restore every broken thing in our lives. And He will do it "in a moment, in the twinkling of an eye" (1 Corinthians 15:52 NKJV). This is where Jesus told us to put our focus. Look up! His redemption is at hand!

So when Jesus tells His followers their redemption is "near," He means He is getting ready to free us from all bondage and restore every broken thing in our lives.

The Birth Pangs of the World

I want to tell you about all the incredible promises God is preparing for you. You have a very bright future, and I often compare the time we are experiencing to that of a couple awaiting the birth of a new baby.

If you have children, then you will remember this time. If you don't have children, then you likely have friends who have shared this experience, or you might be a young person who is excited about the possibility of children in your future. When a couple decides they want to have a baby, the whole experience seems like a flurry of excitement. At first, the wife takes a pregnancy test and shares the good news with her husband. Soon after, everything changes. There is morning sickness followed by aches and pains she has never known before. As the woman moves closer to the pregnancy's full term, she experiences a new kind of excitement, along with fear and increasing physical discomfort. By the time most women reach their ninth month, they are physically miserable and feel the full burden of the infant growing inside them.

However, the woman isn't finished yet. If she opts for natural childbirth, then at some point the labor pains begin. They become more intense and frequent as time goes on. In mortal pain, she screams and cries out for the birth to happen and the pain to be over. Finally, with her anxious and worried husband by her side, and with blood and other fluids pouring from her body, she gives birth! Within a matter of seconds, the new parents can hear the first cries of their newborn baby. Then the doctor or midwife presents the child to the new parents. She or he seems perfect! Everything has changed in only a moment. All the days of pain and discomfort are over, and they are replaced with the unspeakable joy of new life.

When labor started, the new mother probably wondered if she could handle the hours that lie ahead. Those first pains were bad enough, but then they became horrible and incredibly difficult. But that mother also knows the labor pains are the beginning of the end and the end of a beginning. When the pains are their worst, she is even closer to the birth, which is the whole purpose of the pregnancy.

In *Tipping Point* I told readers about all the signs and events happening in the world today, and I described the beginning of the end and the end of the beginning:

Yet what we suffer now is nothing compared to the glory he will reveal to us later. For all creation is waiting eagerly for that future day when God will reveal who his children really are. Against its will, all creation was subjected to God's curse. But with eager hope, the creation looks forward to the day when it will join God's children in glorious freedom from death and decay. For we know that all creation has been groaning as in the pains of childbirth right up to the present time. And we believers also groan, even though we have the Holy Spirit within us as a foretaste of future glory, for we long for our bodies to be released from sin and suffering. We, too, wait with eager hope for the day when God will give us our full rights as his adopted children, including the new bodies he has promised us. We were given this hope when we were saved. (If we already have something, we don't need to hope for it. But if we look forward to something we don't yet have, we must wait patiently and confidently.) (Romans 8:18–25).

I believe that if the world were a pregnant mother, then she has reached full term. We are experiencing something far bigger than a particular social or cultural change. I believe we have approached the biggest event in world history—the return of Christ and the end of the age. If you are a believer, then this is not a reason for alarm. It is a time to soberly consider God's call on our lives and joyously await the Bridegroom. The signs are everywhere. Just as you cannot stop a child from being born without harming the mother or the baby, there is nothing to be done except wait and prepare for Jesus' return.

The Bible speaks more about our current generation than any other generation that has lived or ever will live. We're living in a very severe time. God knows it, and for our sake, He is hastening the end. Just as a doctor or midwife can see when a new mother is about to give birth, we can see that the world is coming to "full term." I am telling you it is all happening right now. The return of Christ is imminent, but you can be prepared. The signs are increasing, the birth pangs are growing stronger, and they are announcing that we are about to be redeemed!

The Bible speaks more about our current generation than any other generation that has lived or ever will live.

In this book, I write about what Adam and Eve lost when they fell. These are the **nine things Jesus will redeem when He returns**:

1. *Perfect bodies.* Adam and Eve lost their perfect, incorruptible bodies, and their bodies died. When Jesus comes again, we will get perfect bodies.
2. *Perfect minds.* Sin and the devil have deluded our minds, but when Jesus returns, He will restore us to perfect sanity and bring us into the full knowledge of God and His Kingdom.
3. *Perfect pleasure.* The first couple lost pleasure. God never intended for people to experience pain or suffering. When Jesus returns, there will be no more pain, and believers will return to Eden, which means 'pleasure.'
4. *Perfect identity.* Our fallenness brought on by sin has caused us to forget who we really are. When Jesus comes back, He

will restore our identities completely as sons of God, the bride of Christ, prophets, priests, and kings.

5. *Total authority.* The first two humans lost the authority God had given them. We have partial authority in this life by which we should be ruling and reigning as kings with the spiritual authority Jesus gave us. When He returns, we will reclaim all authority. We will then come back to rule and reign with Him over the earth.

6. *Perfect home.* The man and woman lost their home. God put them in the perfect Garden of Eden, but when they chose to listen to the serpent and disobey God, they were sent out from their home. Eden will be restored to us when Jesus comes back.

7. *Perfect intimacy.* When Adam and Eve sinned, they lost their intimacy with God. When Jesus returns and we go to heaven, our intimate relationship with Jesus will be completely restored.

8. *Perfect innocence.* When Adam and Eve rebelled, they suddenly realized they were naked, and their guilt caused them shame. When the Rapture occurs, all shame will disappear, and our guilt will be invisible because it will be covered by Jesus' righteousness.

9. *God-directed knowledge.* God wants to be our Father and teach us everything. He would have given Adam and Eve great knowledge if they had been obedient to Him, but they decided to take matters into their own hands. When Jesus comes again, God will reveal everything we need to know, and He will continue to teach us for all eternity.

Isn't it incredible how much our Lord will do in the blink of an eye? The return of Christ is imminent, but you can be prepared. So look up!

A Very Important Question

Before I tell you more about what will happen when Jesus returns, I want to make sure you are ready for it. I have a very important personal question to ask you. In fact, it is the most important question you will ever be asked to answer:

Have you invited Jesus into your heart to be your Lord and Savior?

If your answer is "yes" to that question, then you can skip to Part One.

If your answer is "no" to that question, then I need to tell you that it is very important for you to invite Jesus into your heart. What I am about to tell you in this book will not be good news for you. In fact, it could be very bad news. Unless you surrender to Jesus and have a personal relationship with Him, you will not be ready to meet Him when He comes.

Here are some important Scriptures to help you understand the significance of this major step:

> For by grace you have been saved through faith, and that not of yourselves; *it is* the gift of God, not of works, lest anyone should boast (Ephesians 2:8–9 NKJV).

> ———

> Behold, I stand at the door and knock. If anyone hears My voice and opens the door, I will come in to him and dine with him, and he with Me (Revelation 3:20 NKJV).

> ———

For God so loved the world that He gave His only begotten Son, that whoever believes in Him should not perish but have everlasting life. For God did not send His Son into the world to condemn the world, but that the world through Him might be saved.

He who believes in Him is not condemned; but he who does not believe is condemned already, because he has not believed in the name of the only begotten Son of God (John 3:16–18 NKJV).

Salvation (being saved) is an act of grace we don't deserve. It is a free gift from God that we receive instantly as we open our hearts to Jesus and allow Him into our lives to save us from our sins and become our Lord. God loves you personally and wants to have a personal relationship with you. As you open your heart to Jesus and invite Him in, He will forgive all your sins, give you the gift of eternal life in heaven forever, live in your heart, and personally relate to you. He will also take you with Him when He comes back to gather His people. He does all this because of His great love for you. This love is not one God has for us because we deserve it. He loves us because He created us in our mothers' wombs (see Psalm 139:13–16), and we are His children, made in His image.

Jesus died for us on the cross to pay for our sins and break the power of sin over our lives. He did this because sin was keeping us away from God, and there was no way we could deal with our sin problem on our own. Knowing that we were helpless in our sins, God sent Jesus, His only Son, to die in our place and pay for our sins so they could be removed forever.

When we receive Jesus into our lives, we are laying claim to the forgiveness, freedom, and blessings for which Jesus died and rose again. All these blessings flow from our personal relationship with Him. If you are ready to receive Jesus into your heart at this time, say this prayer to Him:

Jesus, I confess that I have sinned against You, and I repent. I now open my heart to You and ask You to come into my life to be my Lord and Savior. I submit my life to You, and from this day forward I will live to serve You. I believe You have come into my heart and have forgiven me of my sins. I believe I am now saved by your grace. I have the gift of eternal life, and I am now ready for your return. Jesus, I pray You will fill me with Your Holy Spirit and give me the power to change, know You, and live my life for You. Amen!

If you prayed that prayer, then you can be sure that Jesus is now in your heart as the Lord of your life. This is the most important prayer of your life because it changes your eternity. Now, it is also common when you pray this prayer for the devil to try to tell you it isn't real or you are too bad to be forgiven. Don't worry—that happens to almost everyone. Soon you will learn how to discern the voice of the devil and how to overcome him. For now, just know that you are a child of God, a Christian, and a member of God's family. Welcome!

It is important as a new believer to be baptized in water as an act of obedience to Jesus. It is the first thing Jesus commands us to do as new believers as a token of our sincerity and obedience to Him (see Mark 16:15–16; Matthew 28:19–20). If you don't have a home church, then find a Bible-believing church and tell them you would like to be baptized in water. Be committed to church, attend regularly, and get involved. It will be important to your new faith to be around fellow believers who will encourage you in the things of God.

You should also get a Bible if you don't already own one and begin to read it daily. Start in the New Testament, and if you are completely unfamiliar with the Bible, then the Gospel of John is a great book to help you understand who Jesus is and how to have a relationship with Him. Be sure to get a Bible translation you can understand. The New Living Translation is a very good Bible version that is understandable and accurate.

Also, I wrote a book called *Ten Steps Toward Christ: Journey to the Heart of God*, specifically for those who have just given their lives to Christ. I encourage you to purchase and read it. It will show you in detail the important steps to living a victorious and fulfilling Christian life. You can get it on xomarriage.com or Amazon.com. Jesus is coming soon, and I am so happy you will be ready to go with Him when He returns.

PART ONE

Redeemed Bodies

CHAPTER 1

What Has Happened to My Body?

"What has happened to my body?" Have you heard that question? Have you asked it? I know I have. I am now in my 60s, and while God has blessed me with good health, this man "ain't what he used to be." But the truth is, none of us are. The minute you were born is the same minute you began to die. It is incredibly sad when people die, and it's especially tragic to hear about a young person's death or disease. You might ask, *But, Jimmy, isn't that just the human condition?* No. No, it is not. It is not what God designed for us. It was never in His divine plan. Instead of the human condition, it is the *fallen* human condition. So what has happened to our bodies? How did they get this way?

A Perfect World Gone Wrong

The Bible says God created Adam, the first man, and then He created Eve, the first woman (see Genesis 1:26–27; 2:7, 18–25). The Lord placed them in a perfect environment, a home He called the Garden of Eden. At first, everything about creation was perfect, but only for a brief moment in time.

In the garden, Adam and Eve had everything they could ever want or need. God planted fruits and vegetables, and He was the perfect Gardener. Food was plentiful and free for the taking. The man and woman were surrounded by beauty. The garden was also full of animals, but there was no such thing as predator or prey. Lions did lie down with lambs, and no one was harmed. Every creature had a good relationship with every other creature, and they all feasted on the bounty of God's garden.

In that garden God planted many trees, but two played a key role. The Tree of Life would guarantee eternal life to those who ate from it. The Tree of the Knowledge of Good and Evil would help the couple gain wisdom and understanding, but it would also lead them toward evil. Adam and Eve never ate fruit from the first tree. The second tree, however, is a different story.

God was the Master Gardner, but He entrusted Adam with the daily tending of the garden. At first, things went well, but then something terrible happened. God told Adam not to eat the fruit of the Tree of the Knowledge of Good and Evil. Before you think God gave people a lengthy list of "don'ts," I need to tell you it was a very short list. On the contrary, the Lord gave them an exceptionally large list of "dos." Adam named the animals and managed the garden. God told him he could eat whatever he wanted from whichever plant he chose, but there was only one prohibition—that *one* tree. If Adam ate from *that* tree, then he would die *that* day. Adam passed the warning on to his wife.

One day, a day just as wonderful as any other day in the garden paradise, something tragic occurred. Satan, in the form of a serpent, slithered up to Eve. Before you think what happened next was "all her fault," let me remind you that Adam was right there with her. Satan is a professional liar, so you can expect that the first statement the Bible records him saying to be a lie:

> Then the serpent said to the woman, "You will not surely die. For God knows that in the day you eat of it your eyes will be opened, and you will be like God, knowing good and evil" (Genesis 3:4–5 NKJV).

Take a moment to let that statement sink in. This is what God actually said:

> And the LORD God commanded the man, saying, "Of every tree of the garden you may freely eat; but of the tree of the knowledge of good and evil you shall not eat, for in the day that you eat of it you shall surely die" (Genesis 2:16–17 NKJV).

There in the middle of God's garden, the devil had the nerve to contradict the God of all creation. His first lie was about God, and he has been lying about God ever since.

Humans have also been doing the same thing since that time. Rather than believing God's Word, they have chosen to believe the devil's lies. Eve took Satan at his word, and she ate the fruit and then shared it with her husband. Then this happened:

> Then the eyes of both of them were opened, and they knew that they *were* naked; and they sewed fig leaves together and made themselves coverings (Genesis 3:7 NKJV).

God knew what the couple had done, and He went looking for them. When He found them, they were hiding. Then God told them about the results of their choices. The Lord cursed the ground and the serpent, and He told Adam and Eve the severe consequences of their actions. God told them they would die if they disobeyed, but did they die? Yes and no. They did die spiritually that day, but they didn't die physically. Why didn't God just wipe them off the face of the planet at that very moment? Because God loves people and wants to save and restore them. God's very first act of grace was to let Adam and Eve live, albeit in their fallen state. However, their sin brought dire consequences. God killed animals and used their skins for clothing to cover the couple's nakedness. Adam and Eve were now tainted by sin, and they were marked for death, even if God showed His love by not destroying them at that very moment. The Lord did, however, banish them from the Garden of Eden. They would never in this age taste the fruit of the Tree of Life. Death would be their end. Their perfect bodies would never again know perfection.

God's very first act of grace was to let Adam and Eve live, albeit in their fallen state.

You may wonder why you have to pay for the sins of Adam and Eve. But really, you don't pay for their sins. Why is this true? Because their story is *your* story. You have also chosen to disobey God. Adam's and Eve's disobedience to God was the first human sin, and it ruined human nature by passing the desire to sin to every person after them. Yes, we are born into this world as children of Adam and Eve, but we also choose to follow the first human parents in their sinful ways. We are *bent* toward sin. If we think we are without sin, we are only fooling ourselves.

As it is written:

"There are none righteous, no, not one" (Romans 3:10 NKJV).

God did not tempt Adam and Eve, nor has He ever tempted any of us. Out of His love, God created us with a free will, which means we have the choice to obey or ignore His commands. God will never force you to follow Him. In fact, every day He holds back His wrath from us, which is caused by our disobedience. Still, humans continue to disobey God. So from the day Adam and Even sinned onward, every human who has ever lived disobeyed God, except one—Jesus. Through His Son, God planned to save us even "before the foundation of the world" (Ephesians 1:4 NKJV). He has never left us without hope or recourse. He responded to our sin by sending Jesus to save and redeem us.

The Effects of Sin on Our Bodies

Because of Adam's and Eve's sin and humanity's ongoing sins, we live in a fallen world. That is why good and evil coexist in every area of our lives, including our bodies. Everything God created was good, but when Adam and Eve disobeyed, everything within and around them was tainted by evil. The world God created remained, but it was marred by what these humans had done. If you have ever been in a room with warped, funny mirrors, such as in a carnival fun house, then you know you can still see your reflection, but the image is terribly off. That is what happened to the world—you can still see God's hand in creation, but the picture is woefully distorted. Nothing fits correctly anymore, and we constantly see friction, conflict, and destruction. God's good creation is distorted by turmoil and chaos.

God gave two vivid illustrations of the new situation: there would be pain in childbirth, and work would require toil and sweat (see Genesis 3:16–19). The two main illustrations of the change of creation after the Fall are in childbirth and work. Childbirth illustrates the struggle humans would have to encounter to live in this fallen world. Backbreaking work reveals the challenge of survival. Even if we survive, supplies are limited, and obstacles and illnesses prevent us or injure us in our pursuit of a better life. Yes, we were created in the image of God, and He loves us without measure, but we are also fallen and sinful and capable of the worst kinds of sins. We are created in the image of God, but humanity is also capable of the worst sorts of evil.

Nature itself bears the results of sin. I love to be outside and witness the beauty of God's creation. I enjoy the power of the ocean, the mystery of the forest, and the majesty of all the creatures God placed on the earth. Yet I know that is not the complete picture. I have seen the dangers of fire, earthquakes, hurricanes, and other disasters. I know the world has much evil and ugliness because of human sin and disobedience.

Nature itself bears the results of sin.

I also know the effects of sin on our bodies. Sickness and disease have touched every human family because of sin. While we can't trace every illness directly to sin, every human disease, frailty, and calamity come to us ultimately because of the fall of Adam and Eve. Within one generation, the first baby born into the world became the world's first murderer. Cain introduced the first recorded tragedy caused by the sin of his parents, but it certainly wasn't the last. Abel was a victim of his brother's violence, but equally a casualty of his parents' sin. Abel did nothing personally to deserve death, yet he died because of Cain's direct sin and Adam and Eve's indirect disobedience to God's command.

What are the results of sin on your body?

1. *Your genes have been corrupted, which means you are predisposed to certain illnesses and diseases.* Your doctor wants to know your family health history because you are more likely to experience the same physical problems as other members of your family. You may be prone to engage in harmful behaviors or fall into various addictions, such as to alcohol or drugs.

2. *Your own bad decisions contribute to your physical problems.* People know they shouldn't smoke, drink excessive alcohol, or take part in illegal drug use, yet many willingly engage in habits they know are harmful. Are alcoholism and drug addiction sins or sicknesses? The answer is likely both. It begins with a willful choice until the addicted person no longer has any self-control. The same is true with overeating, refusing to exercise, or engaging in risky sexual behavior. Our choices are often reflected in our physical bodies.

3. *Others can make bad choices beyond your control that also harm your body.* Only in the past couple of decades have people come to understand the dangers of secondhand smoke. Sometimes even a faithful spouse contracts a sexually transmitted disease from an unfaithful partner. People are injured every day by thoughtless and reckless drivers.
4. *Some illnesses and physical conditions are the result of both bad choices and corrupt genes.* Heart disease and diabetes usually stem from poor habits coupled with genetic predispositions.

The bottom line is this: sickness is both a direct and indirect result of sin. Because of the disobedience of Adam and Eve, all humanity became sick. In fact, all creation is groaning in sickness. We need healing, and we need a Healer. If you are sick, then is it your fault? Yes and no. There may be no cause and effect because of anything you have personally done, but you and I are sojourners in a corrupt and sinful world. It is undeniable.

Our Bodyguard

You must know there is a huge contrast between the Garden of Eden and the world we know today. When you recognize the difference, it's frightening. Adam and Eve had no experience with disease that we know of except for their causes of death. If you have lived any amount of time, then you know death, disease, and suffering cover the earth. You have heard about wars, or you have been a soldier in or a victim of one. In your own town or city, you know about murder, abuse, and every other kind of human cruelty. You have also experienced tragedies, accidents, and every other awful thing that can happen in this life. If you live long enough, you will experience sickness, weakness, frailty, and, ultimately, death. The apostle Paul wrote,

> Therefore, just as through one man sin entered the world, and death through sin, and thus death spread to all men, because all sinned (Romans 5:12 NKJV).

Death is our ultimate enemy, the Bible says. If you knew you had an enemy, and you knew who this enemy was, then you would do everything in your power to stop or defeat that person or persons. You would get a weapon, install a security system, and maybe even hire a bodyguard. No one would pass unless you knew whether they were friend or foe. Nevertheless, I am here to deliver some very unfortunate news: the enemy is already in your house! Death isn't your only enemy, but the Bible says it is your "last enemy" (see 1 Corinthians 15:25–26). Even so, Jesus will have His victory, even over death.

Do you believe this? Do you believe Jesus will finally and ultimately destroy your last enemy? The writer of Hebrews says,

> For it was fitting for Him, for whom *are* all things and by whom *are* all things, in bringing many sons to glory, to make the captain of their salvation perfect through sufferings (Hebrews 2:10 NKJV).

The Greek word translated here as "captain" is *archegos,* and it means 'supreme champion.' Yes, you do know your last enemy, but you also have the ultimate bodyguard, weapon, and security system. If you have Jesus, then you will defeat this enemy.

God is in the bodyguard business. Do you remember that famous death match between David and Goliath? (If not, I encourage you to read 1 Samuel 17.) The Israelite and Philistine armies stood on opposite hills with a valley in the middle. They agreed to decide the outcome of their war not through a bloody, all-out battle, but by choosing a champion from each side as a representative in hand-to-hand combat, with winner-take-all as the final result. The Philistines chose the giant Goliath as their champion. He terrified the Israelite soldiers, and they believed they had no chance against him. King Saul searched in vain for volunteers, but no one stepped forward. Then a shepherd boy presented himself as Israel's last and only hope. Goliath came into battle with his reputation, but David came under the power and authority of "the LORD of hosts, the God of the armies of Israel" (1 Samuel 17:45 NKJV). Notice David's title for God—he seemed to be the only one from Israel's side who really believed the God of the army could give the army victory. As you know, David emerged from the confrontation as the true champion. His defeat of Goliath has inspired every child who ever attended Sunday school, but David's triumph pales in comparison to the victory of the Son of David who would arrive almost a thousand years later. David conquered Goliath, but Jesus took on sin, death, and the devil himself, and He emerged as the all-time winner and champion.

God is in the bodyguard business.

After Adam and Eve sinned, the Lord spoke directly to Satan:

And I will put enmity
Between you and the woman,
And between your seed and her Seed;
He shall bruise your head,
And you shall bruise His heel (Genesis 3:15 NKJV).

And that is exactly what Jesus did. This prophecy from God directly to Satan is known as the "Protoevangelium," which means it is the first time we see the gospel of Jesus in the Bible. It is a reference to what Satan did to influence Jesus' torture and execution, but it is also the first words about Jesus' victorious resurrection. Satan enlisted men to kill Jesus, but the story did not end on a lonely hill outside Jerusalem. Jesus rose again, and Satan was defeated! Jesus is the ultimate bodyguard. He defeated sin, death, and the devil at His first coming, but none of them will have power over Jesus or His people when He comes again.

Before moving to the next chapter, I want to leave you with one particularly important reminder: You cannot overcome your sinful, fallen nature on your own. Your only hope is to turn to Jesus Christ as your Lord and Savior. He offers salvation to you. It is a free gift given by God's grace if you will merely accept it in faith. It is the first and most important way for you to prepare for His return.

CHAPTER 2

Jesus: The Firstfruits of Our Transformation

In the previous chapter, I told you why our bodies become diseased and die. We live with the results of the disobedience of Adam and Eve, as well as with the consequences of our own sins. We are plagued with imperfections and decay. I don't even pretend to be a scientist, but most of us can remember certain concepts we learned in our high school science class. Do you remember the "second law of thermodynamics?" In its simplest form, scientists in the 1800s recognized that you can't pass heat from a colder physical body to a warmer body. Other scientists took that initial observation and recognized that everything we know in the physical world is moving toward entropy and decay. The biblical origin of this "second law" can be traced to one event:

> Therefore, just as through one man sin entered the world, and death through sin, and thus death spread to all men, because all sinned (Romans 5:12 NKJV).

In fact, the apostle Paul said it spread *not only* to people:

For we know that the whole creation groans and labors with birth pangs together until now (Romans 8:22 NKJV).

Consider the context of what Paul was saying in this verse. Just a few verses before, he wrote:

For I consider that the sufferings of this present time are not worthy *to be compared* with the glory which shall be revealed in us (Romans 8:18 NKJV).

While we may suffer in the present, this is not our home (see 1 Peter 2:11; Hebrews 11:13). Paul is saying we will have a glorious future in a kingdom where death is defeated and all other human suffering ends (see Revelation 20:14). Yes, the actions of Adam and Eve had severe consequences, and we are all living with them—or dying with them! But here is some really good news about those consequences: *they are temporary.* When we lay hold to this promise, we can begin to understand our current troubles with an eternal mindset. They are small and light compared to the greater eternal weight of the glory that is to come (see 2 Corinthians 4:17). We may suffer now, but our heavenly reward is worth the wait. We have been offered salvation and eternal life through the sacrifice of Jesus Christ, who lived, died, and rose again. Through Him we have been redeemed, and that includes the redemption of our physical bodies. When will this happen? When will our bodies be redeemed? It will be at the end of this age. Does that sound like it is a long time away? I am telling you it is closer than you think, and it will happen in an instant. When Jesus comes again, we will receive new, perfect bodies. Sometimes I feel like a game show host giving away new cars to everyone in the audience on a television show: "You get a new body! You get a new body! And you get a new body! Everybody gets a new body!" I say that with one important qualifier: you must be born again. God is going to restore and perfect everything in your life. He will heal everything about you, including your body, mind, will, and emotions.

We may suffer now, but our heavenly reward is worth the wait.

This news is incredibly important. We live in a fallen world that is obsessed with appearances. When people are dying, they will pretend they are fine. When they are poor, they will act like they are rich. When they know they don't appear at their best, they will do their absolute best to put on an appearance. Spend five minutes on social media, and you will understand just how important appearance is to people. With all the photo filters and highly edited stories, everyone looks great. Many people are driving luxury cars, and their kids are going to Ivy League schools. But the truth is, in spite of our best efforts, none of us measure up to the expectations of others or even our own expectations, and it can be overwhelming.

In the real world, people are coping with illnesses or other infirmities. Disabilities challenge those we know and love. On top of those things, all of us are becoming older the longer we live, and the issues of aging are becoming increasingly more pronounced. I can give witness to that fact! But when Jesus returns, we will instantly receive new bodies. You won't become a ghost. No, when the Rapture occurs, you will instantaneously receive the promise of the redemption of your body.

> Not only *that*, but we also who have the firstfruits of the Spirit, even we ourselves groan within ourselves, eagerly waiting for the adoption, the redemption of our body. For we were saved in this hope, but hope that is seen is not hope; for why does one still hope for what he sees? But if we hope for what we do not see, we eagerly wait for it with perseverance (Romans 8:23–25 NKJV).

The Prototype

It was astounding to me when I realized that many people, even believers, don't understand that we will receive new bodies when Jesus returns. How do I know it is possible to receive a new body? Because I know one Man who has already received a new body. Jesus was bodily resurrected. I also know His new eternal body was awesome in nature, and ours will be too.

Jesus said, "Look up, your redemption is near." You might think, *Aren't we already redeemed?* Yes, Jesus died on the cross to redeem us, but we've only received a tiny fraction of the whole package. We only have a small taste of what is to come. But on the day Jesus returns, we will get everything!

You see, Jesus is the *prototype* and *firstfruits* of the full transformation of our physical bodies. He is the whole package. What has happened to Him will also happen to us. Jesus' resurrected body foreshadows what will happen to the bodies of all believers when He comes again.

Jesus is the *prototype* and *firstfruits* of the full transformation of our physical bodies.

But now Christ is risen from the dead, *and* has become the first-fruits of those who have fallen asleep. For since by man *came* death, by Man also *came* the resurrection of the dead. For as in Adam all die, even so in Christ all shall be made alive. **But each one in his own order: Christ the firstfruits, afterward those *who are* Christ's at His coming.** Then *comes* the end, when He delivers the kingdom to God the Father, when He puts an end to all rule and all authority and power (1 Corinthians 15:20–24 NKJV, bold mine).

If Jesus was the first of all those who will be resurrected from the dead, then we need to understand what happened to His body after God raised Him up. We also need to know how our new bodies will be like Jesus' resurrected body. The Gospel of Luke gives this description:

Now as they said these things, Jesus Himself stood in the midst of them, and said to them, "Peace to you." But they were terrified and frightened, and supposed they had seen a spirit. And He said to them, "Why are you troubled? And why do doubts arise in your hearts? Behold My hands and My feet, that it is I Myself. **Handle Me and see, for a spirit does not have flesh and bones as you see I have.**"

When He had said this, He showed them His hands and His feet. But while they still did not believe for joy, and marveled, He said to them, "Have you any food here?" So they gave Him a piece of a broiled fish and some honeycomb. And He took *it* and ate in their presence.

Then He said to them, "These *are* the words which I spoke to you while I was still with you, that all things must be fulfilled which were written in the Law of Moses and *the* Prophets and *the* Psalms concerning Me." And He opened their understanding, that they might comprehend the Scriptures.

Then He said to them, "Thus it is written, and thus it was necessary for the Christ to suffer and to rise from the dead the third day, and that repentance and remission of sins should be preached in His name to all nations, beginning at Jerusalem. And you are witnesses of these things. Behold, I send the Promise of My Father upon you; but tarry in the city of Jerusalem until you are endued with power from on high."

And He led them out as far as Bethany, and He lifted up His hands and blessed them. Now it came to pass, while He blessed them, that He was parted from them and carried up into heaven. And they worshiped Him, and returned to Jerusalem with great joy, and were continually in the temple praising and blessing God. Amen (Luke 24:36–53 NKJV, bold mine).

From this text we can gather *four important facts about Jesus' eternal body.*

1. *Supranatural*

Jesus has a physical body, but it is also supernatural and *supranatural*. His body could be touched; He ate, and He could feel pleasure. His pre-resurrection body could only be in one place at a time. He grew tired and became hungry. He limited Himself and succumbed to suffering at the crucifixion. But His new body was raised up in power. In His resurrected body, Jesus can appear out of nowhere, and He is filled with ability and might from God.

In this text and in John 20:19, 26, Jesus visited His followers in their familiar meeting place. He joined them first on the evening of the resurrection and again eight days later. Both times, with no human explanation, Jesus physically entered the room. Neither text says He walked through walls—He was able to simply enter the room and stand in their midst. On both occasions, "the doors were shut." I don't know exactly how Jesus was able to enter the room with closed doors, but I do know that is a supranatural ability. He no longer had the same physical limitations and weaknesses that all of us still experience.

2. Physical

As I said in the previous point, while Jesus had supranatural and supernatural abilities, He still had a physical body. Why is this an important fact? A heretical sect known as the Docetists rose up in the first-century church even while the apostles were still alive. They derived their name from the Greek word *dokesis*, which means 'to appear' or 'to resemble,' because they taught that Christ only "appeared" or "seemed" to be a real human. They taught He was not really born, did not live a human life, and never suffered or had a physical death. Some of them denied Jesus' human nature altogether. Probably the best modern word for a Docetist would be an "illusionist." They thought Jesus was an illusion, not a real human person. If you are interested in learning more and keeping score, not all Docetists were Gnostics, but as far as we know, all Gnostics had docetic beliefs.[1]

Some later heresies began within the church, but Docetism cannot be properly seen as a Christian heresy at all. It did not come from people in the Church who created a theological error. Rather, it came from philosophers outside the Church. Gnostics accepted the platonic concept of *dualism*. Dualism essentially means that all physical matter is evil, and everything spiritual is good. Salvation comes when people free themselves from the physical and return to only the spiritual. Dualists, for example, could never accept the sentence, "The Word became flesh" (John 1:14 NKJV). After all, how could a perfect God become flesh if flesh itself is evil? Therefore, the only way for a Docetist to accept that Jesus could be a savior was to modify or deny the Incarnation—that God indeed became flesh. He only "appeared" to be human. Others accepted that Jesus had a body, but He could not have been born of a woman. Still others thought Jesus' death on the cross was only an illusion. He only "seemed" to suffer while He miraculously substituted someone else to die on the cross. It was all one big visual deception. Jesus' resurrection also was not real. He was resurrected spiritually, but His bones are still hidden somewhere in the Middle East.

My word for docetic teaching is *baloney!* It wasn't true then, and it will never be true. Can you understand why? Docetists tried to destroy the very meaning and purpose of the Incarnation. The apostle

Paul said that in Christ the fullness of the Godhead dwelt bodily (see Colossians 1:19; 2:9). And the apostle John certainly tried to correct docetic errors (see 1 John 1:1–3; 4:1–3; 2 John 7). He wanted his readers to know that he had seen, heard, and touched Jesus' physical body. Elements of the docetic heresy are still around today, they are still demonically inspired, and they are still wrong.

I need to address a common misconception at this point. Many people will point out that the New Testament tells us to be spiritual and not fleshly, but that is because the word translated "flesh" is used in more than one way in the text, just like we use it in more than one way in English. Sometimes, for example, Paul is referring to the flesh as our sinful nature. In that sense, no, we don't want to live "according to the flesh" (Romans 8:5). However, when John says that God became flesh in Jesus, he is not referring to a sinful nature. John is describing actual physical flesh with blood, bones, and muscles. When God created everything, He said it was "good." That "goodness" is still who we are, minus our sinful nature. In fact, Paul tells us we should take great care of our bodies because they are the "temple of the Holy Spirit" (1 Corinthians 6:19).

Jesus told His followers to touch Him. He wanted every one of them to handle Him. He told them He was not a spirit—He had flesh and bones. Not only is this true, but it is also critically important for you and me. If Jesus is only spirit and never really became human flesh, then what hope is there for us? You may think, *Well, Jimmy, Jesus was perfect. I can't ever hope to be perfect.* Yes, you can! And that is my entire point in this chapter. I want you to understand that very soon, when Jesus returns, you will be made perfect – body, soul, and spirit.

Yes, Jesus was resurrected as a physical body. It was unlike any body you have ever seen, but it was a real body. Jesus became flesh; He was a genuine human. Even more, He is still human, yet without sin. (1 Timothy 2:5) That is the best news you could ever receive. There is hope for you, even while you are a human. When Jesus comes, He will transform your body to be like His, but it will still be a physical body. How is that possible? The apostle Paul explains it:

But someone will say, "How are the dead raised up? And with what body do they come?" Foolish one, what you sow is not made alive unless it dies. And what you sow, you do not sow that body that shall be, but mere grain—perhaps wheat or some other *grain*. But God gives it a body as He pleases, and to each seed its own body.

All flesh *is* not the same flesh, but *there is* one *kind of* flesh of men, another flesh of animals, another of fish, *and* another of birds.

There are also celestial bodies and terrestrial bodies; but the glory of the celestial *is* one, and the *glory* of the terrestrial *is* another. *There is* one glory of the sun, another glory of the moon, and another glory of the stars; for *one* star differs from *another* star in glory.

So also *is* the resurrection of the dead. *The body* is sown in corruption, it is raised in incorruption. It is sown in dishonor, it is raised in glory. It is sown in weakness, it is raised in power. It is sown a natural body, it is raised a spiritual body. There is a natural body, and there is a spiritual body. And so it is written, "The first man Adam became a living being." The last Adam *became* a life-giving spirit.

However, the spiritual is not first, but the natural, and afterward the spiritual. The first man *was* of the earth, *made* of dust; the second Man *is* the Lord from heaven. As *was* the *man* of dust, so also *are* those *who are made* of dust; and as *is* the heavenly *Man,* so also *are* those *who are* heavenly. And as we have borne the image of the *man* of dust, we shall also bear the image of the heavenly *Man* (1 Corinthians 15:35–49 NKJV).

Paul compares our physical bodies to seeds, which are planted and then grow from the ground. Now, here is my question: If I plant a seed in the ground and it begins to grow, is it still the seed? Before you answer, I must tell you it's a trick question. That answer is *yes and no.* Yes, whatever plant grows from the ground still contains that seed. But no, it's not exactly the same as the seed. It's something newer and greater, though it maintains some "seedy" characteristics.

When Jesus gives my new resurrection body to me, I will have a hugely different body to the one I am living in right now, and I am so thankful for that. Nevertheless, there will still be something very "Jimmy-ish" about my new body. If you know me now, you will still know me then. I don't know how you will know me, but you will know me. The disciples knew who Jesus was. How did they know Him? They recognized His voice, and they had a certain feeling about His identity.

Jesus' most significant identifiers were the scars on His hands, feet, and sides (see John 20:24–29). I have a few scars, but does that mean I will have them in heaven? Maybe and maybe not. The reasons I may not have them is because my scars are ugly, and they don't mean anything. However, Jesus' scars are the most beautiful thing you will ever see. They mean everything. They are like the most precious jewels that have ever been found. So we might know some people by their scars, but they won't be ugly, and they won't be disabilities. I can imagine saying,

> Look at that man who was always in a wheelchair. I recognize him as the man who never walked. Yet he praised God every day for giving him life and opportunities to share the Good News with others. He doesn't have a wheelchair anymore, but I can see the beauty and meaning God created in the middle of it all. Glory to God!

I don't know if that is exactly what will happen, but I do know God will take everything we have experienced and turn it for our good if we belong to Him.

Jesus' scars are the most beautiful thing you will ever see.

---

3. Glorious

When I say that Jesus' body is glorious, I mean it is anything but common. The apostle Paul said we will be "raised in glory" (1 Corinthians 15:43). Jesus' body was glorious. It traveled to heaven without a spacecraft or a space suit. His new body was surrounded by a brightness or splendor. The prophet Daniel said this about our resurrected bodies:

Those who are wise shall shine

Like the brightness of the firmament,

And those who turn many to righteousness

Like the stars forever and ever (Daniel 12:3 NKJV).

Jesus Himself said, "Then the righteous will shine forth as the sun in the kingdom of their Father. He who has ears to hear, let him hear!" (Matthew 13:43 NKJV). Jesus' appearance was unlike anything His followers had ever seen. Of Jesus' meeting with Moses and Elijah on the Mount of Transfiguration, the apostle Matthew wrote,

His face shone like the sun, and His clothes became as white as the light (Matthew 17:2 NKJV).

Yes, Jesus has a physical body, but it is also a glorious body, more beautiful and amazing than anything you have ever seen.

4. Eternal

I want to make an incredibly careful distinction between two terms: *immortal* and *eternal*. When something is immortal, it means it will never die. Yes, those things that are eternal are also immortal, but they are not *only* immortal. For example, would you want to continue forever in the world in which you currently live with the body you now have? I will answer for you: No, you would not. You want something different. Jesus was at first a mortal who took on immortality and became eternal. He was not resurrected from the dead to continue on with life "as usual." When I say He was mortal, I mean the eternal God willingly chose to take on flesh in Jesus Christ.

Jesus was born with a body that could die, and I mean *really* die. It was not immortal. Could He have died a natural death from old age? That was not in His Father's plan, but presumably He could have. He was a human, and human bodies are subject to disease, decay, and death. However, Jesus' resurrected body was "imperishable" (see 1 Corinthians 15:42 NIV). Jesus can never be a victim of disease, aging, disability, or death. The only hope we have that our bodies will be imperishable is that Jesus is eternal. He is strong and healthy forever. He will never age or become frail. He is not only youthful, but He is also more mature than any person you have ever known. As a human, Jesus is everything Adam would have been if Adam had never sinned. And He is fully in the image of God forever. Jesus, now and forever, will be ideally human according to God's original design and intention.

The Body of a Champion

When Jesus comes again, Christians will instantaneously be like Him. You now have the promise of God that you will have a supranatural, physical, glorious, and eternal body. You will never age or know disease. You will never die. How do I know this? Because one Man has already done it. He is the "author and finisher of *our* faith" (Hebrews 12:2 NKJV). That means He was knocked down by death and the devil, but they could not knock Him out. He got up again, and because He got up, you will get up as well. Jesus is the champion.

When Jesus comes again, Christians will instantaneously be like Him.

I have already written about 1 Corinthians 15 and Hebrews 2, but I want you to see the link between these two texts:

> The last enemy *that* will be destroyed *is* death. For "He has put all things under His feet." But when He says "all things are put under *Him,*" *it is* evident that He who put all things under Him is excepted. Now when all things are made subject to Him, then the Son Himself will also be subject to Him who put all things under Him, that God may be all in all (1 Corinthians 15:26–28 NKJV).

"You have put all things in subjection under his feet."

For in that He put all in subjection under him, He left nothing *that is* not put under him. But now we do not yet see all things put under him. But we see Jesus, who was made a little lower than the angels, for the suffering of death crowned with glory and honor, that He, by the grace of God, might taste death for everyone.

For it was fitting for Him, for whom *are* all things and by whom *are* all things, in bringing many sons to glory, to make the captain of their salvation perfect through sufferings (Hebrews 2:8–10 NKJV).

Both of these texts remind us that Jesus is the "Second Adam." God gave the first Adam dominion over creation, but he lost it to Satan through his disobedience. The Second Adam took it back, and now all things are under His subjection. Jesus is now at the right hand of the Father, ruling over all creation. However, not all of creation is willing to submit to Him. Jesus is King, but He has some very rebellious subjects, including Satan himself. Satan is the one who had the power over death until Jesus pried it from his hands (see Hebrews 2:14–15).

Any power Satan has ever had was delegated to him. God has always had the ultimate authority over death, and Jesus took away any delegated authority Satan previously had. Jesus defeated the devil and death through His own death. Death could not hold Jesus, because He is the champion or "the captain." Even so, Paul says there is still a final victory to be won, and you can be sure that Jesus will win.

CHAPTER 3

Your New Body

The New Testament provides us with details about how and when we will get our new bodies:

> But I do not want you to be ignorant, brethren, concerning those who have fallen asleep, lest you sorrow as others who have no hope. For if we believe that Jesus died and rose again, even so God will bring with Him those who sleep in Jesus.
>
> For this we say to you by the word of the Lord, that we who are alive *and* remain until the coming of the Lord will by no means precede those who are asleep. For the Lord Himself will descend from heaven with a shout, with the voice of an archangel, and with the trumpet of God. **And the dead in Christ will rise first. Then we who are alive *and* remain shall be caught up together with them in the clouds to meet the Lord in the air.** And thus we shall always be with the Lord. Therefore comfort one another with these words (1 Thessalonians 4:13–18 NKJV, bold mine).

We Do Not Sleep

When Jesus comes again at the Rapture, all true believers—both the living and the physically dead—will be immediately and eternally transformed. This new and glorified physical body is what they will have forever. When Paul says some believers have "fallen asleep," he is not referring to "soul sleep," which is the teaching that when believers die, they simply go to sleep when they are buried and stay that way until Jesus comes. No, their bodies are in the ground, but as Paul says, they are "present with the Lord" (2 Corinthians 5:8). If we die ("the dead in Christ"), then although we are no longer in our earthly bodies, our spirits are present with Jesus immediately upon our death. People might be buried in the ground, buried at sea, or even cremated. Regardless, God knows where they are. When Jesus comes again, our physical bodies will be resurrected and transformed into our heavenly bodies. Our bodies will be reunited with our spirits at that point, where we will continue to be "present with the Lord" in our new gloried and eternal state.

Heaven Has Moved

Where is heaven today? I must tell you that heaven has been moved from the place it was before Jesus' resurrection. In Luke 16, Jesus tells a story about someone He knew or knew about. I believe it is a true story and not a parable. Parables use a story to represent a spiritual truth. This story is not representative; it delivers a direct truth about these two men and the afterlife. Jesus also never used the names of the characters in His parables, but He does name the main person in this story:

> There was a certain rich man who was clothed in purple and fine linen and fared sumptuously every day. But there was a certain beggar named Lazarus, full of sores, who was laid at his gate, desiring to be fed with the crumbs which fell from the rich man's table. Moreover the dogs came and licked his sores. So it was that the beggar died, and was carried by the angels to Abraham's bosom. The rich man also died and was buried. And being in torments in Hades, he lifted up his eyes and saw Abraham afar off, and Lazarus in his bosom.
>
> Then he cried and said, "Father Abraham, have mercy on me, and send Lazarus that he may dip the tip of his finger in water and cool my tongue; for I am tormented in this flame." But Abraham said, "Son, remember that in your lifetime you received your good things, and likewise Lazarus evil things; but now he is comforted and you are tormented. And besides all this, between us and you there is a great gulf fixed, so that those who want to pass from here to you cannot, nor can those from there pass to us."
>
> Then he said, "I beg you therefore, father, that you would send him to my father's house, for I have five brothers, that he may testify to them, lest they also come to this place of torment." Abraham said to him, "They have Moses and the prophets; let them hear them." And he said, "No, father Abraham; but if one goes to them from the dead, they will repent." But he said to him, "If they do not hear Moses and the prophets, neither will they be persuaded though one rise from the dead" (Luke 16:19–31 NKJV).

Jesus said there was a beggar named Lazarus who laid at a rich man's gate. He was sick and wanted help. The rich man who lived there "fared sumptuously every day" (v. 19), but he wouldn't help Lazarus.

Then both men died. The angels carried Lazarus to Abraham's bosom. This was heaven in the Old Testament. But the rich man went to hell. In the torment of hell, he looked across some sort of divide and saw Abraham and Lazarus in Abraham's bosom (close to Abraham's chest). The rich man called over and asked if Abraham would send Lazarus to put a drop of water on his tongue, because the rich man was in agony. But Abraham replied he could not because there was a chasm fixed between them, and neither could go to the other side. They could only look at each other. That place, which included both paradise and hell, was called Sheol. In Hebrew thought of the time, heaven and hell were together in the center of the earth.

However, that's not where heaven is now. Ephesians 4:8 says when Jesus ascended, "He led captivity captive." He both descended and ascended. He emptied Abraham's bosom, taking everyone with Him up to the third heaven, where believers who die go now. The first heaven is our atmosphere around us right now. The second is what we call outer space. And the third heaven is the presence of God.

In 2 Corinthians 12:2–7, the apostle Paul said he didn't know if he was "in the body ... or whether out of the body," but he was "caught up to the third heaven." There he saw things that were indescribable, and he called the place "paradise." On the cross, Jesus said the thief next to Him, "Today, you'll be with Me in Paradise" (Luke 23:43 NKJV).

I can't tell you all the differences between paradise before the resurrection and heaven after, but I can tell you that wherever God is, paradise is there also.

How Will Our Bodies Be Redeemed When Jesus Returns?

The apostle Paul gives more details about our new bodies at the return of Christ in a text we looked at earlier:

There is one glory of the sun, another glory of the moon, and another glory of the stars; for *one* star differs from *another* star in glory.

So also *is* the resurrection of the dead. *The body* is sown in corruption, it is raised in incorruption. It is sown in dishonor, it is raised in glory. It is sown in weakness, it is raised in power. It is sown a natural body, it is raised a spiritual body. There is a natural body, and there is a spiritual body. And so it is written, "The first man Adam became a living being." The last Adam *became* a life-giving spirit.

However, the spiritual is not first, but the natural, and afterward the spiritual. The first man *was* of the earth, *made* of dust; the second Man *is* the Lord from heaven. As *was* the *man* of dust, so also *are* those *who are made* of dust; and as *is* the heavenly *Man*, so also *are* those *who are* heavenly. And as we have borne the image of the *man* of dust, we shall also bear the image of the heavenly *Man*.

Now this I say, brethren, that flesh and blood cannot inherit the kingdom of God; nor does corruption inherit incorruption. Behold, I tell you a mystery: We shall not all sleep, but we shall all be changed—in a moment, in the twinkling of an eye, at the last trumpet. For the trumpet will sound, and the dead will be raised incorruptible, and we shall be changed. For this corruptible must put on incorruption, and this mortal *must* put on immortality (1 Corinthians 15:41–53 NKJV).

When Jesus returns, whether we are dead or alive, we will be transformed to become like Him in our bodies.

Paul says the dead in Christ will rise first. He doesn't mean they will rise on one day and other believers will meet Jesus in the Rapture on the next day. There will be perhaps a millisecond between those who are already dead going to meet Jesus and those who are still alive on earth also being caught up with Him. That means the bodies of your dead loved ones will be first in line when Jesus transforms our bodies. You may remember them as old or diseased, but the next time you see them, they will have bodies like Jesus' body. Their bodies will come out of the ground, gathered up from the ashes, or recovered from the sea to rise and meet their spirits. In ancient Christian tradition, Jesus will return and be seen in the eastern sky. So, even today, many people are buried with their heads to the west and their feet to the east so they will be able to rise up and meet Jesus face-to-face. Jesus said His coming is going to be like lightning beginning in the east and spreading to the west (see Matthew 24:27). Jesus doesn't need our help to find His saints, but it is a beautiful ancient symbol to bury people in this way.

Because you are alive and reading this book, I have some important news for you: Paul says there will be a generation of people who will never die. If you're alive when the Rapture happens, you will be immediately changed. The dead in Christ will rise first, but then we who are alive and remain will be "caught up." The concept of the Rapture is derived from the Greek word *harpazo*, which most English translators render as "caught up." But the word *rapture* comes from the Latin Vulgate, which was Jerome's translation of the Greek New Testament. We get the word *rapture* from the Middle French word *rapture*, which came from the Medieval Latin word *rapturo*, which means 'to seize, such as in a kidnapping.' That word was derived from the ancient Latin word *raptus*, which means 'to carry off.' So we will be seized, caught up, and carried off by Jesus, and it will happen "in the twinkling of an eye." If people blink, then they actually could miss it, but believers won't miss it.

If you're alive when the Rapture happens, you will be immediately changed.

I told you in the previous chapter about Jesus' resurrected body. Even more amazing is the fact that your new body will be like His! It will be **supranatural, physical, glorious, and eternal.** In a moment you will be changed. You will have supranatural and supernatural power, strength, and ability like you have never known before. You will be spiritual, physical, and multi-dimensional. Your body will be glorious, in the same way Adam and Eve's bodies were before sin and the Fall and like Jesus' body after the resurrection. You will receive a new, incorruptible, and eternal body that will remain the same for trillions of years. You will be completely conformed to the image of Christ, who is fully in the image of God without distortion. Through sin, the image of God was distorted in us, even while we still bear His image. Jesus Christ, however, is the Second Adam. In Him, the image of God is perfect, unmarred, and unchangeable, and we will be like Him.

When people on earth are exceptionally beautiful or handsome, there is a temptation for them to fall into pride and vanity. But there is no vanity in heaven—there is only humility. We will all know that we are there only by the love and grace poured out on us in Jesus Christ, not by our own efforts or merits. I believe heaven has no mirrors, only light. We won't be gazing at our own reflections and saying, "Oooh! Look at *this*! Where's the swimming pool? I want to show this off!" We will be focused on Jesus, the only One who is worthy of our adoration and praise.

While I want to tell you the sin of pride is not your destiny, I also want you to know that your body will be perfect in every way. As I told you, Adam and Eve were glorious before they sinned. They were naked, and there was nothing shameful or pornographic about it. The glory of God covered their bodies. As I said, Jesus was on the Mount of Transfiguration with Moses and Elijah. The Synoptic Gospel writers said their garments were transfigured and became "white and glistening," brighter than any earthly launderer could ever get them (see Matthew 17:1–8; Mark 9:2–8; Luke 9:28–36). You see, in heaven, you won't need makeup or beauty products because you will be more beautiful than anything you have ever seen on earth.

You won't need sleep in heaven because your body will never get tired. There's neither day nor night because the Lamb is heaven's light (see Revelation 21:23). You will be perfectly whole and healthy. Your body will never age, nor will you ever get sick or die. You will be "incorruptible," because heaven has no funerals, and there's no mourning and no tears.

You'll never get tired, fatigued, injured, or harmed. You will always feel fantastic and full of energy. You will be able to run at full speed for 100 years and never get out of breath. You will travel at the speed of thought into another dimension of space. Or you will be able to sit, talk, and laugh with the same person for 3,000 years. Time will not run out, because heaven has no expiration date. One of the worst things about earth is we just don't have time for each other, but we will in heaven. Here, people move, or they die—but not there. In heaven, you'll be able to know everyone you want to know.

We'll worship Jesus for a million years with heaven's worship music. Still, we will never grow tired. We'll have perfect voices, great harmony, and impeccable rhythm. We can travel the world and universe, or we can sit, eat, and drink and never get full or gain weight. (I personally can't wait for that!) We will be able to do anything we desire in total freedom without restriction.

We'll worship Jesus for a million years with heaven's worship music.

And let me remind you again: all these changes will happen in the twinkling of an eye, and our bodies will take on the same perfection Jesus already has. Therefore, we need to focus on following Jesus and waiting for His return, because we are not ultimately of this world. Sadly, those who do not believe in Jesus will not ever experience this kind of bodily transformation. Maybe you are currently sick or have a disability. You might be discouraged about the imperfections you currently have in your body. But remember this: Jesus is about to fulfill His promise to us. He will soon come again and redeem our earthly bodies. Lift up your head! Look up! Your redemption is drawing near!

PART TWO

Redeemed Minds

CHAPTER 4

A Changed Mind

I have been in ministry for more than four decades. In all that time, I have learned that almost every Christian family has at least one sad story of a family member, immediate or extended, who has serious problems with addiction, sin, or demonic influence. Sometimes we may try to play it off. Someone will come up to us at a family reunion and ask, "How's your Uncle Joe?" You shuffle your feet and mumble something like, "Well, you know old Joe. You know how he is." Everyone chuckles uncomfortably, and that's the end of that part of the conversation, because everyone *does know* how he is. Uncle Joe has problems, and he's had them for a long time. Ultimately, they may kill him.

Christian counselors do great work. With the help of good training, the Bible, and the Holy Spirit, many lives are changed through their efforts. If you are struggling in an area of your life, I advise you to seek help from a Bible-based Christian counselor or a pastor who has experience in counseling. They can really help you and your family, though, sadly, they can't fix everything.

One of the tools many Christian counselors have employed is Cognitive Behavioral Therapy (CBT). As a therapeutic method, it is neutral when it comes to faith. By that, I mean it can be used by a Christian counselor because there is nothing about it that contradicts the Scripture. CBT has three premises:

1. Psychological problems are based on unhelpful ways of thinking.
2. These ways of thinking are based on learned behaviors.
3. We can learn better ways to think and behave and relieve our negative symptoms.[2]

As I said, there's nothing about these presuppositions that undermines biblical teaching. Many people get helped by CBT. However, some people still succumb to negative thought patterns, which lead to unhealthy emotions and destructive behaviors, even after years of counseling. Sometimes our efforts are just not enough.

When Prayer and Fasting Aren't Enough

Casting out demons is one of the ways people would recognize the Messiah and His followers.

> These miraculous signs will accompany those who believe: They will cast out demons in my name, and they will speak in new languages (Mark 16:17; see also Matthew 12:28; Acts 1:7–8; 1 Corinthians 2:4–5; Romans 15:17–19).

Actually, we are not the ones who have the power to cast out de-mons; it is the Holy Spirit working through us in Jesus' name. Even so, some situations are more difficult than others, and there must be work done by Christians and perhaps even by the person who is demon possessed.

> At the foot of the mountain, a large crowd was waiting for them. A man came and knelt before Jesus and said, "Lord, have mercy on my son. He has seizures and suffers terribly. He often falls into the fire or into the water. So I brought him to your disciples, but they couldn't heal him."
>
> Jesus said, "You faithless and corrupt people! How long must I be with you? How long must I put up with you? Bring the boy here to me." Then Jesus rebuked the demon in the boy, and it left him. From that moment the boy was well.
>
> Afterward the disciples asked Jesus privately, "Why couldn't we cast out that demon?"
>
> "You don't have enough faith," Jesus told them. "I tell you the truth, if you had faith even as small as a mustard seed, you could say to this mountain, 'Move from here to there,' and it would move. Nothing would be impossible" (Matthew 17:14–21).

There are many things to explore and learn from this passage, but one thing is certain: not every demon is easy to expel. The same thing is true about sin and thought patterns. Some are just not that easy to change. They take work on everyone's part—the Holy Spirit's, ours, and the person who is afflicted. Even then, some people just can't seem to overcome the thing that is destroying them.

Recently, a close friend lost an adult child to addiction. Plenty of prayers were offered. All possible types of treatment and counseling were pursued. Everyone, including the young adult, turned to God in this time of trouble. Still, the addiction persisted, and it finally took a beautiful young person's life. This leads to two questions: Where was God in this tragedy? Why did this happen?

First, God was where He has always been, ever present and ever helping. He doesn't walk away from us as long as we turn to Him. God didn't abandon this young adult or the parents. He is eternally committed to them.

So why do bad things still happen? The Bible clearly teaches that sin has tainted everything. Sin is both an act and a condition. We *choose* to sin, and sin affects everything around us. God put a natural order into creation. If we drop something off a building, then the law of gravity says it will hit the ground. If we sin, we set certain consequences in motion. Does that mean everything bad that happens to you is a result of your *personal* sin? Of course, it does not. However, once set in motion, sin leads to destruction and even death. Death is sin's ultimate payday (see Romans 6:23). Because of sin, we live in a world where screws come unscrewed. Adam and Eve rebelled against God, and it had some dire effects. Sin distorted their minds and destroyed their bodies.

In a world such as this, how does anything good happen at all? And what hope do we have? Those are really good questions because sin has really messed up our world. Nevertheless, there is an answer to our dilemma. Good does happen even in this sinful world because there is someone somewhere working for our good. Christians call this Someone "God." He is provident, present, and powerful. He does intervene even in this world to heal, save, and set people free. God can and will change hearts, minds, and bodies if we will allow Him to do it.

Through Jesus' resurrection, the Holy Spirit has been renewing our minds. What we once thought, we no longer think. How we once acted is no longer the way we behave. We are new creatures, part of God's new creation, but we still reside in a world that follows the old ways. Sometimes those old patterns of thinking and feeling override the voice of the Holy Spirit and the authority of God's Word in our lives. We are not what we used to be, but we are not who we are going to be. When Jesus returns, He will transform our minds, and it will happen in an instant.

God Wants Transformation

A few years ago, I delivered a series of sermons under the title *I Changed My Mind*, which was later developed into a short book. God wants us to change our minds. The most important things for us to change are what we think and what we do as a result of our thinking. God gave us a free will, which means we can think and behave according to our own choices. The Bible tells us what we ought to do:

> And so, dear brothers and sisters, I plead with you to give your bodies to God because of all he has done for you. Let them be a living and holy sacrifice—the kind he will find acceptable. This is truly the way to worship him. Don't copy the behavior and customs of this world, but let God transform you into a new person by changing the way you think. Then you will learn to know God's will for you, which is good and pleasing and perfect (Romans 12:1–2).

————

The most important things for us to change are what we think and what we do as a result of our thinking.

————

The apostle Paul is telling us not to follow the world's pattern. He is saying we should not become identical to the world and act the way people do who are not believers. We cannot follow the world's ways of behaving. We are to allow God to *transform* us into new people "by changing the way you think." The Greek word translated "transform" is *metamorpoo*, from which we get the word *metamorphosis*. A metamorphosis is a complete change, like a caterpillar that enters a cocoon and emerges as a butterfly. It is still the same animal, but it has gone through a complete change and has a new beginning. God wants us to have that kind of dramatic change in what we think, feel, and do.

How does God want us to change? Paul says God wants to transform the ways we think. If you are a believer, then God did a great work in you when you accepted Jesus as your Lord and Savior. People probably noticed the transformation. Of course, not everything about you changed in an instant. You might have had a dramatic conversion like Paul on the Road to Damascus, but that's not the way most people are converted to the gospel. It's gradual, but it's also noticeable.

God changes your mind, which is the part of your soul that activates or originates behaviors, such as good works. However, your soul is also influenced by your emotions and your surroundings. God created you to do His will, and Paul says that when God transforms your mind, He gives you the ability to follow it. The more God transforms you, the more you will understand His will for you. In the end, you will know God's will, "which is good and pleasing and perfect"

(Romans 12:2). Every day you walk with the Lord, you know more what He wills, and He transforms you by the Holy Spirit more into His image. Even so, remember, you are still in a world tainted by sin. God is changing you, but you are not yet completely changed. That day is still coming. Many things still influence your mind, so you must choose daily to allow God to mature you. When the Rapture comes, the transformation will be complete because, as Paul explains,

> Now our knowledge is partial and incomplete, and even the gift of prophecy reveals only part of the whole picture! But when the time of perfection comes, these partial things will become useless.
>
> When I was a child, I spoke and thought and reasoned as a child. But when I grew up, I put away childish things. Now we see things imperfectly, like puzzling reflections in a mirror, but then we will see everything with perfect clarity. All that I know now is partial and incomplete, but then I will know everything completely, just as God now knows me completely (1 Corinthians 13:9–13).

How Does God Want to Change Our Minds?

The apostle Paul says God already "knows me completely" (1 Corinthians 13:12). There is nothing more God needs to learn about me. He knew me in my mother's womb (see Jeremiah 1:5). God knows everything about me now, down to the hairs on my head (see Luke 12:7). He knows my innermost thoughts (see Hebrews 4:13). God knows how many days I will live (see Job 14:5). You may have heard your pastor say that Jesus was thinking about *you* while He was on the cross. I have heard someone make fun of that idea. Why would Jesus think about *me*? I will tell you why: Jesus is God. If He knows your birth, your last day, your every thought, and how many hairs you've got, then you can believe you were on His mind when He died for you. You were most certainly in God's thoughts. There is not a secret, a need, or a pain He does not know.

Your Attitude

Your attitude is a settled way of thinking or feeling about someone or something that will often show in your behavior. Your attitude can come from several sources, such as your family, your education, your feelings, and your experiences. We often think in certain patterns due to our up-bringing, education, experiences, and emotions. Before you can change your mind about anything, your attitude must change. Except for your salvation, your attitude will affect your life more than anything else.

Except for your salvation, your attitude will affect your life more than anything else.

The New Testament tells us how to have the right attitude:

May God, who gives this patience and encouragement, help you live in complete harmony with each other, as is fitting for followers of Christ Jesus. Then all of you can join together with one voice, giving praise and glory to God, the Father of our Lord Jesus Christ (Romans 15:5–6).

———

So then, since Christ suffered physical pain, you must arm yourselves with the same attitude he had, and be ready to suffer, too. For if you have suffered physically for Christ, you have finished with sin. You won't spend the rest of your lives chasing your own desires, but you will be anxious to do the will of God (1 Peter 4:1–2).

The apostle Peter tells us how to have the right attitude toward suffering by using Jesus as our example.

Attitude is also seen in your body's posture, which demonstrates your mental state. When I preach, I watch the responses people make with their faces and bodies. I have a good idea what they are thinking by how their bodies are responding. Attitude also relates to the orientation of an aircraft relative to the direction of flight. I am a pilot, so when I am flying, I adjust the plane's attitude to be nose-up, nose-level, or nose-down. The plane's attitude indicates a lot about how well a plane is traveling and the direction it is going.

The people you surround yourself with will influence your attitude because attitudes usually travel in groups. Certain families and businesses have attitudes. If I walk into a Chick-fil-A restaurant, I expect a certain level of interest, courtesy, and service that I may not get from another fast-food establishment. I notice different airlines have their own unique attitudes, both good and bad. The Bible tells us not to conform to the world's attitudes, and you don't have to bend your attitude to those around you, especially if they don't have a positive attitude. Instead, we should fit our thinking to God's perfect will—His attitude.

When you consider how you have acted or reacted in the past, think about how you have behaved. Have you been grateful, gracious, and positive? Or have you been ungrateful, rude, and negative? Have you chosen forgiveness or bitterness? Your attitude influences your present, but it will also determine your future. If you have a bad attitude, then it will very likely prevent you from enacting God's plans for your life.

You choose your attitudes. Do not think they are caused by other people or your circumstances. Some people think they can change their attitudes if they only change their environment or circumstances, but it simply isn't true. Think about how the apostle Paul responded to his arrest and beating in Philippi in Acts 16. He could have become angry and bitter at being thrown into prison. However, at midnight he was praising and worshipping God. If he counted on his circumstances to give him the right attitude, then Paul was never going to get the right circumstances. Instead, he let his relationship with the living God shape how He would respond.

You choose your attitudes.

Happiness is a choice. You might choose misery because others have made you miserable, but you don't have to react that way. You can choose happiness right now. Allow the Holy Spirit to transform you and give God gratitude for who He is and what He is doing in your life. If you want to be miserable, then God will allow you to do it. But if you want to be happy, then the choice is yours too.

God will reward good attitudes, but He will also discipline us when we have bad ones. Like a good parent, He wants to reach you before your bad attitudes develop into bad habits. God will always love you, and because He loves you, He will discipline you:

God opposes the proud but gives grace to the humble (James 4:6).

Pride is an attitude, and God will oppose you if you become prideful. He will still love you, but He will also discipline you. God is not going to allow His children to keep traveling down the wrong path. Choose humility because it is the only way to succeed:

Humble yourselves before the Lord, and he will lift you up in honor (James 4:10).

God waits for us to change our attitudes so He can bless and honor us. He really loves you, but that means He loves you enough not to leave you alone with a bad attitude. You will know discipline is over when you learn your lesson because God wants you to see how your attitudes affect your behavior. One day, if you are a believer, you will serve God and reign with Him. He wants to grow you up to be like Him, so He's going to address your attitudes now.

Attitudes precede and predict your future. A good attitude leads to success, favor, and promotion, just as a bad attitude will precede failure, disfavor, and demotion. When you face difficulties, don't let your emotions or someone else's opinion determine your attitude. God's

Word is the best source and indicator for the attitude you should have. King David always looked to the Lord, even in the worst times. In the book of Psalms, he shows us how we are to respond to hard times. If your own experiences weigh you down and distort your vision, then turn to the Word of God. It will tell you about God's plans for you and help you adopt the right attitude for your circumstances. Even when people around you are more gifted, talented, or attractive, you attitude is the key to your success, and God's Word is the key to your attitude.

I know you try; I really know you do. Your attitude isn't perfect, and neither is mine. God wants us to respond to the world around us with faith and trust in Him, but we continue to allow our circumstances, our sinful flesh, and the devil to influence us. Keep relying on the Holy Spirit. I promise a new day is coming when you will be transformed instantaneously. Jesus will return to rapture the Church, and we will all be changed. Nevertheless, God does not want you to wait for that day before you show any concern about your attitude. He wants you to be conformed to the image of Christ. Jesus endured great suffering while maintaining a godly attitude. He is changing you now, and He will change you completely when He comes again.

Your Views of Success

How does the world view success? It depends on who you ask. Some people look at wealth and financial prosperity as the key indicators of success. As long as they have enough money to buy anything they want, they think of themselves as successful. Some think of popularity as a sign of success. They will sell their souls for popularity.

They count followers and "likes" on social media the same way other people count their dollars. Still others think power and influence define success for them. If they achieve a high rank with enough power, then they believe they have arrived. There are people who mark success based on their relationships, which is not a bad thing, except when those relationships happen outside the Bible's moral standards. Many people seek success through their intellects and educational accomplishments. Others see success in those who have special gifts or talents, such as artistic or athletic abilities. And then there are some people who believe they have become successful when they live in peace and safety, which again is not a negative goal, but Jesus teaches us that our security is in our heavenly Father (see Matthew 6:25–34).

Jesus teaches us that our security is in our heavenly Father.

When you think about how the world defines success, none of the options are evil in and of themselves, but you can still be a failure even if you have all of them. The world strives after all these things because it thinks they are what make us successful. However, none of these fit God's definition of success. I do not want to have all the world's standards for success only enter eternity and discover that I failed in my striving to succeed.

How then should we define success? Jesus Christ is the only true example. He did not meet the world's standards during His earthly ministry. Jesus was popular for a time, but in the end, He was executed on a cross. The authorities despised Him. Jesus did not have strength or security according to the world's standards. The prophet Isaiah says there was nothing about Him in the natural that was unusually attractive (see Isaiah 53:2). Jesus wasn't wealthy. He was even buried in a borrowed tomb. Yet Jesus was the most successful person to ever live.

Don't fall for the world's view of success. It will cause you to think you are a success when you're really a failure and a failure when you are truly a success. You may hold your children to worldly definitions of success, and yet you ignore their spiritual condition. Raise your children to love God more than anything else. If you do, then they will succeed. Wrong views of success will cause you to make poor decisions about the direction of your life. Many of the most valuable people in society do not get paid millions of dollars, such as police officers, firefighters, teachers, members of the military, and other similar professions. They sacrifice wealth for the sake of a more noble calling. If you do everything the world tells you to do to succeed, then you will miss the deeper fulfillment of following God's plan for your life. He wants the best for you, so do your best for Him.

Jesus is coming again—very soon. He told us to how to prepare for His return. You do not know God's timing, so you should always be ready. How can you be ready? First, you only have one option while you are still living, and that is to follow Him. If you know Jesus, then you will go to heaven, but if you don't, then you will go to hell. If you are alive when the Rapture occurs, Jesus will take you with Him if you have made Him your Lord and Savior. He will not care about your money, fame, or education. He will only see that you have given your heart to Him. I implore you not to let anything get in the way of your relationship with Jesus Christ. Do not neglect Him until it is too late. If you know Jesus, then live for Him and treat others with love. You will have everything you need for success on earth *and* in heaven. All things will be fully revealed and rewarded when He comes again.

Your Response to Worry and Anxiety

Anxiety is a state of unease or nervousness about an event, person, or problem that is out of your control. If you can't control it, then you begin to feel anxious about it. Worry happens when you mentally dwell on a difficulty or trouble. It often becomes chronic and ongoing. Of the two, worry is usually a milder emotion related to something specific, while anxiety is consuming and more general. However, these two emotions relate to each other, and they also have connections to fear, which I will discuss later in this chapter.

Paul told the Philippian believers not to be anxious (see Philippians 4:6). In the US, 40 million adults have been diagnosed with anxiety disorders.[3] Psychological distress can actually reduce your life expectancy.[4] Jesus told His followers not to worry about their lives, or what they would eat, drink, or wear (see Matthew 6:25). He told them not to even worry about tomorrow, because tomorrow has its own set of troubles (see Matthew 6:34).

The root of all worry and anxiety is the same—it is an *orphan spirit*. God absolutely loves being our Father. Jesus began His instructions about worry by telling us that God cares for us as a Father. God loves and adores you. He knows everything you're facing, and He wants to be present with you in every circumstance.

Worry and anxiety are neither normal nor inevitable. Yes, they are common, but you do not have to take them on as a believer. We often give in to worry because we think it is normal. However, it steals from us, our families, and our joy. It puts a barrier in our relationship with our Father. We worry because we allow anxiety into our lives. God wants to give us authority over those feelings. He would not ask you not to worry or not to be anxious if it were impossible.

God will give you the power to overcome those emotions. First, you must begin to see worry and anxiety as adversaries; they are the enemy. The devil wants to put things into your life to intimidate you. Attack worry and anxiety every day. Don't sit passively and let them rob you. Second, turn your thoughts into prayers. Pray until victory comes (see Philippians 4:6–7). Wake up every morning and tell God what is bothering you. Thank Him that He loves you, hears you, and will answer you. The enemy wants you to think you are alone, but he is a liar. Your Father is available to you for every circumstance. Third, stand in faith and confess God as your loving Father. He is your answer to worry and anxiety. Will you still fail to address worry and anxiety at times? Yes, you will. Even so, respond in faith. When Jesus returns, all worry and anxiety will cease, but until then, take your concerns to your Father.

Your Feelings of Insecurity

We experience insecurity because we lack confidence or have anxiety about ourselves. We can experience insecurity in many different ways. I believe all of us encounter insecurity because of circumstances in our lives. Some people respond by turning to God, while others turn away from Him. When you encounter insecurity, you can allow either God or the devil to work in your life. You might choose to become insecure, falsely secure, or secure in Christ Jesus. He is the only real cure for insecurity.

Why do people feel insecure? Or what makes people feel secure? One of the most popular ways for people to find security is in money. In fact, we use the term "securities" to talk about financial instruments. Money is not a bad thing in itself, but if you think money is what makes your secure, then you will be disappointed. Jesus talked about the "deceitfulness of riches" (see Matthew 13:22; Mark 4:19). Money is important, and it can be a blessing, but only Christ can make you truly secure. Paul told the Philippians,

> Not that I was ever in need, for I have learned how to be content with whatever I have. I know how to live on almost nothing or with everything. I have learned the secret of living in every situation, whether it is with a full stomach or empty, with plenty or little (Philippians 4:11–12).

If Jesus is in your life, then you can have security regardless of how much money is in your bank account.

Some people find security in their appearance. Even believers can fall into this trap. We want to look our best, but all of us will age, and our looks will eventually change. Some of the most beautiful people suffer from low self-esteem. The beauty industry itself can be quite brutal and exploitive in the way it treats women. Real beauty is not only in appearance.

Another major cause of insecurity comes from "comparing up." Some people will drive into a parking lot and immediately notice nicer cars than the one they are driving. Many of those same people feel tormented by that experience. I recommend occasionally comparing down, which means becoming aware of those who have not experienced the same blessings you have. Give God thanks for what He has allowed you to have. Even better, give up the habit of comparison.

God wants believers to think differently from the world. Psalm 91 provides God's antidote for insecurity:

> Those who live in the shelter of the Most High
>> will find rest in the shadow of the Almighty.
> This I declare about the LORD:
> He alone is my refuge, my place of safety;
>> he is my God, and I trust him (vv. 1–2).

In verse 2, the psalmist says the Lord is our refuge and place of safety, and we should trust in Him. Where you turn will be your security. If you turn to God, then you will recognize that money, relationships, and other people are not your sources of security.

The psalmist continues by telling of God's great promises:

> For he will rescue you from every trap
>> and protect you from deadly disease.

He will cover you with his feathers.

> He will shelter you with his wings.

> His faithful promises are your armor and protection.

Do not be afraid of the terrors of the night,

> nor the arrow that flies in the day.

Do not dread the disease that stalks in darkness,

> nor the disaster that strikes at midday.

Though a thousand fall at your side,

> though ten thousand are dying around you,

> these evils will not touch you.

Just open your eyes,

> and see how the wicked are punished.

If you make the LORD your refuge,

> if you make the Most High your shelter,

no evil will conquer you;

> no plague will come near your home.

For he will order his angels

> to protect you wherever you go.

They will hold you up with their hands

> so you won't even hurt your foot on a stone.

You will trample upon lions and cobras;

> you will crush fierce lions and serpents under your feet!

(Psalm 91:3–13).

The psalmist knows his security is in God. The Lord promised to be with him, protect him from harm, and trample down his enemies. This is a man who does not have to live with fear and insecurity, because God will fight for him.

The psalm ends with God as the source of security:

The LORD says, "I will rescue those who love me.
    I will protect those who trust in my name.
When they call on me, I will answer;
    I will be with them in trouble.
I will rescue and honor them.
I will reward them with a long life
    and give them my salvation" (Psalm 91:14–16).

"I will give them my salvation." That is God's promise to us even now. When Jesus returns, we will see Him for who He is. He will be our salvation, and all insecurity will melt into the security we have in Him.

Your Relationship with Fear

Next to the command to love, "Do not fear" is one of the most frequent commands in the Bible. God does not want us to live in fear. He did not create us to fear. He created us to live in peace. God created us in peace, and Jesus is the Prince of Peace. However, the devil wants us to live in fear.

God does not want us to live in fear. He did not create us to fear. He created us to live in peace.

In the Garden of Gethsemane, the night before Jesus' death, Jesus was in agony (see Luke 22:39–47). The Greek word *agonia* means 'great fear or distress.' In that moment, Jesus felt more fear than any human being has ever experienced. Luke says that Jesus' sweat became "like great drops of blood" (v. 44). The medical term for this condition is *hematohidrosis,* which is a rare condition in which small blood vessels leading to the sweat glands rupture under conditions of intense stress. Jesus experienced real fear, but He also defeated it. Jesus actually shows us how we can have victory over fear.

Why did Jesus experience fear in the garden, and why did He experience fear at all? First, Jesus could identity with us as human beings. He is both fully God and fully man. As a human, Jesus identifies with us:

> So then, since we have a great High Priest who has entered heaven, Jesus the Son of God, let us hold firmly to what we believe. This High Priest of ours understands our weaknesses, for he faced all of the same testings we do, yet he did not sin. So let us come boldly to the throne of our gracious God. There we will receive his mercy, and we will find grace to help us when we need it most.
>
> Every high priest is a man chosen to represent other people in their dealings with God. He presents their gifts to God and offers sacrifices for their sins. And he is able to deal gently with ignorant and wayward people because he himself is subject to the same weaknesses (Hebrews 4:14–5:2).

Jesus was tempted in every way that we are, yet He was without sin. What tempted Him in the Garden of Gethsemane? When Jesus entered the garden, He instructed His disciples,

Keep watch and pray, so that you will not give in to temptation. For the spirit is willing, but the body is weak! (Matthew 26:41).

Jesus was hinting to them about what would soon happen. He was showing extra concern for them in anticipation of an especially stressful and traumatic event.

Three times Jesus prayed and told the Father that He really didn't want to go through with what was about to happen. In the end, He said to the Father,

Yet I want your will to be done, not mine (Luke 22:42).

Jesus acted above His fears. As His followers, we should follow His example and act above our fears. Fear will always be present to some extent, but Jesus is our High Priest who understands every circumstance we face. Our loving Father promises to give us victory through the Holy Spirit. Jesus knows exactly how we feel. He experienced fear in the garden to identify with us so that we could identify with Him.

Second, Jesus knew what He was about to experience on the cross. He died the most painful and grisly death imaginable, and He knew every single detail of what was about to come. At Gethsemane, He went before the Father three times and asked God to remove Him from the situation. Immediately, an angel came and strengthened Him after Jesus yielded to the will of His Father. Luke says Jesus then prayed even *more* earnestly. Only then did He sweat blood. His stress was at its highest level. Jesus knew everything He would suffer, yet He did it for our sake.

Third, Jesus felt fear because Satan, the real spirit of fear, launched a full-scale attack against Him. Fear is not something—it is *someone*. You must understand this about the nature of the devil: He is an opportunist who will assault you when you are at your weakest and most vulnerable. When you are hurting, he presses in and tries to do his worst. Jesus was weak and troubled in the Garden of Gethsemane, so Satan thought it was an opportune time to come at Jesus with a spirit of fear. But Paul writes,

> For God has not given us a spirit of fear and timidity, but of power, love, and self-discipline (2 Timothy 1:7).

The devil can't control your thoughts, but he can certainly influence them. On the other hand, God will never use fear to control your life.

God will never use fear to control your life.

Not all fear is bad. The Bible refers to the *fear of the Lord*, which means a deep reverence for God. This is a positive emotion rather than a negative one. However, most fear is not of God. The writer of Hebrews says,

> Because God's children are human beings—made of flesh and blood—the Son also became flesh and blood. For only as a human being could he die, and only by dying could he break the power of the devil, who had the power of death. Only in this way could he

set free all who have lived their lives as slaves to the fear of dying (Hebrews 2:14–15).

Ultimately, all fear is the fear of death. You may think you have a fear of snakes, but you really have a fear of dying from a snake bite! If you think about it, then you will realize all fears come from the fear of death. We fear those things that can harm us, and the ultimate harm is death.

The good news is if you are a believer, then you will never die. The fear of death is a deception Satan uses to keep people in bondage. As a believer, you will never experience a moment of death. Unless Jesus takes you in the Rapture, your body will die, but one day God will reunite it with your spirit. The instant your eyes close on earth, they will open in heaven. The moment you go numb here, your senses will come alive there. When you take your last breath here, you take your first breath there.

When the devil tries to put the fear of death in you, understand that it is just a demonic spirit trying to give you a negative view of the future so you will make fear-based decisions. Faith comes from the Spirit of God. It tells you about a positive future, so you will make faith-filled decisions that God will honor. Faith gives you hope, and hope does not let you down (see Romans 5:5).

God wants you to be able to tell the difference between types of fear (see 1 John 4:1). You must be able to discern between good and bad fear. I have been telling you about demonic, paralyzing fear, but there is also good fear, such as when you look up and a car is coming straight toward you in oncoming traffic. When fear is good, it is circumstantial. If a car is coming into your lane, then once it moves over, the fear passes. Bad fear does not end. It will constantly torment you and cause you to think something bad is always ready to happen. Good fear will protect you, but bad fear will paralyze you and make you unable to respond in a useful way. Good fear is constructive, and it will lead you to do the right thing. Bad fear will confuse your judgment and give you a fatalistic attitude. Good fear will empower you to do seemingly impossible acts in difficult situations. Adrenaline will make you able to perform almost superhuman deeds. On the other hand, bad fear will enslave you. You are a child of God, but your soul's enemy wants to do everything possible to make you a slave to fear.

Persistent fear is born of the devil, but lasting peace comes from God. Peace is the opposite of fear. Isaiah says, "There is no peace for the wicked" (Isaiah 48:22). That is why the devil has no peace. If you rebel against God, then you will not be able to have peace, even if you try. Peace is God's property, but the devil lives in the land of fear. When God is present, there is peace; when the devil is present, there is fear. Fear does not mean you are demon possessed, but that the devil is trying to influence you to do the wrong thing. Fear is expecting the devil to move; faith is expecting God to move. As I said earlier, you choose your attitude. You can fix your eyes on the devil or on God.

**Peace is God's property, but the
devil lives in the land of fear.**

Do you want to overcome fear in your life? Then do what Jesus did. Jesus felt fear in the Garden of Gethsemane, but He was open and honest with His Father. The devil wants you to keep secrets, but God wants the truth from you. Jesus said, "Father, I feel the fear. I don't want to do this." The truth will actually make you free. When you are honest with God, the Holy Spirit can help you deal with your fears. Submit your fears to Him because they are real even when they are not right. Then allow the Spirit to help you to act above them. When Jesus prayed to His Father, He acted above His fears and submitted His will to the Father's. An angel came to strengthen Jesus, and God will come to minister to you as well. Focus on God's presence and love. How big is the devil? Even more, how big is your God? Remember, the Lord is omnipresent; the devil is not. The universe cannot contain our God. Satan is just a created being. Jesus rejoiced because of God's presence. On the way to the cross, Satan was telling Jesus that He had disappointed His Father and that He was a huge failure, However, Jesus knew His Father would not leave Him in the place of death. In the same way, God is always present with you. When you open your eyes to the spiritual realm, fear will disappear.

The author of Hebrews says angels are ministering spirits sent to render aid to God's people (see Hebrews 1:14). An angel ministered to Jesus in the Garden of Gethsemane. Do you realize there are angels all around you? You cannot see these spirits with your physical eyes, but as a believer, you can have spiritual eyes to walk by faith and not by sight. When you walk by faith with the Lord before you, you cannot be moved. Choose the attitude of Jesus in the Garden of Gethsemane. Then you will know the truth—and the truth will set you free.

Why Do Our Minds Need Transformation?

When Jesus comes again, He will transform your mind completely. If that is so, then why do you need to concern yourself with how you think and feel right now? In the book of Romans, Paul says we are changed—transformed—by the renewal of our minds (see Romans 12:2). If that is all going to happen in an instant with the Rapture, then you might think you don't need to be concerned about it in the present. However, Paul also says that God created us for good works (see Ephesians 2:10).

When we become followers of Jesus, the Holy Spirit begins to transform us into the likeness of Christ (see 1 Corinthians 2:16). God created humans in His image, but sin marred our likeness to Him. As God renews our minds, we become more and more the people He designed us to be. The apostle John says, "Those who say they live in God should live their lives as Jesus did" (1 John 2:6).

I do not believe your mind will reach perfection in a world tainted by sin. You will still need the Holy Spirit to help you define success. You will still have to cast your cares on Jesus. When you experience trials, read James chapter 1. Make your requests known to God. God will give you the power to take more control of your life so you can overcome worry and replace it with *peace*. Acknowledge your need for God. Turn to Him, confess your weakness, and pray for His perspective. Trust in God's grace. Embrace your weaknesses and remember that tribulation produces *strength* and *hope*, which provide *security*. Identify and admit your fears and submit them to God. Focus on God—He is always present with you, and He loves you. I pray the power of the Holy Spirit will rest on you so you will know the riches of Jesus as your source of sanity, confidence, and power.

When Jesus returns, your mind will be completely transformed. You will know that you are a success because the riches of God's grace will be real and present for you. All fear and anxiety will disappear. You will never worry again about your security because you will be held in the arms of your Savior. All fear will cease as you join the resurrected Lord in the air. Why do I tell you these things about your mind in a book about the Rapture? Because in this world our minds are under constant assault. We need to know that not only can we overcome in this life, but also the end of our warfare is very near. When Jesus returns, our minds will be eternally redeemed and forever at perfect peace! Look up because your redemption is drawing near!

PART THREE

Redeemed Pleasure

CHAPTER 5

How We Were Meant to Be

As I told you in the introduction, you were redeemed the day you invited Jesus into your heart and life to become your Savior and Lord. One day in the future, you will be with Him in a beautiful, pleasure-filled heaven. You will experience real comfort and blissful rest with your senses heightened. In heaven you will not lack for anything. All pain and fear will be in the past. The presence of God will surround you. All these things will begin on the day Jesus returns.

Who are we as humans and what is our essential nature? These seem like high-minded questions, and they are, to an extent. One branch of metaphysics, which is part of the larger study of philosophy, is called *ontology*. Ontology is the study of the "nature of being." In layperson's terms, ontology asks the question about who we are as humans in the very nature of our being. Christians who study ontology ask these deep questions: *How did God create us? What was His divine plan for us from the very beginning?* Why are these important questions? Because God created Adam to be and do certain things, and when Jesus, the "Second Adam," returns, He will restore us to God's original intent.

Even more, God has called believers to live in the present as He originally intended *in the beginning* and according to the way He will eternally redeem us *when Christ returns*. In this way, ontology is intimately related to eschatology, the study of "end things." What God originally created humans to be is what we will be when the Kingdom comes in its fullness. For example, as people who have been redeemed, we cannot intentionally live in disharmony with others.

God has called believers to live in the present as He originally intended *in the beginning* and according to the way He will eternally redeem us *when Christ returns*.

Before Adam and Eve sinned, they lived in perfect harmony in the perfect Garden of Eden. *Eden* means 'pleasure and delight.' They would never have known pain or suffering if they had simply obeyed God. When Jesus returns, we will be perfectly at peace with God and others. The Bible begins and ends in a perfect garden. Then how should we live now? The apostle Paul gives this answer:

> If it is possible, as much as it depends on you, live peaceably with all men (Romans 12:18 NKJV).

I understand we cannot always live in perfect harmony with others, but as redeemed people, we should do our utmost to live peacefully.

All through Romans chapter 12, Paul tells the Roman church how to live as "Kingdom people," or people who have already been redeemed. They are not to be "conformed to this world" but be "transformed" (resurrected) people (vv. 1–3). That is the *very nature* of your being now that you are in Christ Jesus.

If you are a parent, then your children will sometimes challenge your instructions with two words: "Why not?" You have a few choices in how you will respond to this protest. You can simply say, "Because I said so." I know I said this when my children were younger. It is the shortest and most efficient answer, though not always the most effective. You can also respond by having a longer discussion or argument about the reasons you have given this particular prohibition. That strategy has its own drawbacks, because not everything is open to question and discussion. Instead, try this: "You are not going to do that *because that is not the kind of people we are.*" You probably don't realize that you will have just made an ontological argument for why your child should obey. You are telling your child that in his or her *very nature*, as a member of your family, disobedience is not who he or she really is. Your child may choose to disobey, but they will do it knowing that they are acting outside of their nature as a member of your family. Paul is telling us how people should act in God's family, by their *very nature*. We were created to be holy and obedient and to follow our Father's purpose, but we often act contrary to whom God created us to be.

Do you know your Creator wants good for you? He wants you to be the person He created you to be. In fact, God's divine intention was never for humans to sin or suffer at all. He wanted us to be obedient and enjoy the full benefits of His presence. God is a good parent—the best parent in the universe. What good parent would ever want their children to feel pain, loss, or suffering? I can speak for myself: I would take on mountains of pain before I would want to see my kids or grandkids hurt. God is a far better Father than I will ever be, so He also doesn't want His children to suffer.

————

Do you know your Creator wants good for you? He wants you to be the person He created you to be.

————

From where, then, did human suffering originate? The biblical answer is unmistakably clear: Adam's and Eve's sinful rebellion ushered pain and suffering into the human race. God created them to be like Him, in His image (Genesis 1:26–27). However, the first humans chose to act in disobedience, contrary to their created nature. God describes the results of their fateful actions:

> To the woman He said:
> "I will greatly multiply your sorrow and your conception;
> In pain you shall bring forth children;
> Your desire *shall be* for your husband,
> And he shall rule over you" (Genesis 3:16 NKJV).

The phrase translated "your desire *shall be* for your husband" means a wife will want to dominate her husband, but he will dominate her. There will be a constant battle for control in the relationship. The wonderful peace and harmony Adam and Eve had in their relationship was now gone as they vied for control.

The Lord continued:

Then to Adam He said, "Because you have heeded the voice of your wife, and have eaten from the tree of which I commanded you, saying, 'You shall not eat of it':

"Cursed *is* the ground for your sake;
In toil you shall eat *of* it
All the days of your life.
Both thorns and thistles it shall bring forth for you,
And you shall eat the herb of the field.
In the sweat of your face you shall eat bread
Till you return to the ground,
For out of it you were taken;
For dust you *are,*
And to dust you shall return" (Genesis 3:17–19 NKJV).

At that moment, pain and suffering joined themselves to the human race. Ever since that time, people have experience four types of pain and suffering:

1. *Emotional pain:* rejection, loss, failure, verbal abuse, emotional abuse, divorce
2. *Physical pain:* illness, accidents, violence, death
3. *Mental pain:* confusion, deception, lies, ignorance, poverty, spiritual attacks, mental illness
4. *Relational and family pain:* dysfunction, rebellion, break-ups, betrayal, unmet needs, dominance

Adam and Eve could neither conceive of nor calculate the disastrous consequences of their sinful decision. But here is the good news: Jesus is returning soon, and on that day, you will never again experience pain. He is redeeming our pleasure. He is giving back Eden.

CHAPTER 6

Times of Perplexity and Lawlessness

Look again at what Jesus says about His return:

> And there will be signs in the sun, in the moon, and in the stars; and on the earth distress of nations, with perplexity, the sea and the waves roaring; men's hearts failing them from fear and the expectation of those things which are coming on the earth, for the powers of the heavens will be shaken. Then they will see the Son of Man coming in a cloud with power and great glory. Now when these things begin to happen, look up and lift up your heads, because your redemption draws near (Luke 21:25–28 NKJV).

Jesus is saying people will be perplexed when they witness the signs and experience the distress before He returns. To be perplexed means they will have no answer. *Perplexity* is intense puzzlement and confusion at the complexity of a situation. Does this sound familiar to you? It should, because that is what is happening in the world at the present moment—there are problems with no answers, and no one is able to step forward and solve them.

Jesus also says the end will happen in one generation. In just a single generation, we will see all these events fulfilled. He says, "Assuredly, I say to you, this generation will by no means pass away till all things take place" (Matthew 24:34 NKJV). So when you see these things start happening, you will know the end is near. The end doesn't happen over a period of 200 to 300 years—Jesus said the generation that sees these things start happening will see *all things* fulfilled. Jesus was not speaking about His own generation during His time on earth, because everyone in that generation died. I believe Jesus was talking about *our* generation.

You may be pulling out your old history book and looking at all the cataclysmic events that have happened since the time of Christ. You're wondering how this generation stands apart from all those that went before. I will readily admit that each generation has had natural disasters, disease, famine, despots, and dictators. Some of those evil leaders were so bad that people wondered if they were the Antichrist. They might have had the *spirit* of the Antichrist, but they weren't the real thing. He is still to come. Yes, every generation has had *some* signs, but the end generation will have *every* sign.

How long is a generation? In Psalm 90:10 Moses wrote:

The days of our lives *are* seventy years;
And if by reason of strength *they are* eighty years (NKJV).

Israel became a nation again on May 14, 1948. That means we have passed 70 years since that event. I don't set exact dates for when the end will come, but Jesus said the generation that sees the beginning of these things will see the end. By my best count, the end times are happening even now. What we see occurring in Israel today is one of those signs.

Yes, every generation has had *some* signs, but the end generation will have *every* sign.

I do not know exactly how long we have left before Jesus returns, but we are seeing all the signs pointing to His arrival. For example, Jesus says, "Because lawlessness will abound, the love of many will grow cold" (Matthew 24:12 NKJV). He is telling us that human depravity and rebellion against God are going to rise to a deafening crescendo. *Lawlessness* doesn't mean kids won't obey their teachers, drivers will break speed limits, or taxpayers will cheat the IRS. Those things certainly are lawless, but they aren't what Jesus means. He is speaking about *rebellion against God*. Of course, rebellion against human authority grows out of rebellion against God, but while those two are related, they are not synonymous. The Greek word for "lawlessness" in this passage is *anomia* ('without law'), and it specifically refers to *rebellion against God*.

Lawlessness as Misplaced Love

The apostle Paul describes the days leading up to the coming of Christ like this:

Let no one deceive you by any means; for *that Day will not come* unless the falling away comes first, and the man of sin is revealed, the son of perdition (2 Thessalonians 2:3 NKJV).

Another way to translate the phrase "falling away" is *apostasy*. Paul is saying people will turn away from the truth. He wasn't referring to the way the world often rejects God; he meant that people in the Church will reject the truth of God's Word. We are witnessing this happen right now in our generation.

Paul gives an even fuller description of lawlessness in his second letter to Timothy:

But know this, that in the last days perilous times will come: For men will be lovers of themselves, lovers of money, boasters, proud, blasphemers, disobedient to parents, unthankful, unholy, unloving, unforgiving, slanderers, without self-control, brutal, despisers of good, traitors, headstrong, haughty, lovers of pleasure rather than lovers of God (2 Timothy 3:1–4 NKJV).

Paul's list is extensive. How many of these things do we see in our current generation?

Paul lists 18 negative actions that will typify human behavior before Jesus returns. Halfway through the list, Paul says people will be *unloving*. What makes that particular behavior so interesting is he says they will be "lovers," but they will love something other than God or people. In fact, the behaviors he lists are unloving toward God, others, or both. The Greek word translated "unloving" in this passage is *astorgoi*, which means 'without natural affection.' They don't even have the love that normally should accompany human existence. They don't love their families, and they certainly don't love God. Consider the number of parents killing their children and children killing their parents today. Stories such as these were unheard of 30 or 40 years ago, but they're commonplace today.

People do love themselves, though. Boasting, pride, blasphemy, disobedience, unthankfulness, unholiness, slander, lack of self-control, brutality, hating goodness, betrayal, stubbornness, and haughtiness all share a close connection. All of them operate as if *I* am the most important person. It's as if we are saying, "You don't matter. God doesn't matter. I am the only one who matters." Our culture has built a whole industry around this list of vices. Spend an hour on social media, and you will see what I mean. Some people have even made a living off doing nothing except promoting themselves and focusing on these behaviors. We call them "social influencers." They haven't accomplished anything except to be noticed through self-promotion. Not all social influencers are bad. In fact, some use their influence for good. But those who engage in these sinful kinds of vices have proven that our culture elevates those who openly engage in sin.

Think about how much our contemporary culture focuses on self-love. People are told to love themselves unconditionally because that is the only way they will be healthy, happy, and whole. We should love ourselves but not to the exclusion of loving God and others. Jesus didn't say that love of self was the greatest commandment or one "like unto it" (see Matthew 22:36–40 KJV). He told us to love God and others. We should know who we are in God's eyes, but we should not think of ourselves more highly than we ought to think (see Romans 12:1–3). Paul is writing about those who lift themselves up and ignore God. We don't really need to be encouraged to love ourselves, nor do we need to hate ourselves.

We should know who we are in God's eyes, but we should not think of ourselves more highly than we ought to think.

We should see ourselves as we really are, which is how God sees us. We are sinners who have been saved only by the love, grace, and righteousness of Jesus Christ. The Greek term Paul uses here is *philautos,* which means 'self-loving or self-centered.' Believers are never encouraged to become self-centered or self-focused. The first minute you decide to become the center of your own existence is the same minute you choose to destroy your relationships with God and others. "Lovers of self" may head up Paul's list because it is the essence of every other sin. Once we take our eyes off God and put them on ourselves, we open the door for our flesh to take over.

People also love money. According to a survey conducted by Dave Ramsey, "Money fights are the second leading cause of divorce, behind infidelity."[5] Money problems stoke worry, conflict, and even crime. How we relate to money says more about us than we think. Paul wrote,

> For the love of money is a root of all *kinds of* evil, for which some have strayed from the faith in their greediness, and pierced themselves through with many sorrows (1 Timothy 6:10 NKJV).

You don't have to possess a lot of money to be a money-lover. Many people who don't have much money are as obsessed with it as those who do. Our society often marks the value of people by how much they possess. The Bible repeatedly warns us not to show favoritism or esteem others based on how much they own, but most people in our culture ignore that admonition.

You can have money, but you must guard your heart. Jesus said,

> No one can serve two masters; for either he will hate the one and love the other, or else he will be loyal to the one and despise the other. You cannot serve God and mammon (Matthew 6:24 NKJV).

Mammon was the Syrian deity of wealth and riches. Jesus was warning His followers that they could be worshipping a demonic idol if their focus became money and greed. I must tell you that we are living in a culture of idol worship.

People love pleasure. This type of pleasure Paul lists is not the kind God intended for us in creation. The Lord wanted us to find pleasure in Him. Others bring us pleasure because of their connection to Him. Paul is writing about those who find pleasure in sinful and thoughtless behavior, which ignores God and misuses others.

We are seeing these sinful, unloving behaviors exhibited in our everyday lives. People seek peace and pleasure in everything except a relationship with the Lord. It's distressing and disturbing. However, Paul does not list these vices to discourage us. He is saying we are one step closer to the return of Christ. Jesus wants His followers to get excited because He is about to restore all things for those who believe. Right now, we only have a small portion of what Jesus redeemed for us on the cross. But one day soon, we will get everything back that was stolen by sin and Satan. On the day Jesus returns, He will redeem us and make all things new.

CHAPTER 7

Pleasure in Paradise

In Revelation 21:1–4, John writes:

> Now I saw a new heaven and a new earth, for the first heaven and
> the first earth had passed away. Also there was no more sea. Then I,
> John, saw the holy city, New Jerusalem, coming down out of heav-
> en from God, prepared as a bride adorned for her husband. And I
> heard a loud voice from heaven saying, "Behold, the tabernacle of
> God is with men, and He will dwell with them, and they shall be His
> people. God Himself will be with them *and be* their God. And God
> will wipe away every tear from their eyes; there shall be no more
> death, nor sorrow, nor crying. There shall be no more pain, for the
> former things have passed away" (NKJV).

Pleasure Redeemed on the Cross

In the vision the apostle John received from Jesus, he saw a new
heaven and new earth, and there was no more ocean ("no more sea").

There will also be no more death, sorrow, crying, or pain. If you have ever been fearful of Jesus' return, John's words should encourage you. You don't need to hang on desperately to this life. Please understand, the world in which we now live is a torture chamber compared to what God has in store for us in the new heaven and new earth. This vision is incredibly good news for believers!

When Jesus comes again, all pain will cease, but there's even better news:

> You will show me the path of life;
> in Your presence *is* fullness of joy;
> at Your right hand *are* pleasures forevermore (Psalm 16:11 NKJV).

God wants you to know that ending pain is not enough—He wants you to experience exquisite pleasure with Him for all eternity. God's initial desire when He created the Garden of Eden and placed humans in it was for them to experience the spectacular pleasure and joy of His presence. Sin caused pain, but that was not God's divine aim. He wants to give you pleasure beyond anything you can possibly understand while you're still living on this earth. The Bible promises it. Paul writes,

> But as it is written:
>> "Eye has not seen, nor ear heard,
>> Nor have entered into the heart of man
> The things which God has prepared for those who love Him" (1 Corinthians 2:9 NKJV).

God wants you to know that ending pain is not enough—He wants you to experience exquisite pleasure with Him for all eternity.

I know it's hard for us to wrap our heads around. Heaven is so far beyond what we know on this earth that it's impossible for us to comprehend the blessings and pleasures we will experience there. About himself, Paul also writes,

> It is doubtless not profitable for me to boast. I will come to visions and revelations of the Lord: I know a man in Christ who fourteen years ago—whether in the body I do not know, or whether out of the body I do not know, God knows—such a one was caught up to the third heaven. And I know such a man—whether in the body or out of the body I do not know, God knows—how he was caught up into Paradise and heard inexpressible words, which it is not lawful for a man to utter (2 Corinthians 12:1–4 NKJV).

As much as Paul is trying to translate his heavenly experience to the believers in Corinth, there are no words to explain it. All he can tell them is Paradise is so much better than anything they could experience here. He's saying it's so good that talking about it is probably illegal!

Jesus was nailed to the cross and placed between two men who were being executed for crimes they committed. The Roman authorities had convicted them as thieves, although they may have simply defied the occupying government. One of the men mocked Jesus and died with ridicule on the tip of his parched tongue. The other, however, knew there was something different and supernatural about the man dying next to him.

> Then he said to Jesus, "Lord, remember me when You come into Your kingdom."
> And Jesus said to him, "Assuredly, I say to you, today you will be with Me in Paradise" (Luke 23:42–43 NKJV).

God created the Garden of Eden as a paradise, but humans lost it because of sin. When Jesus comes back, we are returning to Paradise.

Paul says he can't express everything he has experienced and knows about Paradise, but that doesn't mean we don't know anything. The Bible gives us glimpses of our future, and we can know at least *five elements of Paradise.* In fact, these five aspects must exist for it to qualify as Paradise. Without them, a place might be great, but it isn't Paradise. These are the five things you will experience in heaven when you arrive there:

1. *Beauty.* You will never be able to call an ugly place "Paradise." In heaven you will experience beauty beyond anything you can imagine.
2. *Comfort.* You will find true comfort and deep rest that will flow through all your senses.
3. *Pleasure.* In heaven you will experience every sense of your heavenly body exploding.
4. *Plenty.* You will have everything you need and more than enough. It will be free because Jesus already bought it for you. You will never worry about lack because you will never run out.

5. *Safety.* You will live in perfect peace and fear nothing. Nothing can interrupt heaven, and no harm can come to you. You will be safe there.

Heaven is a place of complete beauty, comfort, pleasure, plenty, and safety, while hell is a place of ugliness, discomfort, torment, lack, and fear. You will never find a greater difference between anything you can find on earth as you will in the contrast between heaven and hell. In fact, as Paul says, you can't even find anything in this world that you can adequately compare to the riches and pleasures of heaven. You may think you've experienced some very wonderful things on earth that you don't want to leave behind. Nevertheless, when you arrive in heaven, those things will appear as next to nothing. Not only will you no longer have any pain, but you'll also look back on this life and realize nothing here compares to anything else in heaven. Paul says there are no human words for it. The devil will be in hell, and there is nothing he can ever do to harm people ever again.

You will never find a greater difference between anything you can find on earth as you will in the contrast between heaven and hell.

Have you ever considered that every pleasure you can find here on earth has a downside to it? It's true. If you eat too much, then you gain weight, your health deteriorates, and you can even die from the results of overeating. If you rest too much, then you get lazy and you never accomplish anything. If you cross sexual parameters that are outside God's design, then you will experience emptiness, treat others as objects, and even destroy your marriage and family. If you stay in the sun too long, then you'll get a sunburn and maybe skin cancer. If you spend too much money, then you'll be without the things you need in the future, go broke, and end up in poverty. Every good thing you know in this life may be misused in ways that are contrary to God's will, and the results can be devastating. But in heaven there is no such thing as too much. You will be able to do anything you want to do, and there's no downside.

More Than We Can Imagine

Take a moment to dream with me. Now, before you do, let me add this disclaimer: these are the images I have in my mind about heaven, but just as the apostle Paul says words are inadequate to describe it, my mind also cannot conceive of everything God has in store for us. I don't know that everything in my imagination is accurate or even real; in fact, I think heaven is far better than I could ever wrap my natural mind around. Even so, I want to expand your view of heaven and encourage you to think about it in a different way. So allow yourself to contemplate the wonders of heaven with me for a few moments:

The highlight of heaven is God's presence. He is at the center and focus of everything in Paradise, the New Jerusalem. As you enter to heaven, you immediately join all other believers of all the ages in God's glorious presence. There you worship Him with a perfect voice. Heaven's music fills the air with melodies thousands of times more lovely than any sounds you have ever heard. In God's presence, you experience the fullness of joy as your heart explodes with happiness and delight. After just a short million years, you are still worshipping the One who died for you, yet you've never grown bored, tired, or distracted.

After the second million years in the Lord's presence, you join your friends at Paradise's banquet table. Heaven's angels serve the meal, and you eat the most indescribably delicious food for another 15,000 years. The table conversations are incredible, and fun and laughter fill the room. You eat and eat, yet you never gain weight, feel full, become ill, need to take a restroom break, or think you have to stop. You don't have to save food for anyone else, because the more you eat, the more food the angels bring to the table.

Then you leave the table and decide to go to your mansion. Only one second later, you arrive at your gorgeous 500-acre estate. At your heavenly home, you will meet all your family for an incredible reunion. One of the angels leaves to gather your loved ones. When your relatives arrive, the angels arrange everything perfectly, and they serve you and your family for another 5,000 years. You eat, play games, share memories, and enjoy each other in an atmosphere of laughter and love. No one gets hurt feelings or does anything harmful. Everyone is mature, sensitive, godly, loving, and affectionate toward each other. On your back porch there are no ants, mosquitos, or other insects. The sun doesn't burn your skin, and no one gets injured. You don't have to pay for anything. In fact, you don't need money or any other property to trade because everything you want is immediately provided by the angels.

As the family reunion draws to a close, someone suggests going on an adventure. So you leave your mansion with your loved ones and take a 14,000-year journey to explore the new earth. There are no vicious animals. You can immediately travel to any place you want to be. The world is a paradise, and there's amazing thrill after thrill. You can climb the highest mountain without feeling fatigued or needing oxygen. You can swim under water for 100 years without needing to breathe or feeling tired. No dangerous sharks try to attack you, and nothing can harm you. There are no deserts remaining on earth. There's no such thing as going to a "bad" place because God has redeemed every place. Nothing tragic has ever happened anywhere you go. The old earth of sin and corruption is gone.

When your tour of the new earth ends, everyone is pleased and enthusiastic. One of your family members says, "I was exploring the universe with a group of my friends earlier, and we found a galaxy 300 million light years away. It was incredible!" Everyone agrees they would also like to see this galaxy, so you decide to go. One second later, all of you are there. For the next 30,000 years, your group explores that galaxy and its stars. You share great experiences together, seeing things beyond description. Everything you witness is far different from anything you've ever seen before, and it's extremely fun and interesting. Your mind takes in information, and everything makes sense.

Next, you all decide to return to your mansions. With no need for rest, you make a visit to the Hall of Pavilions, where you meet the great men and women of the Bible. They are heroes to you, but they tell you Jesus is the only true Hero. Even so, you're still in awe of them. All 12 disciples have their own pavilions, and so do the apostle

Paul, Mary (the mother of Jesus), King David, Daniel, Esther, and all the other people of the Bible you loved before you ever met them in person. In each pavilion, you meet a new person of the Bible, and you spend time talking with them intimately and getting to know them.

In each pavilion, you are able to relive the actual events of the Bible with those people who were there when they happened. It's a technology beyond anything you've ever known. In Noah's pavilion, you watch him construct the Ark and see how God rescued him from the Great Flood. In Elijah's pavilion, you witness his faith as he trusts God to defeat the prophets of Baal. You get to watch King David fling a stone in the air and God direct it straight to Goliath's forehead. Then you are present as Mary gives birth to Jesus. You watch Him grow up, see Him perform miracles, and listen to His teaching. You linger in the Hall of Pavilions for 40,000 years, seeing fascinating event after event.

After these experiences, you have an overwhelming desire to be in the presence of God and worship Him. In the blink of an eye, you are kneeling at His throne. As you worship Him, He looks straight at you and smiles. Suddenly, you realize an angel has taken you by the hand and is leading you toward the throne. Now you are face-to-face with the living God. Immediately, you know He loves you personally. He shows you affection and speaks words of affirmation and blessing over you. You can do nothing other than worship Him for seven million more years. You praise Him with a clear voice, and no distraction or fatigue ever overtakes you. Beauty after beauty, glory after glory, and joy after joy fill your days. Every day is more amazing than the day before. God is infinite, and as the Architect of your heavenly home, He can only make a marvelous Paradise.

I'll remind you again, that's heaven according to Jimmy. I can't tell you I got that straight from the Bible, but there's nothing I have written here that contradicts the Bible. It's my imagination. The purpose for sharing my description is just to mess up your hairdo. I want you to think differently. Heaven is bigger and better than you've ever thought or can ever think in this world.

I was trying to lead a friend to the Lord one day, but he said he didn't want to go to heaven. I asked him where he thought he would go when he died. He wasn't sure, but it wasn't heaven. He said he didn't want to go because he didn't want to float around on a cloud playing a harp for all eternity. Does what I described sound like that? Of course, it doesn't.

Read these words from Paul again:

> But as it is written:
>> "Eye has not seen, nor ear heard,
>> Nor have entered into the heart of man
>> The things which God has prepared for those who love Him"
> (1 Corinthians 2:9 NKJV).

Do you see what I am saying? Even if my vision of heaven isn't directly from the Bible, understand that heaven is even better than that. You won't experience physical or relational pain. You'll never again have hurt feelings. We will all be mature and loving to each other.

You may have heard of Don Piper. He died as the result of a car accident and spent 90 minutes in heaven. He documented his experience in the book *90 Minutes in Heaven, a True Story of Life and Death.*

He details the light, colors, and profound happiness he experienced. Here is some of what Piper wrote:

> Everything I experienced was like a first-class buffet for the senses. I had never felt such powerful embraces or feasted my eyes on such beauty. Heaven's light and texture defy earthly eyes or explanation. Warm, radiant light engulfed me. As I looked around, I could hardly grasp the vivid, dazzling colors. Every hue and tone surpassed anything I had ever seen. With all the heightened awareness of my senses, I felt as if I had never seen, heard, or felt anything so real before. I don't recall that I tasted anything, yet I knew that if I had, that too would have been more glorious than anything I had eaten or drunk on earth. The best way I can explain it is to say that I felt as if I were in another dimension. Never, even in my happiest moments, had I ever felt so fully alive. I stood speechless in front of the crowd of loved ones, still trying to take in everything. Over and over I heard how overjoyed they were to see me and how excited they were to have me among them. I'm not sure whether they actually said the words or not, but I knew they had been waiting and expecting me, yet I also knew that in heaven there is no sense of time passing.[6]

The things Piper witnessed in heaven were endlessly and overwhelmingly beautiful. He says everyone there was ecstatic to see him and had been anticipating his arrival.

I want you to know that you are only a twinkling of an eye away from that. You and I are going to a place that's indescribable, a place with the greatest joy and pleasure you can possibly imagine. Sadly, people who don't receive Christ will not go there. Instead, they will be in hell, the worst place of which we could ever conceive. Hell is a real place, and everyone should know that. If you don't know Jesus, then I can tell you there is no better time than now to receive Him as your Lord and Savior. If you are a believer, there is no time better than now to share the Good News about Jesus with someone who does not yet believe.

CHAPTER 8

How Could God Send Anyone to Hell?

As I wrote in the previous chapter, hell is real, and no one would ever want to go there if they knew how awful it really is. How, then, could a loving God send people to hell, the ultimate place of suffering and torment? If you are a believer, you have either been asked this question, or you will be asked it. You need to be ready with an answer when you talk with unbelieving friends and loved ones.

Free Will and the Consequences

God has given the incredible gift of free will to every human who has ever been on earth. Nevertheless, that gift comes with responsibilities for us to use it according to God's design, and there are consequences when we don't. When God extended free will to Adam and Eve, He informed them that He was putting a tree in the Garden of Eden from which they could not eat. They could freely eat from every other tree, but one was off-limits. With their free will, they could choose obedience and blessings or disobedience and curses. As you know, they chose the latter. They consciously rebelled against God and His command. That rebellion is what we call "sin." Adam and Eve were without excuse because God had warned them of the consequences.

God has given the incredible gift of free will to every human who has ever been on earth.

Later, God chose a people through Abraham. Once the Lord delivered His people from Egypt, He took them on a journey that would ultimately lead them to the Promised Land. On the way there, He gave specific and elaborate instructions about how to obey Him. If they did what He commanded, then everything would go well for them. However, if they disobeyed, then all sorts of awful consequences would follow. The Lord was setting before them life and death, blessings and curses. He told them that if they chose life, then they and their children would live (see Deuteronomy 30:15–20). But you know the story: they chose death. Their wilderness voyage was one long series of constant rebellion against God. He warned them of what would happen if they rebelled, but they disobeyed Him anyway.

You may be thinking, *Well, Jimmy, I think people are good enough, and everyone should get to go to heaven.* I understand what is going on in your mind. But are you saying there should be no difference between a loving parent and a child abuser? A murderer and a medical doctor? A thief and a diligent worker? A drunkard and an Olympic athlete? An atheist and a missionary? A cynic and a believer? Hitler and Abraham? The apostle Peter and Judas? Osama bin Laden and SEAL Team 6? Abraham Lincoln and John Wilkes Booth? Or Martin Luther King Jr. and the Ku Klux Klan? Now, if any of those people chose to follow Jesus, their sins are covered by His righteousness, but without Jesus there are huge differences. If there is no difference, and everyone finally gets saved in the end, then that's chaos and meaninglessness. God has given us the gift of free will, but it comes with consequences for misusing it. He gave that same free will to Adam and Eve. He told them they would die, but they disobeyed Him anyway. We are still dealing with the consequences. You can't have free will without the potential of consequences for your choices. If there are no consequences, then life has no meaning and there is no true justice.

You can't have free will without the potential of consequences for your choices.

You might say, "Well, Jimmy, I'm all for universalism. I want everyone to be saved."

(Universalism is the belief that God will save all people regardless of their beliefs or behavior.) That's fine. You can want that, and I can appreciate that you love people. But the real question is, does God want that? He loves people, and He's provided a way for every person to avoid hell. Even if someone thinks universalism is a great concept, it's a moot point, because the Bible teaches God will *not* finally save everyone, because not everyone will choose God. I am going to go with the Bible's version of reality. All roads do not lead to the same destination. And free will means we can freely choose the path of destruction. Consequences are real, and they mean something.

At the dawn of Creation, our loving God extended this precious gift of free will. He desires for us to use it to love and obey Him—that's why there was only one bad tree in the Garden of Eden and thousands, if not tens of thousands, of good trees that included no prohibition. God did not stack the deck against the first humans. The cards were in their favor. They had only *one* choice that they could make against God, but that is precisely the one they made. They experienced the consequences, and we are still suffering with them. Even after such a fateful choice, God didn't take free will away from the human race. I have it, and so do you. Nevertheless, He also didn't remove the consequences that come from using that will to disobey Him. I have done it, and so have you. All of us have chosen to rebel against God, so our sins only compound the consequences.

Only One Way

There is only one way to heaven and only one responsible way to exercise our free will: choose Jesus Christ as Savior and Lord. This isn't God's first rodeo. It is not as if this is the first time God has thought through the problem of sin. He made the choice for all humans to go to heaven, and His plans are perfect. But we must choose Jesus! He is *the* way, *the* truth, and *the* life and no one comes to the Father except through Him (John 14:6).

There is only one way to heaven and only one responsible way to exercise our free will: choose Jesus Christ as Savior and Lord.

God's Initial Design

God created the first two humans to love and obey Him. As I said previously, that is our ontology—our very being. That was His initial design for humanity. If they had followed His command, then they would have lived with Him forever in His perfect garden. However, their rebellion had roots even before they were created. Ezekiel 28 tells how God created perfection long ago in eternities past even before He made the world. Before God made the angels, nothing existed except for God. Then He created a very high order of beings we know as angels, which included Lucifer, whom we now know as Satan. He placed them in the heavenly garden, which God called the first "Eden" (see Ezekiel 28:13). Lucifer was a covering cherub in the presence of God. He had musical instruments built into his body and was a worship leader in heaven. Lucifer, whose name means "light bearer," reflected the glory of God like the moon reflects the sun. The Lord chose for all of them to be present there with Him.

One day, Lucifer became puffed up with pride and decided he wanted to take God's place in the universe. He began to behold his own beauty, fell in love with himself, and led one-third of the angels in heaven in a rebellion against the Lord. God had allowed them all to live in His presence, and they chose to step away from Him. It's hard for believers to understand that there are beings who would reject God, even as they stood in His presence. But that has occurred ever since Satan declared war in heaven.

Sometime later, although we don't really know how long it was, God created everything that we know. He made humans in His image and placed them within the Garden of Eden here on earth. Then one day, they encountered Satan, and he led them to rebel against God just as he had done. They traded a piece of forbidden fruit for their relationship with Almighty God. They slapped Him in the face, turned their backs on a relationship with Him, and gave up heaven in an attempt to be the rulers and gods of their own lives. As a result, their relationship with God was irretrievably broken. God had an initial plan for humans, but He allowed Adam and Eve to assert their free will and choose to listen to Satan tell lies about God's commands.

God's Rescue Operation

Before God ever removed Adam and Eve from the Garden of Eden, He had already established a plan to rescue them. He told Eve that one day her descendant would overcome Satan and restore humanity to its rightful place (see Genesis 3:15).

At first, God chose a man named Abraham. From Abraham, God made His people, Israel, and from Israel, God chose Mary to be the virgin mother to His very own Son, Jesus. Jesus lived the perfect, sinless life. He taught truth, performed miracles, cast out demons, and told people the Good News about God's rescue plan to save all humanity.

As a reward for Jesus' good works, humans put Him on trial, mocked Him, and executed Him in shame. Even so, God intervened and raised Jesus from the dead. Because of Jesus' sacrifice, all humanity is now invited to receive the gift of salvation and eternal life. Every person is given the free will to choose Him as Savior and Lord, call on Him as the Mediator between them and God the Father, and trust Him to present them to God as blameless and righteous. Every human has the promise of heaven if they will only believe and receive Jesus. The ultimate sin that will lead to the ultimate penalty is to refuse the grace of God through Jesus Christ. Hell is entirely avoidable, but it is also entirely real. Without God's grace, hell is inevitable. God doesn't send anyone to hell unless they choose to go there themselves by rejecting Him.

God always wanted a relationship with humanity. Adam and Eve used their free will to spoil His initial design for people, so God sent His Son to restore and redeem them. Because He knows everything, God knew they were going to sin. He didn't create them to sin, want them to sin, or tempt them to sin, but He prepared to deal with their sin before the foundation of the world (see Ephesians 1:4). God was completely aware that they would use their free will to sin against Him. Even so, He was already laying out His rescue plan. It was a plan that would cost God the most precious possession He will ever have, His own Son.

So before you decide universalism is a great idea, I regret to inform you: *there will not be another plan.* At its best, universalism is a sentimental idea that is really misplaced compassion. At its worst, it makes a mockery of the sacrifice Jesus made for us on the cross. If we embrace universalism, we do so in error, and we risk other people not hearing about the only way God has established to save us and keep us out of hell.

Why Would Anyone Refuse God?

The apostle John quotes Jesus in the book of Revelation:

> Behold, I stand at the door and knock. If anyone hears My voice
> and opens the door, I will come in to him and dine with him, and
> he with Me (Revelation 3:20 NKJV).

When it comes to offering us salvation, Jesus is the perfect gentlemen. He stands outside the door and knocks, but He won't kick down the door. He has the ability to break in, but that's not in His character. Jesus wants us to choose Him of our own free will. You see, He values His relationship with us, and He wants it to be one of mutual love rather than coercion. So He knocks on the door of every single person's heart, but those doors must be opened from the inside.

Many people wonder why a loving God would ever send anyone to hell. However, I have a question in response: Why would any sane and reasonable person reject and refuse the grace of such a loving God? He is incredibly loving, and He died on the cross so no one would have to go to hell. Why would anyone turn away from that?

**Why would any sane and reasonable person reject
and refuse the grace of such a loving God?**

Jesus actually answers this very question:

For God so loved the world that He gave His only begotten Son, that whoever believes in Him should not perish but have everlasting life. For God did not send His Son into the world to condemn the world, but that the world through Him might be saved.

He who believes in Him is not condemned; but he who does not believe is condemned already, because he has not believed in the name of the only begotten Son of God. And this is the condemnation, that the light has come into the world, and men loved darkness rather than light, because their deeds were evil. For everyone practicing evil hates the light and does not come to the light, lest his deeds should be exposed (John 3:16–20 NKJV).

Why would anyone reject God's love and light? It is because some people love evil and darkness. That is the choice they have made. God desires that no one would perish, but we must come to Him of our own choice.

When someone asks, "Why would a loving God send someone to hell?" they are essentially saying, "I refuse to accept a higher moral authority than myself, nor will I take responsibility for the consequences of my choice." That is precisely what Lucifer said to God, but so did Adam and Eve and the people of Israel. History is littered with the sad results of people who rebelled against God.

As for me, I choose not to rebel against God. I have thrown open the door and welcomed Him in with thankfulness and joy. I am totally and completely giving the Lord control of my life. I know He created me, died for me, and gave me new life. I cannot repay Him, but I will gladly serve Him for all eternity. And I believe that because of His grace, I will experience the pleasures of heaven forever.

PART FOUR

Redeemed Identity

CHAPTER 9

Who Are You?

Not long ago, I heard the story of a 1980s rock musician who recently visited Indonesia. Walking down a city street, he came upon a cigarette vendor. This woman had a variety of cigarette brands she was selling from an usherette tray that hung from straps around her neck. The rocker is a non-smoker, and it had been many years since he sung on stage, but as he drew closer to the vendor, he could see she was wearing a t-shirt that bore the name and emblem of his band that was once semi-famous several decades ago. He was both surprised and excited to see this "fan" halfway across the world. So he said to her, "Hey, I was the lead singer of that band on your shirt." The vendor was nonplussed and paused in her sales pitch before she blurted out, "So are you going to buy cigarettes or not?" The retired singer thought he had found perhaps his one true admirer in all of Indonesia, but in effect she was saying, "I don't care who you are. I just got dressed today. Either buy something or move along. I've got a job to do."

That humbling and humorous incident reminded me of something Luke recorded in the book of Acts:

A group of Jews was traveling from town to town casting out evil spirits. They tried to use the name of the Lord Jesus in their incantation, saying, "I command you in the name of Jesus, whom Paul preaches, to come out!" Seven sons of Sceva, a leading priest, were doing this. But one time when they tried it, the evil spirit replied, "I know Jesus, and I know Paul, but who are you?" Then the man with the evil spirit leaped on them, overpowered them, and attacked them with such violence that they fled from the house, naked and battered (Acts 19:13–16).

As you can see from this story, the demons in Ephesus were as impressed with the seven sons of Sceva as the cigarette vendor in Indonesia was with the once-famous rocker. "I know Jesus, and I know Paul, but who are you?"

This would be a good time to tell you one way language in the church has changed in the last 75 years. If you listen to 10 sermons by a variety of evangelical pastors in the US this week, I can guarantee at least one will use the phrase "your identity in Christ." I have used it myself, even recently. It might surprise you to find out this phrase was seldom, if ever, used in any Christian books or sermons before the 1950s. It will probably really surprise you to learn the phrase is never used in the Bible. So where did it come from? The term had its origins in secular psychology of the mid-1900s as a way for people to explore their personalities, gifts, and strengths. It was picked up by Christian communicators as a way to express our need to understand who we are in Christ. Is there anything wrong with using it? The answer is both "no" and "yes."

Let me start by saying that I will continue to use the phrase "your identity in Christ" because it helps communicate to a contemporary audience the need to discover everything you can about yourself under God so you can offer your best in service to Him. I know one of the deepest issues believers face in finding freedom and inner healing lies in how they understand who they are in relationship to Christ. The devil tells us many lies about ourselves, and we need to know the truth. What it does not mean, however, is that you can take a personality, spiritual gifts, or strengths test and suddenly declare that you are called and prepared for a certain type of ministry. To understand who you truly are in Christ, let me tell you that the popular phrase "your identity in Christ" replaced the biblical phrase: "your *union* in Christ."

The devil tells us many lies about ourselves, and we need to know the truth.

You see, your identity matters, but it is only spiritually relevant if it is connected to Christ or in union with Him. Why did the demons in Ephesus not recognize any authority in the sons of Sceva? They didn't know those would-be exorcists because those men didn't know Jesus. The sons of Sceva tried to act with authority when they had none. Essentially, the demons were saying, "If you want to speak to us with authority, then we don't know who you are. We only know Jesus and His true followers." If you want to know who you are, then you need to know who God is and why He sent His Son, Jesus, so that you could be in eternal union with Him. In that sense, I want to help people find their identities, but even more I want them to know their identities *in* Christ. I want them to be in union with Him.

Understanding who we are in Christ means we must first understand who He is.

How does this issue of our identity relate to the Rapture when Jesus returns to gather the believers here on earth? The apostle John gives us the reason:

> Dear friends, we are already God's children, but he has not yet shown us what we will be like when Christ appears. But we do know that we will be like him, for we will see him as he really is. And all who have this eager expectation will keep themselves pure, just as he is pure (1 John 3:2–3).

God has already claimed us as His children, but we don't see everything clearly yet. When Jesus comes back in the Rapture, we will know exactly who God is and who we are in union with Him. What we do in the meantime is wait eagerly, prepare for His return, stay away from sin, and learn everything we can from and about Him. We will see and understand Him perfectly on the day Christ returns, and our eyes will be opened completely to our identity in Him. Right now, we must learn who God is and who we are in Jesus Christ. We are not left guessing. The Bible tells us who God is and who we are, and the Holy Spirit confirms it for us.

So who is God? There are many ways to describe who God is and who God is not. The entire Bible tells us who He is. However, there are *five ways the Bible describes God*, which run throughout the Bible, from Genesis to Revelation. If we can understand these five ways God reveals Himself, then we will better comprehend our identity in union with Him.

1. **God is a Father.** He is intimately present for us. He is a Father, and we are His sons.
2. **God is a Bridegroom.** He wants us to be ready for Him when He comes, and He wants to have a deep, personal, and loving relationship with us. He is a Bridegroom, and we are His bride.
3. **God is a Messenger.** He freely delivers the gracious good news of His truth to us, and He wants us to tell others what He has said. God is a Messenger, and we are His prophets.
4. **God is a Person.** He wants to give us access to Himself so we can receive forgiveness, bring others into His presence, and glorify Him. He is a Person, and we are His priests.
5. **God is a King.** He is the Ruler of all Creation who gives authority to His sons. God is a King, and He has made us kings to reign with Him.

Finding Your Identity in Christ Jesus

"I don't know who I am anymore." You may have heard those words from someone who has gone through a life crisis, such as a divorce or the death of a loved one. When the person to whom you are closest is no longer in your life, it's an extremely unsettling experience because something precious has been lost. That person has walked through many trials with you, shared many laughs, and dreamed common dreams. The loss of that person is the loss of shared history. Their mere presence reminded you daily of who you are, what you know, and what you've experienced.

If our hearts feel that much pain because of the loss of a primary relationship, can you imagine what it must have felt like for Adam and Eve to be barred from the Garden of Eden? Who are they now that they no longer walk with God in the cool of the day? Who are they now that they are no longer directly in God's presence, hearing directly from Him, or ruling the world on His behalf? Not only did they lose their special place in the Garden of Eden, but now Satan and all his minions stand as their constant accusers. Isn't that just like the devil to lead them astray and then get in their faces to tell them how worthless they are?

In the previous chapters, I addressed the philosophical and theological concept of ontology as it relates to us as humans. Who did God create us to be? What is the very nature of our being? Why are these questions so important in a book that discusses what will be redeemed about us when Christ returns? If we know who God created us to be, who Jesus is, and how God wants us to live in this world, then we can see how He is planning to transform us in the Rapture. He wants to take us back to the Garden.

Let me state it another way with *four important truths about our identity*:

1. God created Adam and Eve with a distinct identity to be what He wanted them to be and for them to do His will.
2. The choice to sin distorted Adam and Eve's identity, so God began to restore it through Abraham and Israel.
3. Jesus Christ is the Second Adam, and He restores God's original intent and design for humanity.
4. Jesus Christ restores our relationship with God and enables us to reclaim our identity now both as individuals and as the

Church. He will perfect that identity when He comes again because it is then that we will know Him perfectly.

Who are we now that we are in Christ? Let me begin by telling you some of the ways the New Testament describes believers. This is not an exhaustive description, because for you to understand who you are in Christ, you would need to read the entire Bible, listen for the Holy Spirit's voice, and join a fellowship of believers who will constantly remind you of who you are. Nevertheless, here are some important verses to help you see yourself the way that God sees you if you are in Christ.[7]

So now you Gentiles are no longer strangers and foreigners. You are citizens along with all of God's holy people. You are members of God's family (Ephesians 2:19).

You are not a stranger in God's house. You belong to Him and to all His people. Remember, you are now part of the family and a legitimate son of God.

———

And God will generously provide all you need. Then you will always have everything you need and plenty left over to share with others (2 Corinthians 9:8).

Since you are God's son, He will take care of you and give you everything you need in Christ. Everything belongs to God, so He can provide all you need.

———

> For the Lord your God is living among you.
>> He is a mighty savior.
> He will take delight in you with gladness.
>> With his love, he will calm all your fears.
>> He will rejoice over you with joyful songs (Zephaniah 3:17).

Your Father takes great delight in you. He doesn't merely tolerate you; He rejoices in you. He throws a great celebration when you join His family. He will correct you when you do wrong, but that is so you will become more like Him.

———

> For God made Christ, who never sinned, to be the offering for our sin, so that we could be made right with God through Christ (2 Corinthians 5:21).

Jesus made you right with God. You did nothing to earn what Jesus did for you. You take on His goodness and righteousness because He died for you, and you are now in right standing with your Creator. You can approach God without fear, and you can also bring others to Him as His ambassador. God gives you the power to live right and invite others to become right with Him.

———

> Make allowance for each other's faults. and forgive anyone who offends you. Remember, the Lord forgave you, so you must forgive others (Colossians 3:13).

God has forgiven you. You are His son, and He does not hold your past sins against you. Since you have been forgiven, you have the power and responsibility to forgive others. If God has given grace to you, then He expects you to extend His grace to others.

———

For we are God's masterpiece. He has created us anew in Christ Jesus, so we can do the good things he planned for us long ago (Ephesians 2:10).

You are not here by accident; God created you for a great purpose. He had plans for your life even before you were in your mother's womb. Your first responsibility is to know God and give glory to Him. Jesus has delivered you from sin through His sacrifice. As a son of God, you can walk with confidence and authority because you belong to Him.

———

This means that anyone who belongs to Christ has become a new person. The old life is gone; a new life has begun! (2 Corinthians 5:17).

God has made you a new creation in Jesus Christ. All the old ways of defining yourself are now gone. Your way of seeing the world is forever changed. You are God's friend, and He is yours. He knows you as a beloved son, not as a slave, sinner, or enemy. Jesus paid for your sin in full, and He restored you to your Creator.

Our Identity from Garden to Garden

The Scriptures I just shared with you give you some very basic information you need know about your relationship with God, but I want to take some of those themes a little deeper. If we want to know who God is and who He intends us to be, then we need to go all the way back to the beginning. The roles God gave to Adam played out throughout God's relationship with Israel, in the identity of Jesus, and ultimately in the eternal identity of those who follow Jesus as Savior and Lord. Related to the five ways I said the Bible describes God are *five ways* the Bible describes Adam, Israel, Jesus, and members of the body of Christ: *sons of God, marriage partners, prophets, priests, and kings.* In this section, I will tell you how the first four ways of looking at our identity apply to every person who is a believer. Then in the next section on "Redeemed Authority," I will discuss the fifth way of looking at our identity—our kingship under Christ.

If we want to know who God is and who He intends us to be, then we need to go all the way back to the beginning.

Typology and Identity

Bible scholars often use the word *typology* to show patterns that run through the Bible. The writers of the Bible use certain "types" to describe how God works to save people. Many types are very clear in the biblical text. For example, Adam was the first man, and now Jesus is the Second Adam because He is the first person fully living in God's new creation. This is why the Church is called the New Israel. Some of these typologies we talk about so frequently, we don't even recognize when we use them. Probably the most common one we use is "Old Testament" and "New Testament." The word *testament* means "covenant or agreement," so we think of the Old Testament as God's initial agreement with His people and the New Testament as the new and renewed covenant God has made to include everyone who becomes a follower of Jesus Christ.

In these chapters on our identity when Jesus returns, I will start with Adam. He is the initial type, and he was meant to fulfill God's original intent for humanity. For example, I will show how Adam was a priest, but he failed in his priestly role because of sin. God chose priests in Israel, but they too became corrupt. Jesus establishes Himself as our High Priest forever. Then He makes all believers priests, and we are now part of a royal nation of priests. When Jesus returns, we will continue in our role as priests, although we will have greater access to God at that time.

In the beginning, God gave Adam several ways to understand himself. These are parts of Adam's identity, which were meant to reflect God's glory. Throughout the rest of the Bible, the writers often return to Adam as God's original type or prototype. The man is the fountainhead for every other type of person we see in the Bible, including Jesus. God made Adam in His image and intended for Adam and Eve to forever be in His likeness and image. Nevertheless, sin tainted and distorted the person God originally created Adam to be. Adam passed down the image of God to every person, but we also inherited the distortion caused by sin. Adam's role and identity are significant because God placed within him all the possibilities and promises of the wonderful relationship we *could* have with God if only we had a way to deal with sin. Jesus is the new Fountainhead. Now, because of what Jesus has done through His life, death, and resurrection, every person compares themselves to these two "Adams." We know we are like the original Adam in creation, but we also know we can be like Jesus. He is the "author and finisher" of the entire matter (see Hebrews 12:2 NKJV). He fixes everything Adam broke.

Adam was God's first earthly son, the first bridegroom, and he served in the offices of prophet, priest, and king. I will explain all of this more fully in the following pages. As part of God's rescue mission after Adam and Eve sinned, He created the corporate firstborn son, Israel. With the exception of Abraham, God did not allow any individual within Israel to hold all three offices of prophet, priest, and king. Jesus Christ came as the last and Second Adam, who then created a new spiritual race out of all those who believed in Him. He is God's Son, Bridegroom, and the eternal Prophet, Priest, and King. He is now conforming all believers to Himself. We are called to be sons of God and the bride of Christ, and we have been given the offices of prophet, priest, and king. For us to understand who we are in Christ, we must first understand who Adam is in Creation, who Israel is in God's rescue plan, and who Jesus is. Then we will know what God has called us to be and do, and we will know what our role and identity will be when Jesus returns to take us with Him.

CHAPTER 10

We Are Sons of God

If you want to know who you are in the Lord, then I will begin by telling you about *God's four sons*. When I say God has four sons, I am talking about the way God addresses Adam, Israel, Jesus Christ, and all believers who are part of His Church. I also am not over-looking how God refers to various people in the Bible as His sons, such as kings, but these I mention are the four primary sons of God in the Bible.

You probably have noticed that I have repeatedly referred to be-lievers as "sons of God." *This is intentional.* Did you realize women in the Bible are never referred to as "daughters of God"?[8] Never. Not once. If you look up books about "daughters of God" on amazon.com, you will find over 1,000 of them with that phrase somewhere in the title, which is interesting because the Bible never uses it. Now, I am not saying you shouldn't think of yourself as God's daughter if you are a woman, but I am saying that if you don't also see yourself as a son, then you are missing something very important.

Is this use of both "son" and "daughter" something Bible transla-tors missed? No, the Greek word *adelphoi* can mean both 'brothers' and 'sisters,' but *huioi* means 'sons.' It's tempting to add "daughters" when we see "sons of God," but the writers used "sons" for a reason. Was God trying to exclude women? Some critics of the Bible make claims such as this, but actually it is quite the opposite. The use of "sons of God" is a big deal. It means that the writers of the Bible were elevating women by including them as "sons." Why do I say this?

In the ancient world, only sons received an inheritance. The only way for a woman to gain wealth was to marry someone who had it. Daughters received nothing. If the writers of the Bible had said we are "sons and daughters of God," then women would have considered their current cultural situation and thought, *Well, I guess in the Kingdom of God, I still get nothing. I might be included, but I won't get an inheritance. It doesn't sound so great to me.*

When the Bible calls both men and women "sons of God," something profound is happening. It's a major statement about the worth of women in God's eyes. Keep that in mind when you see the term "sons of God" in the Bible. In God's Kingdom, women are sons too!

In God's Kingdom, women are sons too!

Look at what the apostle Paul says:

I mean that the heir, as long as he is a child, is no different from a slave, though he is the owner of everything, but he is under guardians and managers until the date set by his father. In the same way we also, when we were children, were enslaved to the elementary principles of the world. But when the fullness of time had come, God sent

forth his Son, born of woman, born under the law, to redeem those
who were under the law, so that we might receive adoption as sons.
And because you are sons, God has sent the Spirit of his Son into our
hearts, crying, "Abba! Father!" So you are no longer a slave, but a son,
and if a son, then an heir through God (Galatians 4:1–7 ESV).

Do you see what has happened? All of us—both men and women—
were slaves to sin and the world. But God sent His own Son to pay
the price for us to be adopted as sons of God. We aren't just sons, but
very intimate sons. We can cry out, "Abba! Father!" *Daddy!* Can you
believe it? This is an amazing inheritance!

Look at one more passage of Scripture from Paul:

For all who are led by the Spirit of God are sons of God. For you did
not receive the spirit of slavery to fall back into fear, but you have
received the Spirit of adoption as sons, by whom we cry, "Abba!
Father!" The Spirit himself bears witness with our spirit that we are
children of God, and if children, then heirs—heirs of God and fellow heirs with Christ, provided we suffer with him in order that we
may also be glorified with him (Romans 8:14–17 ESV).

You don't have to fear anymore. The Creator of the universe is your
Dad, and you are His son. Even if we experience suffering in this
world, we should anticipate the great inheritance that Jesus has won
for us. So I will say again, it is good for both men and women to be
a son of God. Jesus bought us out of slavery, our Father adopted us,
and now we get a full inheritance. If you are shouting for joy as you
read this, I don't blame you!

Adam, Son of God

Maybe you are surprised to hear Adam described as a "son of God." Where do we get this concept? I want to show you why it's important to read the entire Bible. We miss important insights if we only read select parts. Genesis describes Adam in this way:

> Then God said, "Let us make human beings in our image, to be like us. They will reign over the fish in the sea, the birds in the sky, the livestock, all the wild animals on the earth, and the small animals that scurry along the ground."
> So God created human beings in his own image.
> > In the image of God he created them;
> > male and female he created them (Genesis 1:26–27).

Notice what God says: "In our image, to be like us." That is the way God defines Adam.

Watch what happens in Genesis 5 after Cain murders Abel and God gives Adam and Eve another son:

> When Adam was 130 years old, he became the father of a son who was just like him—in his very image. He named his son Seth (Genesis 5:3).

Do you see what happened? Genesis uses the same description for Seth's relationship to Adam as God used for Adam's relationship to Himself. In fact, in Hebrew, they are the very same words. The writer of Genesis uses "image" and "likeness" to refer to sonship. Seth was Adam's son because he bore Adam's image and likeness. Adam bore God's image and likeness; he was God's son. In case you think these verses are stretching it too far, let me say that in his Gospel, Luke refers directly to Adam as "son of God" (see Luke 3:38). Adam was God's son. Some of the greater truths of the Bible are hidden in its genealogies.

Since the Bible clearly says Adam is the son of God, what does it mean? One of the main purposes of the Bible's genealogies is to show a direct lineage to an even greater person, such as Abraham. Adam is unlike any other person in a genealogy because he is traced directly to God. We should not think, however, that God only became a Father when Adam was created. Paul writes, "When I think of all this, I fall to my knees and pray to the Father, the Creator of everything in heaven and on earth" (Ephesians 3:14–15). Prior to any humans, God was Father. His Fatherhood defines who He is in an eternal Trinity with Son and Spirit.

John 3:16 says Jesus is God's one and *only* Son, so what does that title mean for Adam? Jesus was born of Mary without any man being involved, so Jesus is both the eternal God, Son of God, and second person of the Trinity. However, Jesus is also biologically God's Son by the seed of the Holy Spirit—God in human form.

Adam was not born. God created him directly, which means Adam did not have a biological mother. Luke calls Adam "son of God" because God alone is the one who brought him into the world. Only Adam and Jesus can claim God as their Father in the biological sense.

The apostle Paul calls Jesus "the last Adam" (see 1 Corinthians 15:45). Paul is not saying Jesus is only a spiritual Adam; he means that Jesus came as a human to earth the same way Adam did. Paul refers to Leviticus 25, which states that if a man falls into debt or his property is confiscated, his next of kin must buy back or redeem what he forfeited. So Paul is saying Jesus came to earth as a true human. He is Adam's next of kin, and He has the authority to buy us back.

When Luke finishes listing the genealogy of Jesus and refers to Adam as "son of God," he immediately moves into the temptation of Jesus in the wilderness. The connection between these two passages is not a coincidence. There is a huge difference between how Adam and Jesus encountered and responded to temptation. Adam did not obey God, but Jesus obeyed only God. There is a deep connection between faithful sonship and resisting temptation.

Israel, God's Son

The people of Israel are called the son of God and even the firstborn son (see Exodus 4:22; Jeremiah 31:9; Hosea 11:1). If faithful sonship requires resisting temptation, then how did Israel fare? God delivered Israel from Egypt and tested the people for 40 years. Did they trust God to keep His word? Did they believe God would provide for them? What happened when they were faced with the worship of false gods rather than the one true God? Of course, if you know the story of the Exodus and Israel's wandering in the wilderness, you know they failed miserably.

Israel was repeatedly disobedient to God's covenant with them. Bible scholars have called Israel's situation in the book of Judges a "sin cycle." It goes like this:

1. The people choose idolatry.
2. The people are enslaved or made to suffer.
3. The people show great sorrow and cry out to the Lord.
4. God delivers them.
5. They start sinning all over again.

While this sin cycle is true of the time of the judges, it is also true for all of Israel's history. The cycle continues to repeat. The people took many years to reach the Promised Land, but then subsequent generations sinned and got kicked out of the land during the Babylonian Exile. Like Adam, they disobeyed God and were displaced because of it (see Deuteronomy 4). When we read Israel's story, and we read about Adam's sin, we can see parallels to our own lives. We are sons of God like Jesus, but with one great exception: Jesus didn't sin. Jesus always did the will of His Father.

Jesus Christ, Son of God

I have told you both Adam and Israel are types of sons of God, and Jesus Christ is the Son of God. One of the primary ways we know Jesus is a different kind of Son of God is that when faced with temptation, He never yielded to it. Jesus always did exactly what the Father wanted Him to do.

Nevertheless, there is an even more important truth we are proclaiming when we say Jesus Christ is the Son of God—**Jesus is God.** How can I make this claim with such certainty? Consider what the New Testament says.

For in Christ lives all the fullness of God in a human body (Colossians 2:9).

———

Though he was God,

he did not think of equality with God

as something to cling to (Philippians 2:6).

———

And now in these final days, he has spoken to us through his Son. God promised everything to the Son as an inheritance, and through the Son he created the universe. The Son radiates God's own glory and expresses the very character of God, and he sustains everything by the mighty power of his command. When he had cleansed us from our sins, he sat down in the place of honor at the right hand of the majestic God in heaven (Hebrews 1:2–3).

———

But to the Son he says,

"Your throne, O God, endures forever and ever.

You rule with a scepter of justice" (Hebrews 1:8).

———

In the beginning the Word already existed.

The Word was with God,

and the Word was God (John 1:1).

———

So the Word became human and made his home among us. He was full of unfailing love and faithfulness. And we have seen his glory, the glory of the Father's one and only Son (John 1:14).

The message of Jesus as the Son of God was so important to the first believers that it was the first sermon Paul preached after his conversion.

Saul stayed with the believers in Damascus for a few days. And immediately he began preaching about Jesus in the synagogues, saying, **"He is indeed the Son of God!"**

All who heard him were amazed. "Isn't this the same man who caused such devastation among Jesus' followers in Jerusalem?" they asked. "And didn't he come here to arrest them and take them in chains to the leading priests?"

Saul's preaching became more and more powerful, and the Jews in Damascus couldn't refute his proofs that Jesus was indeed the Messiah (Acts 9:19–22, bold mine).

Of all the topics Paul could have preached about, why is it that Jesus' identity as the Son of God was so important that it was the very first message the apostle delivered? The New Testament gives four essential answers to that question:

1. We cannot have eternal life without the Son of God (see 1 John 5:12).
2. For us to have a relationship with God the Father, we must confess Jesus as the Son of God (see 1 John 2:23).
3. Our only hope of ever being reconciled to God is through the Son (see Romans 5:10).
4. Our only hope of life beyond this life is through the Son (see Galatians 2:20).

As you can see, having faith in Jesus as the Son of God is not one important belief among many other beliefs. It is what you must *first* believe.

What does it mean to "believe Jesus is the Son of God"? Jesus is fully man, but He is also much more than a man. He is not a high-ranking angel who came to earth as a human. Jesus is fully man and fully God. Jesus Christ is not a created being—He is coequal and co-eternal with God the Father and God the Holy Spirit. Adam is a son of God, in that God is his origin. Adam is created, but Jesus is begotten. That means Jesus is of the same nature as God. We might, for example, make something like a chair or a painting. We would say we created it. But a son is something we beget. Jesus, the Christ, is begotten and not created. There was never a time when He was not. There was a time when the Son was not yet a man, but there was never a time when He was not God. Now Jesus is forever both fully God and fully man. He shares God's divine nature from all eternity past to all eternity future.

As you can see, having faith in Jesus as the Son of God is not one important belief among many other beliefs. It is what you must *first* believe.

God the Father has a unique and special love for Jesus. God loves us because He adopted us as sons. However, we are only adopted as sons because of what Jesus has done.

We also pray that you will be strengthened with all his glorious power so you will have all the endurance and patience you need. May you be filled with joy, always thanking the Father. He has enabled you to share in the inheritance that belongs to his people, who live in the light. For he has rescued us from the kingdom of darkness and transferred us into the Kingdom of his dear Son, who purchased our freedom and forgave our sins (Colossians 1:11–14).

Jesus is our Elder Brother, and it is through His inheritance that we also will receive our inheritance. God directly confirmed that Jesus was His Son twice during Jesus' ministry: at His baptism and on the Mount of Transfiguration. There is an eternal love between God the Father and God the Son, and we benefit from that love.

Jesus is our Elder Brother, and it is through His inheritance that we also will receive our inheritance.

Our Identity as Sons of God When Jesus Returns

So far, we have talked about Adam as God's son who disobeyed and Israel as God's son who also gave in to temptation. Then we talked about Jesus as the Son of God. He was tempted but did not sin. As Son of God, He is also God. Through His death on the cross, Jesus makes us able to become sons of God who receive a full inheritance because of the sacrifice of Jesus, our Elder Brother.

If we know we are sons of God right now, then what will change in our understanding when Jesus comes to take us in the Rapture? The answer can be boiled down to two concepts: *assurance and inheritance*. We will receive full assurance that we are sons of God, and we will receive our inheritance of eternal life.

Assurance

Sometime in your life you have probably heard of John Bunyan's *Pilgrim's Progress* (the full original title was *The Pilgrim's Progress from This World, to That Which Is to Come*). Sometimes pieces of the book are assigned in school, and there have been a variety of cartoons suitable for children made about the book. Bunyan wrote the book in 1678 while in England's Bedford jail for preaching the gospel. This Christian allegory is considered one of the most important works of theological fiction ever written. It tells the story of the Christian's life, with all its ups and downs, until we go to be with the Lord in heaven. What you probably don't know is Bunyan wrote another book before this one, titled *Grace Abounding to the Chief of Sinners*. The earlier book is not written in allegory form; it is a memoir or testimony of Bunyan's own personal pilgrimage to find assurance of his salvation in Jesus Christ. You can find free digital versions of the book online.

If a secular psychologist were to read *Grace Abounding*, I am sure they would think Bunyan needed medication for anxiety, depression, or some other mental malady. Repeatedly, he describes feeling terror and torment that he is eternally damned with no hope of salvation. Then, through prayer, worship, or the encouragement of other believers, Bunyan will have a breakthrough and feel a glorious rush of God's love and assurance, only to be back in the "slough of despond" the very next day. The book can be a very frustrating reading experience as you witness his high highs and lower lows. In the end, Bunyan does receive assurance of his salvation, but the pilgrimage is a roller coaster ride. Those of us who have read it feel a bit sorry for this great hero of the faith and greatly relieved when it's finally over.

Here is the reality of our situation: almost every believer has moments of doubt and despair. I have been a pastor for a long time, and I cannot count the number of people who have come to me wondering if they are "really saved." It is a very common torment. It was so widespread that the apostle Paul needed to address it. I can tell people every time I preach that God loves them and wants to save them forever, but we are sinners living in a fallen world. Doubt creeps into our hearts, and the devil is always ready to stand and accuse us. That is why Paul tells believers,

For his Spirit joins with our spirit to affirm that we are God's children (Romans 8:16).

Don't think the Holy Spirit has to keep reassuring us because He thinks it's a great hobby. He gives us assurance because we *need* it. The Spirit knows that the world and the devil will keep shouting at us and saying we are worthless, so He speaks even louder into our hearts and reminds us that we belong to our Father. We are His sons.

When Jesus comes for us in the Rapture, all doubt will cease. Our Elder Brother will speak to us clearly and directly. He will only need to tell us *once*, and we will *believe Him*! Doubt and fear have no place in God's Kingdom. They don't come from God, and He will not give them even an inch in His eternal Kingdom. You will never again wonder if God loves you. You will have an eternal Sabbath rest in the assurance that God is your Father, and you are His son.

The Spirit knows that the world and the devil will keep shouting at us and saying we are worthless, so He speaks even louder into our hearts and reminds us that we belong to our Father. We are His sons.

Inheritance

Paul continues in Romans 8:

> And since we are his children, we are his heirs. In fact, together with Christ we are heirs of God's glory. But if we are to share his glory, we must also share his suffering.
>
> Yet what we suffer now is nothing compared to the glory he will reveal to us later. For all creation is waiting eagerly for that future day when God will reveal who his children really are. Against its will, all creation was subjected to God's curse. But with eager hope, the creation looks forward to the day when it will join God's children in glorious freedom from death and decay. For we know that all creation has been groaning as in the pains of childbirth right

up to the present time. And we believers also groan, even though we have the Holy Spirit within us as a foretaste of future glory, for we long for our bodies to be released from sin and suffering. We, too, wait with eager hope for the day when God will give us our full rights as his adopted children, including the new bodies he has promised us. We were given this hope when we were saved. (If we already have something, we don't need to hope for it. But if we look forward to something we don't yet have, we must wait patiently and confidently) (Romans 8:17–25).

What is our inheritance as sons of God? There are many things we receive when God adopts us, but Paul tells us the most obvious and important part of our inheritance: death has no hold on us, and we will have eternal life. Even if we suffer in this world, it will all melt away in our memories the moment we see Jesus. Because of Adam's sin, all his sons have suffered. Because Jesus suffered, all God's sons will be redeemed.

In that exact second when we look into Jesus' face, we will know we have eternal life and death can never touch us again. We will have new bodies without disease or decay. God began this process when we were saved, and He will complete it on the day Christ returns.

CHAPTER 11

We Are the Bride of Christ

There are three marriage partnerships I want to bring to your attention. I use the term "marriage partnership" because Adam, God, and Jesus are bridegrooms, while Eve, Israel, the Church, and individual believers are brides.

BRIDEGROOMS	BRIDES
Adam	Eve
God (YHWH)	Israel
Jesus	The Church & Believers

Just as I did in the previous discussion on sons of God, I need to say that the bride of Christ includes both women *and* men.[9] You may wonder how men can relate to Jesus as their Bridegroom, but we don't run from the language of the Bible simply because it makes us a little uncomfortable. Both men and women can have intimacy with Jesus, but it doesn't mean it is sexual. Marriage is one of the best ways to describe that relationship. In true intimacy with another person, we know each other deeply, we talk and laugh, and we have the same heart. If you are married, you know what I am talking about. I can look at Karen across a room, catch her eye, and immediately, we know what the other is thinking. That is what our relationship with Jesus is designed to become.

Male believers usually want to think of themselves in heroic terms—they are strong, tough, independent, and adventurous. But as they begin to walk with the Lord, they also discover in time that they are falling in love with Jesus over and over again. Women crave intimacy and security, and it makes it easier for them to think of themselves in a heart-to-heart, passionate relationship with the Lord. But men should not run from this image. If you are a male believer and reading this chapter, I encourage you to experience the presence of the Lord. There is a hunger within you that only He can satisfy. I would hate for you to wait until you get to heaven before you ever experience a secure, intimate, and real relationship with Jesus. If you are a believer, you are part of the bride of Christ. Allow Jesus to pursue you, just as you pursue Him. One day, He will gather you into His arms and keep you safe for all eternity. As I said, daughters of God are sons, and sons of God, male and female, are also brides.

As I said, daughters of God are sons, and sons of God, male and female, are also brides.

Adam as Bridegroom

Then the LORD God said, "It is not good for the man to be alone. I will make a helper who is just right for him." So the LORD God formed from the ground all the wild animals and all the birds of the sky. He brought them to the man to see what he would call them, and the man chose a name for each one. He gave names to all the livestock, all the birds of the sky, and all the wild animals. But still there was no helper just right for him.

So the LORD God caused the man to fall into a deep sleep. While the man slept, the LORD God took out one of the man's ribs and closed up the opening. Then the LORD God made a woman from the rib, and he brought her to the man.
"At last!" the man exclaimed.

"This one is bone from my bone,
and flesh from my flesh!
She will be called 'woman,'
because she was taken from 'man.'"

This explains why a man leaves his father and mother and is joined to his wife, and the two are united into one.

Now the man and his wife were both naked, but they felt no shame (Genesis 2:18–25).

Adam is the first bridegroom. God takes a rib from Adam's side to create the first woman, Eve. Adam awakens to see what God has done, to which he exclaims with joy,

"This one is bone from my bone,
and flesh from my flesh!"

Adam is very pleased with what God has done, and he sees in her a reflection of himself. It is as though they are two halves of the same whole.

God could not have created a being any more different from Adam—Eve was his mirror image. God could not have created a being any more the same than Adam—they were like missing pieces of each other's puzzle. Adam was downright poetic when he met her for the first time, and men have been using their words to impress women ever since. You may remember this dialogue from the movie *Dead Poets Society*:

John Keating: Language was developed for one endeavor, and that is ... Mr. Perry?

Neil Perry: To communicate.

John Keating: No! To woo women!

And that, my dear female friends, is more truth than I should probably tell![10]

Israel, God's Bride

Repeatedly throughout the Old Testament, various prophets depict Israel as God's bride (for example, see Jeremiah 31:32). God has a deep love for Israel and makes covenants with her, but Israel proves herself to be a faithless wife to the point that several prophets refer to her as an "adulteress" and even as a "prostitute":

> Israel treated it all so lightly—she thought nothing of committing adultery by worshiping idols made of wood and stone. So now the land has been polluted (Jeremiah 3:9).

> ———

> But you thought your fame and beauty were your own. So you gave yourself as a prostitute to every man who came along. Your beauty

was theirs for the asking. You used the lovely things I gave you to make shrines for idols, where you played the prostitute. Unbelievable! How could such a thing ever happen? (Ezekiel 16:15–16).

God has a deep love for Israel and makes covenants with her.

In case you think that is the most salacious part of Ezekiel 16, I recommend reading the entire chapter. God calls Israel a "degenerate harlot" (see v. 30 NKJV). The Lord is not pleased with Israel's flirtations with other nations and their idols. God loves Israel, and He will always love her, but just before the Babylonian Exile, He goes as far as to issue a bill of divorce to her (Jeremiah 3:8). The reason the Old Testament prophets depict the relationship between God and Israel as a marriage is because marriages are formed by solemn covenants (see Malachi 2:14). When Israel betrays God, the wound is on the same level as what humans experience when a spouse is unfaithful.

Jesus, the Bridegroom

In the New Testament, the Church is depicted as Christ's bride. The apostle Paul made the connection between the marriage of a man and a woman and the marriage of Jesus and the Church:

For husbands, this means love your wives, just as Christ loved the church. He gave up his life for her to make her holy and clean, washed by the cleansing of God's word. He did this to present her to himself as a glorious church without a spot or wrinkle or any other blemish. Instead, she will be holy and without fault (Ephesians 5:25–27).

———

For I am jealous for you with the jealousy of God himself. I promised you as a pure bride to one husband—Christ (2 Corinthians 11:2).

The reason the New Testament writers compared the relationship between Jesus and the Church as a marriage is because of the solemn covenant made in marriage vows. Both Israel and the Church joined in a covenant with God. The writer of Hebrews says,

But now Jesus, our High Priest, has been given a ministry that is far superior to the old priesthood, for he is the one who mediates for us a far better covenant with God, based on better promises.

If the first covenant had been faultless, there would have been no need for a second covenant to replace it (Hebrews 8:6–7).

A covenantal marriage is monogamous and exclusive between one man and one woman. In the same way, God wants an exclusive relationship with His people, and He will do what is necessary to protect that relationship. God says, "I am jealous for you" (see Exodus 20:5).

God wants an exclusive relationship with His people, and He will do what is necessary to protect that relationship.

I told you how God opened Adam's side, removed a rib, and created Eve. I do not think it is a coincidence that the apostle John includes this incident in his Gospel:

> It was the day of preparation, and the Jewish leaders didn't want the bodies hanging there the next day, which was the Sabbath (and a very special Sabbath, because it was Passover week). So they asked Pilate to hasten their deaths by ordering that their legs be broken. Then their bodies could be taken down. So the soldiers came and broke the legs of the two men crucified with Jesus. But when they came to Jesus, they saw that he was already dead, so they didn't break his legs. One of the soldiers, however, pierced his side with a spear, and immediately blood and water flowed out (John 19:31–34).

Just as God wounded Adam's side to create his bride, Jesus' side was wounded, and the Church was born. Blood and water flowed from Jesus' side. I do not know if there is a direct connection between the piercing of Jesus' side with water baptism and the Lord's Supper, but I will say this: when you are baptized and water flows, you publicly vow that you are now part of the bride of Christ. When you take communion and symbolize Christ's blood with the wine, you are renewing that vow as you remember the blood that was poured out for you as a sign and seal of God's eternal covenant with you. The next time you witness a baptism or take part in the Lord's Supper, remember you are married to Christ as His bride, and the marriage license is signed in His blood.

Both Jesus and Adam were wounded to form their brides. And just like Adam, Jesus is delighted in His bride. Adam looked at Eve and saw a mirror image of himself; Jesus looks at His Church and longs to see His image in her. He wants nothing more than to be one with His bride.

Our Identity as Bride When Jesus Returns

In ancient Israel, a bride did not know the exact time her groom would come to take her permanently to his home, nor did the groom know himself. The groom's father set the timetable, but it was based on completion of a few tasks. All the preparations for the wedding had to be finished, and the bridal chamber where the new couple would consummate their union had to be prepared. Only the father could say when these tasks were sufficiently done. Jesus referred to this tradition when He spoke of His own return:

> However, no one knows the day or hour when these things will happen, not even the angels in heaven or the Son himself. Only the Father knows. And since you don't know when that time will come, be on guard! Stay alert! (Mark 13:32–33).

In Israel, bridegrooms usually came to retrieve their brides sometime near the midnight hour. Trumpets, probably shofars, were blown to signal the approaching bridegroom. The groom's party would follow him through the streets shouting to proclaim and celebrate the groom's procession to the home of the bride's parents. By the light of burning torches, the groom's entourage would wind its way through the streets in a noisy, makeshift parade.

Meanwhile, the bride would receive word of the groom's imminent arrival.

> At midnight they were roused by the shout, "Look, the bridegroom is coming! Come out and meet him!" (Matthew 25:6).

All the members of the bride's household are now on their feet, and lamps are ignited. This gives the bride just a few extra moments to prepare herself. Several times the New Testament describes Jesus' return as quick and unexpected.[11] Once she has heard that the bridegroom is coming, the bride's only appropriate response is to prepare herself with urgency.

A procession would then head back to the bridegroom's home accompanied by musicians, singers, dancers, friends, family, and the bride's attendants (see Jeremiah 33:11). Once they arrived, the groom would check under the bride's veil to make sure he had the right bride. She would wear an exquisitely beautiful dress and fine jewels. She would be beautiful, and she would know she is loved.[12]

This ancient Jewish wedding description is but a dim shadow of what will happen when Jesus, our heavenly Bridegroom, returns for His beloved Church. God the Father will give the signal, and Jesus will appear to gather His bride from the ends of the earth. We will hear a shout and the sound of a trumpet. Light will split the sky. It will happen quickly, but just at the right time. For those who are prepared, we will welcome His coming with great joy, but there will be those who are left with no time to make ready.

For the Lord himself will come down from heaven with a commanding shout, with the voice of the archangel, and with the trumpet call of God. First, the believers who have died will rise from their graves. Then, together with them, we who are still alive and remain on the earth will be caught up in the clouds to meet the Lord in the air. Then we will be with the Lord forever. So encourage each other with these words (1 Thessalonians 4:16–18).

Today, if you are a believer in Jesus Christ, you know intellectually that you are His bride, and you may even know it in the depths of your heart. But until the Bridegroom comes, the bride cannot fully know the joy that comes from being totally present in body with the One she loves. God has an endgame, and it has always been to love us with an everlasting love. As the bride of Christ, what will be your new experience when you see your Bridegroom face-to-face in the Rapture? You will experience many emotions, and your mind will race with all the sights and sounds, but there are *two heightened experiences* you will have as the bride when you see Jesus: *intimacy and security*. As a believer, you know these experiences now, but when Jesus comes, they will be more real for you than they have ever been before. We will be closer to our Bridegroom than we have ever felt before, and we will feel more secure and safe in His presence than anything we have ever experienced. While the people who remain on earth will be going through the worst tribulation in human history, we will be marrying our Lord Jesus at the Marriage Supper of the Lamb. We will hear the clear passion of His voice as He says,

Rise up, my darling!

Come away with me, my fair one! (Song of Songs 2:10).

God has an endgame, and it has always been to love us with an everlasting love.

Intimacy

Sometimes we need to be reminded that God is an eternal Trinity of Father, Son, and Spirit. God is three Persons who have always been united in a dance of ongoing, intimate love. We will never be able to fully understand that love because it is beyond human comprehension. God has an intimacy within Himself that is deeper than any human relationship. God is fully complete within Himself. He does not need us, but He created us, and He loves us. He did it because He *is* love.

God exists to love, and love must have an object to extend itself to. He created humans for no other reason than to love them and for them to love Him. We are the only creatures suitable for the kind of intimacy God had in His divine mind. He did not need us, but He wanted us very much. In a way, it was not good for God to be alone, just like it was not good for Adam to be alone.

God exists to love, and love must have an object to extend itself to.

So God, who is Spirit, went beyond the spiritual realm and created a physical realm. In that realm, He made people so He could have an intimate relationship with them. God always wanted to make a being like Himself, in His image and likeness, so He could become one with that creature. He wanted to reproduce His love in and through them. He breathed His Spirit into Adam, and the first human's very life came from God's very breath. He made you in His image to represent and reflect Him. He wanted to know you intimately before you were even in your mother's womb. He loved you, and He wanted you to return that love to Him.

Jesus Christ is the Word of God in creation. He was there from the beginning, calling all humans, including you, to be His eternal bride. The Christ wanted to walk with us, talk with us, and live with us forever. We were created for an intimate relationship with Him so we would know and love Him in His fullness. God always wanted us to grow into a mature intimacy with Him.

As I have said, earthly marriage foreshadows the marriage we will have with Jesus, the Bridegroom. He left God the Father and God the Spirit to join with humanity so that one day He would become "one flesh" with us. When He comes again, we will take on our identity as His bride completely and eternally. It begins now, but it will be fully consummated on the day Jesus returns. Marriages here are earth are only a shadow of the "real" marriage we will have with Jesus. We should not look at human marriage and say, "Our marriage with Jesus will be like that." Instead, we should look at our marriage to Jesus the Bridegroom and pattern our earthly marriages after that.

But the person who is joined to the Lord is one spirit with him (1 Corinthians 6:17).

Security

In the Garden of Eden, God made Eve and brought her to Adam. On the day Jesus returns, God will join us individually and collectively as the Church with our eternal Bridegroom. God made you for this. You were created for intimacy with the God of the universe. So what would ever cause us to feel insecure in our relationship with Jesus Christ? That answer is one word: *sin*.

Sin can be defined as missing your purpose or missing the mark. If God created you for a loving relationship with Him, then sin is anything that destroys your relationship. On the day of the Rapture, sin will no longer have a place in your life. All that will be left is you and your Bridegroom.

If God created you for a loving relationship with Him, then sin is anything that destroys your relationship.

Think about your human relationships, particularly your romantic relationships. Have you ever felt insecure in a romantic relationship? Almost all of us have. Why did it happen? Usually, it is because someone violated the relationship in one way or another.

I have been working to strengthen and restore marriages for many years, and I am always surprised when a spouse says something like, "I don't know why my spouse wants a divorce. I didn't do anything wrong." Then when I begin to explore the situation with that person, I find sometimes, but not always, they have been neglecting their spouse or choosing something above them. You see, sin isn't always about the bad things we do. Often, it is simply choosing something else rather than an intimate relationship with Jesus. I have told the story many times how I chose to golf rather than spend time with my wife and family, almost destroying my marriage. Is there anything wrong with golfing? Of course not. However, there is something very wrong with choosing golf over your spouse—or choosing anything else over your spouse for that matter.

You destroy your intimacy with Jesus when you prioritize something above Him. The Bible calls that "idolatry." God will give you the desires of your heart, but you have to seek Him first (see Matthew 6:33). If you have willfully chosen to walk away from God's love, no wonder you feel insecure in your relationship with Him. No one else can protect you and provide for you. In fact, if you walk away from Him, then you open yourself up to stronger attacks from the enemy. If you want security, then stay by Jesus' side.

I am secure in my relationship with Jesus Christ, but I also know I will feel completely secure when I look into His face. Yes, you can have security now, but it will pale in comparison to the assurance you will feel when you are in His presence. His love for you is unconditional. Even if you have walked away from Him, He stands waiting for you. And on the day He returns, nothing again will ever again come between you and your Bridegroom.

CHAPTER 12

We Are Prophets

Most of us remember the telephone game we played as children. We sat in a circle, and someone started with a sentence or even a whole story. They would whisper it into the ear of the person next to them. Then that person would pass on what was heard to the next person and the next and so forth until it reached the final person in the circle. That final person would then repeat what they had heard. Seldom did the final version resemble the original. God does not play the telephone game. He delivers His messages to His human messengers, and they are responsible for repeating them clearly. Those who accurately repeat God's messages are prophets.

When most people think of the role of a prophet, they think of someone who foretells the future, and that is certainly what some prophets do in the Bible and in the modern Church. However, that is not the only function of a prophet, and it is usually not the primary one. The Hebrew word for prophet is *navi*. The root meaning of *navi* is 'mouth.' A *navi* hears from God directly and then accurately delivers these words to others. In a sense, a prophet is God's mouthpiece. One of the first explicit references to a prophet in the Old Testament occurs in Exodus 7:1–2:

Then the LORD said to Moses, "Pay close attention to this. I will make you seem like God to Pharaoh, and your brother, Aaron, will be your prophet [*navi*]. Tell Aaron everything I command you, and Aaron must command Pharaoh to let the people of Israel leave his country."

Those who accurately repeat God's messages are prophets.

In this passage, Moses hears directly from God and then tells Aaron what God has said. Aaron is to deliver the message to the Pharoah. The role of the prophets is twofold:

1. Hear from God.
2. Speak what God has said.

Moses and Aaron worked as a prophetic duo to hear God and deliver His messages.

The prophet becomes a channel to deliver what God is saying to others; a prophet is a conduit for God's direct message. A *navi* is someone who spends time with God in some way that gives them the ability to speak God's clear message.[13] A prophet is a person to whom God reveals His secrets and the organ through which God speaks to people.

Adam, the Prophet

Given the previous description of a prophet, how can we refer to Adam as one of them? Jewish, Christian, and even Islamic sources refer to Adam as God's first prophet. Adam did not predict the future, so he would not fit that description. Nevertheless, Adam did speak on behalf of God, and he was the first human to do so.

What does Adam do in Genesis that would qualify him as a prophet? Bible scholars point to the naming of the animals:

> So the LORD God formed from the ground all the wild animals and all the birds of the sky. He brought them to the man to see what he would call them, and the man chose a name for each one (Genesis 2:19).

How does this verse speak to Adam's prophetic role? Only the Creator has the prerogative to name His creation unless He delegates that task to someone else. Adam did not create the animals, nor did he create anything else. Still, the Lord gave Adam the privilege of choosing their names. In this sense, Adam spoke on God's behalf. This is the reason Adam can rightfully be called a prophet.

Prophets in Israel

As a people, all of Israel did not fulfill the prophetic function, partly because of their ongoing disobedience and rebellion against the Lord. Judaism considers Abraham as Israel's first prophet, and Isaac and Jacob followed in his footsteps. After that, however, Israel's prophets usually had a conflicted relationship with the people. A prophet, by God's design, does not always have to deliver bad news, but most of Israel's prophets found themselves doing just that. Why was that the case? Remember, a prophet is someone who first must have a relationship with God to hear Him before delivering His message. If that relationship is clouded by sin and idolatry, then it's going to be difficult to get close enough to God to hear Him clearly. Most Israelites couldn't draw near to God because of the sin in their hearts.

When the people disobeyed God, He chose obedient men and women to hear Him and deliver His messages to the rebellious nation. God called these prophets and filled them with His Spirit so they could deliver His word to the people. They were the original "whistle-blowers," telling God what the people were doing and then telling the people God's response.

Moses was the first prophet to speak both God's truth and judgment. Moses led the people out of Egyptian slavery, but they continued to turn against God. Moses drew close to the Lord to hear His message and then deliver it to the people as a way to bring them back from their rebellion. More prophets came forward in the years that followed, including Deborah, Samuel, Nathan, Elijah, and many others. They kept telling a rebellious people what God was saying.

Israel's priests filled a different role. They served as mediators between the people and God, but they were also given the responsibility to teach God's law to the people. However, Israel's priests were prone to disobedience and corruption. At times, they even led the people to worship false gods. God sent prophets when the priests did not remain faithful to the law and led the people into idolatry. When Israel's judges and kings ruled unwisely and unjustly, God spoke through the prophets and warned of the consequences of ongoing sin.

One of the greatest tragedies that puzzles readers of the Bible is how God loved Israel, yet the people persisted in following after the gods of their pagan neighbors. Occasionally, Israel followed the most unthinkable practices of idolatry, including giving their children to be sacrificed to idols or allowing their young women to become prostitutes in pagan temples (see 2 Chronicles 28:4). How could they turn away from God in such evil ways? Their sin led them to exploit the poor, neglect the widows, abandon the orphans, and disregard the strangers to whom they were supposed to extend hospitality. They cheated people in the marketplace, extorted each other in their businesses, and stole as a daily routine. Kings and other leaders destroyed the people. Religious leaders acted in the most unholy ways imaginable. So God sent prophets to warn the people. They were God's last attempt to call the people to repentance. In many cases, the prophets were the last people in the land who still listened to God's voice and spoke His words.

When we think of prophets, our minds often go to these heroic individuals of the Old Testament. But is this God's ideal model for a prophet? No, it is not God's original intent for prophets to speak words of judgment. God desires for His people to live in righteousness and holiness. If Israel had obeyed God and listened to His voice, then it would have been a nation of prophets that declared more and more of the goodness, promises, and blessings that can only come from the Lord. God would speak through them from "glory to glory" (see 2 Corinthians 3:18 NKJV), and the people would respond in joyful obedience. Sadly, that is not what happened in Israel, but it is what God originally intended.

If Israel had obeyed God and listened to His voice, then it would have been a nation of prophets.

Jesus, God's Ultimate Prophet

As I have said, Israel's prophets often spoke about God's judgment, but that does not mean all their words were bad news. They did tell of a future when God would right all wrongs and restore peace and prosperity. When Jesus came into the world, He fulfilled all the functions of the Old Testament prophets. He told about the future, healed the sick, performed miracles, and spoke all the words God gave Him to say.

Jesus often told His followers He would die and rise again. He spoke about Judas's betrayal and how Peter would deny Him three times before the crucifixion. Jesus told His followers how the owner of a donkey would prepare it for His ride into Jerusalem on Palm Sunday. When Jesus said something would happen, it happened. He spoke words of truth from God.

When Jesus said something would happen, it happened.

Jesus not only spoke the words God told Him to say, but He also *is* the Word of God. Remember, prophets hear God and then deliver what God has said to the people. Jesus is God's Word delivered directly to all humanity. He is God's ultimate Prophet.

In the beginning the Word already existed.
  The Word was with God,
  and the Word was God.
He existed in the beginning with God.
God created everything through him,
  and nothing was created except through him.
The Word gave life to everything that was created,
  and his life brought light to everyone.
The light shines in the darkness,
  and the darkness can never extinguish it (John 1:1–5).

———

So the Word became human and made his home among us. He was full of unfailing love and faithfulness. And we have seen his glory, the glory of the Father's one and only Son (John 1:14).

God is still raising up prophets today. How do we know if someone is a true or false prophet? In Numbers 12:6, God says He reveals Himself to prophets in visions and speaks to them in dreams. Jeremiah offers a further requirement:

So a prophet who predicts peace must show he is right. Only when his predictions come true can we know that he is really from the Lord (Jeremiah 28:9).

Jeremiah is saying that what a prophet predicts must come true if the prophecy is authentic. The book of Deuteronomy echoes that requirement:

> I will personally deal with anyone who will not listen to the messages the prophet proclaims on my behalf. But any prophet who falsely claims to speak in my name or who speaks in the name of another god must die.
>
> But you may wonder, "How will we know whether or not a prophecy is from the LORD?" If the prophet speaks in the LORD's name but his prediction does not happen or come true, you will know that the LORD did not give that message. That prophet has spoken without my authority and need not be feared (Deuteronomy 18:19–22).

Over the years, I have heard that the only requirement of a true prophet is that the prophecy comes to pass, but the New Testament gives a further requirement: Jesus is the criteria by which all truth can be verified. Moses said there would be a prophet to come that would not only hear from God but would also be *just like* God:

> Moses continued, "The LORD your God will raise up for you a prophet like me from among your fellow Israelites. You must listen to him" (Deuteronomy 18:15).

Jesus is *that* Prophet. He is just like God because He is God. Moses' prophecy is fulfilled in Jesus:

Long ago God spoke many times and in many ways to our ancestors through the prophets. And now in these final days, he has spoken to us through his Son. God promised everything to the Son as an inheritance, and through the Son he created the universe (Hebrews 1:1–2).

Jesus is a Prophet, the ultimate Prophet, and the fulfillment of all true prophecy. He is the One to whom we should listen.

Our Identity as Prophet When Jesus Returns

Again, a prophet is a person who hears God and then speaks accurately what God has said. There are many ways to hear God as a Christian, but there are two primary sources in this present world:

1. The Bible
2. The Holy Spirit

The Bible and the Holy Spirit are mutually confirming. As we read or hear God's Word, the Holy Spirit will help us understand it, and He will confirm our understanding. As we hear from the Holy Spirit, the Bible will be the measuring rod by which we can confirm that the Spirit truly spoke. When I say the Bible is one source to hear from God, I mean that we may read God's Word for ourselves or hear it read or spoken. A preacher can deliver the Word of God, and the Holy Spirit will help us weigh what has been said (see 1

Corinthians 14:29). The Holy Spirit may speak to us in visions, dreams, impressions, or through the words of other believers. In every case, the Spirit will confirm that we have correctly received God's Word, and God's Word will confirm what the Spirit is saying.

The Bible and the Holy Spirit are mutually confirming.

Ephesians 4:11–13 lays out the fivefold ministry of the Church with prophets as one of the five callings for believers. Does that mean there is a special prophetic office that includes or excludes particular believers? The answer is both "yes" and "no." Some individuals have an evident calling on their lives to interpret the Scriptures, listen to the Spirit, and accurately deliver God's messages. However, their calling is in a matter of degrees, and it does not exclude other believers from the prophetic function. All believers are called to listen for God's voice and then commissioned to deliver clearly what He has said. If you have been saved, then you are called to listen to and deliver what God tells you. It is a prophetic function for you to fulfill. God calls all believers to admonish, counsel, nourish, and encourage fellow believers through the Spirit and the Word.

On the Day of Pentecost, Peter quoted Joel 2:28–29, which predicts the day when all believers will act as prophets (see Acts 2:14–36). In fact, Jesus said believers are in an even greater position than the prophets of the Old Testament and John the Baptist (see Matthew 11:9–11). New Testament prophets teach, admonish, and exhort so others will not be overwhelmed by sin. We are called to encourage believers to love others and do good deeds (see Colossians 3:16; Hebrews 3:13; 10:24–25).

A New Testament prophet always encourages and strengthens. At times, they will deliver difficult messages of correction along with calls to repentance, but they never offer them in a way that destroys. Prophets build up with the Good News of Jesus Christ, which may include warnings, but never condemnation.

At this point, you're probably wondering how we will claim our identity as prophets when Jesus comes again in the Rapture. Let me remind you once more that we live in a world corrupted by sin. Our churches must constantly remind us how to hear God and train us how to use our tongues. Even the most mature believer must keep vigilant to hear and be disciplined to speak. Sometimes, even when we give it our best effort, both our ears and our tongues fail us.

When Jesus comes again, we will no longer hear with distortion, and our mouths will constantly break forth in praise of our God and King. This is how we will continue our prophetic role for all eternity.

Repaired Ears

Have you ever done something and later regretted your decision, even when you thought you made the right choice? You found yourself saying something like, "I guess I didn't hear the Lord right on that one." I know I have. The problem wasn't that God was unclear; rather, our hearing was distorted. There are many reasons we hear wrong, even when we are doing our very best to listen to what God is saying. We might be struggling with sin we have not confessed. Perhaps we replaced God's voice with our own wishful thinking. Sometimes the enemy gives a counterfeit message. I do believe the Holy Spirit speaks clearly and loudly, but I also know our own thoughts can get in the way of our hearing sometimes. The world is full of distractions, which is why we must constantly stay in God's Word, pray regularly, and listen for God's voice. Even with all those efforts, we live in a fallen world, and we make mistakes. Our spiritual ears need repair and redemption.

When Jesus returns, we won't need to question the source of messages any longer. We will hear directly from our Shepherd. His sheep know His voice (see John 10:27–30), but for now, other voices tend to get in our way. In an instant, we will see Jesus and never mistake another voice for His again. The melody of His sound will echo in our ears for all eternity, and we will never grow tired of hearing Him.

Renewed Voices

Why, then, would anyone but Jesus need to say anything? It's a valid question, and the answer lies in Creation. God spoke everything, including humans, into existence by the power of His Word. If He had only wanted to hear His own voice for all eternity, then He would not have made anything. Our God wants to speak to us, and He has given us the authority to repeat what He says.

As believers, we are commanded to proclaim the Good News. Does that mean when Jesus returns, we have nothing left to say? No! The gospel is eternal. We will be speaking and singing God's message without end. God will continue to speak, and we will echo His voice. He made Adam with that ability and purpose, but sin ruined man's connection to the Source. When Jesus returns, the Source will be recovered for us. God has made you an eternal prophet. You will listen to Him, and you will repeat what He has said in endless praise forever and ever.

Our God wants to speak to us, and He has given us the authority to repeat what He says.

CHAPTER 13

We Are Priests

"Who's in charge here?" You may not have asked that question outright, but it runs through most of our minds when we visit a new church. Is it the pastor or a group of elders? Does the church have congregational governance, or is there an authority structure outside the church? I have my own opinions about how a church should be governed, but I'm not going to address all those details here. However, I will say if you're going to be a part of a church, then you'd better figure out how the government and power structures work, or you will end up having a difficult time there.

At least since the split between the eastern and western churches (Eastern Orthodox and Roman Catholic) in AD 1054, this question gets asked with great frequency and even greater differences of opinion. During the Protestant Reformation, Luther, Calvin, and the Anabaptists all questioned the legitimacy of the papacy specifically and the authority of bishops and priests more generally. The reason the question about who is in charge happened around the idea of the priesthood is because the Catholic Church developed a hierarchical system of government throughout the Middle Ages that excluded laypeople from having a say about how the Catholic Church would operate. Unchecked power allowed priests, bishops, and even the pope to engage in corrupt practices that spiritually extorted more wealth and prevented the people from accessing the Scriptures. By the time of the Reformation, great dissatisfaction with the Catholic Church and the papacy was already present throughout Western Europe. The Reformation was only a response to a problem that was already brewing.

The Protestant Reformers began to articulate a doctrine that had been absent from the western church for several centuries. It was not a new teaching; it has its basis in both the Old and New Testaments, though it received new emphasis. The Reformers called this freshly articulated doctrine *The Priesthood of All Believers*. It was revolutionary for two reasons:

1. It challenged the power structures in Europe that gave spiritual and secular (political) authority to priests and bishops.
2. It gave all believers the right and authority to approach God for themselves and others and to interpret Scripture for themselves.

One of the earliest accusations the Reformers received from their Catholic detractors was that they had no priests. The Reformers responded, "Oh, but we do. We are all priests. What we really don't have is laypeople. We're all ministers here." Martin Luther said, "This word priest should become as common as the word Christian" because all believers are priests under God. Luther thought God had even given the plowboy or the milkmaid priestly work to do.

————

"We are all priests. What we really don't have is laypeople. We're all ministers here."

————

How would our lives change if we really treated our fellow believers as priests? If we would teach that every occupation is really ministry, then it would encourage Christians to connect their convictions to their daily lives at home, at work, and in society. We wouldn't think of our pastor as the "resident holy person," because we would recognize God's calling for all of us to be holy. In fact, we would still honor those who follow God's call into professional ministry, but that vocation would be given no more esteem than God's calling to be a teacher, farmer, doctor, store clerk, or law enforcement officer. Every person would fulfill the role of priest. Our churches would be stronger if we lived as though the priestly calling fell upon all believers.

In the New Testament, a priest was never a formal office in the church. The Holy Spirit selected other roles for leaders in the church, but priest was not one of them. For example, the early church had apostles, preachers, teachers, pastors, elders, and so on. It did not, however, have specific individuals chosen as priests, because all believers became priests the moment they were baptized.

The Priesthood of All Believers has significant implications for how Christians live before God and with each other. The concept that every believer is a priest, regardless of any other occupation, revolutionized the Church as we know it today. Over time, it even had an influence on the Catholic Church and can be seen in some of the ways Catholics operate today.

As I said, the Priesthood of All Believers has its basis in the Bible. In the Old Testament, God intended for all the people of Israel to be priests. At Sinai, He declared,

"And you will be my kingdom of priests, my holy nation." This is the message you must give to the people of Israel (Exodus 19:6).

The prophet Isaiah wrote about a day when

You will be called priests of the LORD,
    ministers of our God.
You will feed on the treasures of the nations
    and boast in their riches (Isaiah 61:6).

Through Jesus Christ, God accomplished His plan to make all believers priests:

And you are living stones that God is building into his spiritual temple. What's more, you are his holy priests. Through the mediation of Jesus Christ, you offer spiritual sacrifices that please God (1 Peter 2:5).

———

But you are not like that, for you are a chosen people. You are royal priests, a holy nation, God's very own possession. As a result, you can show others the goodness of God, for he called you out of the darkness into his wonderful light.
    "Once you had no identity as a people;
        now you are God's people.

Once you received no mercy;

> now you have received God's mercy" (1 Peter 2:9–10).

The apostle John referred back to God's promise in Exodus 19:6 twice:

> He has made us a Kingdom of priests for God his Father. All glory
> and power to him forever and ever! Amen (Revelation 1:6).

> ———

> And you have caused them to become
>> a Kingdom of priests for our God.
>> And they will reign on the earth (Revelation 5:10).

The concept of the priesthood of all believers occupies an important place in the Bible. It has great implications for our personal and public lives, as well as for our roles in the church and in our occupations.

Adam, the Priest

God made Adam in His image to reflect His character. Adam was crowned with honor and glory:

> Yet you made them only a little lower than God
>> and crowned them with glory and honor (Psalm 8:5).

God had already told Adam to govern the earth (see Genesis 1:28), but then He gave Adam the authority of a priest. Many Bible scholars have noted that there are connections between the Garden of Eden and the Temple. All the universe is God's temple, and the garden was His sanctuary. God gave Adam priestly instructions for serving in His garden-temple:

> The Lord God placed the man in the Garden of Eden to tend and watch over it (Genesis 2:15).

The most important phrase related to Adam's priestly role in this verse is "to tend and watch over." (In the King James Version, the directive is "to dress it and to keep it.") Why would gardening have anything do with the priesthood? And how does this phrase relate to the priesthood? The answer to these questions lies in two Hebrew words: *abad* ('to tend') and *shamar* ('to watch over'). They are used here together in Genesis 2:15 and in one other place in the entire Bible:

> They will serve Aaron and the whole community, performing their sacred duties in and around the Tabernacle. They will also maintain all the furnishings of the sacred tent, serving in the Tabernacle on behalf of all the Israelites (Numbers 3:7–8).

In this version, they are translated as 'performing their sacred duties' or 'maintain' (*abad*) and 'serve' or 'serving' (*shamar*). This pair of words is used in Genesis 2:15, and when they are placed together again twice in Numbers 3:7–8, they refer to priestly work in the Tabernacle. This usage is not coincidental.

God gives Adam the role of priest, and Adam becomes the prototype for every other priest in the Bible. When Israel finally had official priests, there was a connection to what God intended for Adam to do in Eden—tend and watch over. When the Israelites heard Moses read the Genesis account of Creation in the wilderness, they likely would have recognized he was using priestly words to describe Adam's role—to tend and to watch over.

Of course, we know Adam sinned, and his priestly role was corrupted because of his disobedience. God barred him from the garden-temple. Just how far did Adam fall? Consider this: God ordained Adam as a priest, but then because of Adam's sin, sacrifice became necessary, including the blood of God's own Son.

God made Adam a priest for two reasons:

1. To have direct access to God
2. To tend and watch over God's garden-temple

Now priests must take on a third role—they must *shed blood to atone for sin.* After Adam and Eve sinned in Genesis 3, the rest of the Bible is an account of God's rescue plan. God was searching for someone who could stand before Him and make peace with sinful humans.

> If only there were a mediator between us,
>> someone who could bring us together.
> The mediator could make God stop beating me,
>> and I would no longer live in terror of his punishment.
> Then I could speak to him without fear,
>> but I cannot do that in my own strength (Job 9:33–35).

No human priest in all Israel could become that mediator, that go-between. Only Jesus could do what no other priest could do.

**Only Jesus could do what
no other priest could do.**

Priests in Israel

I have been a pastor and a member of churches that use the term *anointing*. When we use this word, we usually mean it in one of two ways. First, we often speak of actual, physical anointing with oil that is done by someone placing a small amount on a finger or their hand and touching someone's head or hands with it while praying. Sometimes I have seen this done when we pray for people who are sick, pray for deliverance from demonic influence, ask God for a special blessing on someone, or install someone into an office or ministry position. Second, we use the word anointing to talk about the special manifest presence of the Holy Spirit in someone's life. We will see someone exercising their spiritual gifts with power and say, "That person has the anointing." I can't tell you exactly how you know someone has a special anointing, but when you see it, you know it.

If you have not been in a church that frequently uses this word, it may sound strange to you. In Bible times, anointing was not a frequent event, at least in the Old Testament. Anointing was part of a ceremony to install someone into an important role or office. It was used similarly to the way we inaugurate a president into office in the US, except it had more religious significance. It was a public symbol that an individual was chosen by God for that office, and everyone recognized it. It was also a way to ask God for a special blessing on that person. In the Bible, anointing someone to a new office was a major event because all the positions that used anointing in the Bible were for life.

In Israel, three different offices received an anointing ceremony: prophets, priests, and kings. Sometimes prophets did not go through a formal anointing ceremony, but occasionally they did. Israel did not have official priests prior to Moses and the Exodus. Before that, the firstborn son usually took on the priestly role for a household, although there were a few traveling priests who went from one settlement to another. Household priests constructed altars, interceded for others, and offered sacrifices. For example, Abraham did all these tasks (see Genesis 12:7–8; 13:4, 18; 18:22–33; 22:1–18). While Abraham never assumed the official title of a priest, he served all the priestly functions.

The official priesthood in Israel began at Mount Sinai. It was there God selected Aaron's sons to serve Him at His altar. These Aaronic priests were placed between God and the people, which gave the sons of Aaron a special position because they could approach God. They had *access*. Whenever we see Old Testament passages that refer to approaching God, there is usually a priest involved because they were given that privilege. No one could draw near to God's altar without authorization, or else there were dire consequences.

Moses told the priests how they were to gain access to the altar and serve in the Tabernacle. They worked as mediators, enabling

God to dwell with Israel and Israel to approach God. In the book of Leviticus, priests are instructed on the use of blood around the altar, told to teach the people about the Law, commanded to purify the house of God, and directed to communicate God's blessings. Priests had a major role in stewarding God's house. When they followed God's instructions, the people received God's blessings, but when they did not obey, God came in judgment. Like the history of Israel's struggle with sin, the story of the priesthood is a sad cycle of failure, judgment, repentance, and deliverance.

Even before the time of the judges, priests in Israel were often unfaithful. The complete failure of the priesthood, however, happened early in Israel's monarchy during the reign of King Saul. Eli, the priest at the Tabernacle in Shiloh, had two wicked sons, Hophni and Phineas, who followed him into the priesthood. Their evil deeds invited God's judgment and their deaths, which a young Samuel prophesied (see 1 Samuel 2:31–35). The priesthood in Israel would never fully recover after Eli's sons were killed. In fact, Hosea specifically blamed the priesthood for Israel's unfaithfulness, saying Israel sinned in the same way Adam had done (see Hosea 6:7–9). The priests did not teach the people God's law, so all Israel sinned, which led to terrible consequences (see Hosea 4:6). The Old Testament ends with God expressing His anger at the priesthood (see Malachi 2:3). Ezekiel summed up the sad state of the priesthood in Israel when he said their sin caused the glory of the Lord to depart from the Temple (see Ezekiel 8–10).

The story of God's rescue plan required the redemption of the priesthood. When Hophni and Phineas were killed, God pledged to establish a new priesthood:

Then I will raise up a faithful priest who will serve me and do what I desire. I will establish his family, and they will be priests to my anointed kings forever (1 Samuel 2:35).

This verse is the first time God promises a faithful priest who will have a family of priests to serve forever. Throughout the remainder of the Old Testament, God was building up Israel's expectation for this new priest who would atone for Israel's sins and bring the people into the Lord's presence. There were brief times of repentance and revival in Israel, but also much failure. God would need to raise up a new priest who could not be corrupted. The Lord spoke through the prophet Zechariah and promised a new priest who would also serve as king:

Tell him, "This is what the LORD of Heaven's Armies says: Here is the man called the Branch. He will branch out from where he is and build the Temple of the LORD. Yes, he will build the Temple of the LORD. Then he will receive royal honor and will rule as king from his throne. He will also serve as priest from his throne, and there will be perfect harmony between his two roles" (Zechariah 6:12–13; see also Psalm 110).

The Law of Moses did not allow a single individual to serve as both priest and king, but God was going to issue a new covenant and establish a royal priesthood. Jesus would be that High Priest and King. It took Jesus' death on the cross for us to be able to approach God without fear. He is now our High Priest and King, and He sits at the right hand of His Father, giving us access to God. He does not fail, because God the Father Himself has invited Jesus to join Him on His throne.

"They will have their own ruler again,

and he will come from their own people.

I will invite him to approach me," says the LORD,

"for who would dare to come unless invited?" (Jeremiah 30:21).

———

**It took Jesus' death on the cross for us to
be able to approach God without fear.**

———

Jesus, Our High Priest

The most frequently quoted Old Testament Scripture related to Jesus Christ's high priesthood is found in Psalm 110:4:

The Lord has taken an oath and will not break his vow:

"You are a priest forever in the order of Melchizedek."

The writer of Hebrews presents a full explanation of Christ's priesthood in chapter 7. All the priests in the Old Testament came from the tribe of Levi, but not Jesus. He is not in the old order or line of priests. He is in a new line: the order of Melchizedek. Jesus is a sinless priest, while all priests before Him disobeyed God. Because He was without sin, He offered Himself as a sacrifice, unlike the other priests who offered the blood of animals. The other priests had to offer regular, ongoing sacrifices, but Jesus died once for all time.

The priesthood of Jesus Christ is of a higher order than all other priests. In fact, He fulfills the role of the priest, and there is no need for another. How did Jesus become the High Priest for all time? His life, death, resurrection, and exaltation by God the Father qualified Him. Jesus Christ lowered Himself to become like us, laying aside His glory. He is the perfect Son of God, which proves that He alone has the authority and superiority to be our Priest. Hebrews 5 gives an account of Jesus' high priesthood, which is established and confirmed by His Sonship. Then Hebrews 7 explains how Jesus is a priest after the order of Melchizedek. He alone has the right to sit at God's right hand because He lived a perfect, sinless life. Jesus has made a new and better covenant (see Hebrews 7:12) and sealed it by His blood (see Hebrews 8:1–10:25). There is no need for any more sacrifices because Jesus is the final sacrifice to atone for our sins. This was God's rescue plan from the time Adam and Eve sinned in the Garden of Eden.

The priesthood of Jesus Christ is of a higher order than all other priests.

Our Identity as Priests When Jesus Returns

Adam was God's first human priest, but he did not obey God, so the priesthood was corrupted. God's royal priesthood was recovered by

Jesus Christ. However, Jesus' priesthood alone is not the end of the story. God's plan all along was to reproduce priests through His Son. When Jesus ascended to His Father's right hand, He sent the Holy Spirit to anoint every believer for priestly service. In the same way that special offices were recognized by anointing in the Old Testament, now all believers have been set apart for priestly service. The Holy Spirit has made the Church a holy nation and all believers a royal priesthood. Jesus now has a whole family of royal priests. He cleansed us by sacrificing His own blood and anointed us by His Holy Spirit.

The Holy Spirit has made the Church a holy nation and all believers a royal priesthood.

Many Bible scholars believe the book of Hebrews was originally delivered as a lengthy sermon. If that is the case, then the preacher began by declaring that Jesus is God's royal, priestly Son (see Hebrews 1:13). When he gets to the close of his sermon, the preacher returns to the same theme by telling his listeners that those of us who came into union with Christ by faith were adopted as sons of God (see Hebrews 12:1–18) and heirs of God's Kingdom (see Hebrews 12:19–29), and now we are qualified to offer sacrifices of praise (see Hebrews 13:1–19). Thus, all believers are part of Jesus Christ's royal priesthood. While we are here on earth, He has given us special authority in our priestly role. First, as royal priests, *we declare God's glory*. Of course, there are individuals who will be given the unique calling to be preachers and teachers, but all believer-priests are called to proclaim the Good News of Jesus Christ until He returns. We will need the Holy Spirit to empower us for proclamation in whatever career God calls us to serve.

Second, we are God's *ambassadors of reconciliation*. Priests in the Old Testament served as agents of reconciliation between God and the people. Now, through Jesus Christ, we are called to intercede with God on behalf of others. One of the greatest corrections made by the Protestant Reformers was that official priests alone should not have the prerogative to go to God on behalf of the people since all believers are part of the priesthood. However, many Christians have taken the Reformers' concerns to mean, "I can go to God for myself, and I have no need for anyone else." That claim is only partially true. We are called to be priests to each other. Paul wrote to Timothy,

> I urge you, first of all, to pray for all people. Ask God to help them; intercede on their behalf, and give thanks for them. Pray this way for kings and all who are in authority so that we can live peaceful and quiet lives marked by godliness and dignity. This is good and pleases God our Savior, who wants everyone to be saved and to understand the truth (1 Timothy 2:1–4).

James wrote,

> Confess your sins to each other and pray for each other so that you may be healed. The earnest prayer of a righteous person has great power and produces wonderful results (James 5:16).

You do not need to find a person with the official title of "priest" before you can confess your sins, nor do you have to confess all of your sins to other believers. But there are times when we are struggling when we need the priesthood of other believers to agree with us for freedom and deliverance. We all need other believers to help us in our walk with Christ. God is the one who started the process of reconciliation in your life, but He still involves believers in the process of forgiveness and reconciliation:

> And all of this is a gift from God, who brought us back to himself through Christ. And God has given us this task of reconciling people to him. For God was in Christ, reconciling the world to himself, no longer counting people's sins against them. And he gave us this wonderful message of reconciliation. So we are Christ's ambassadors; God is making his appeal through us. We speak for Christ when we plead, "Come back to God!" (2 Corinthians 5:18–20).

Jesus has called you to be a reconciling priest—His ambassador—who calls out to others, "Be reconciled to God!"

**God is the one who started the process
of reconciliation in your life,
but He still involves believers in the process
of forgiveness and reconciliation.**

I mention these first two tasks because one of them will change when Jesus returns, and the other will no longer be necessary. In your priestly and prophetic role, you will declare the glory of God for all eternity. However, you will no longer need to be a minister of reconciliation when Jesus returns. In the Rapture, all sin will cease, so forgiveness will be unnecessary. Jesus' blood covers our sin once and for all time. Then how do we exercise our priestly identity when Jesus returns? These next two aspects of our role as priests are both for this world, and we will continue operating in them even after the Rapture.

Access

In the Old Testament, both the Tabernacle and the Temple had a special room called the Holy of Holies. Only the high priest could enter that room and only once per year. Inside the Holy of Holies rested the Ark of the Covenant. This special holy box contained various artifacts from Israel's beginning, including Aaron's rod, some manna, and the tablets of the Ten Commandments. God's manifest presence rested upon the Ark's top, called the Mercy Seat.

The moment Jesus died, the curtain separating the Holy of Holies was torn by God's own hand from top to bottom (see Matthew 27:51). Now every believer has direct access to God through Jesus Christ. We can approach God's throne of grace with boldness (see Hebrews 4:16).

Because of Christ and our faith in him, we can now come boldly and confidently into God's presence (Ephesians 3:12).

Nevertheless, we still live in a world tainted by sin, and our own hearts and minds often keep us from approaching God without fear. We know that prayer works, but sometimes we lose confidence in our own access to God. We know the Lord has won many victories before us, but when times get difficult, we sometimes forget that God's power and love are available to us regardless of merit. That is what grace is about. And God's grace through Jesus' blood is what gives us complete access as His priests to His throne of grace and mercy!

When Jesus returns, you will never forget that again. Your access to God will be so real and evident that you will never again shrink away from Him. You will not fear His wrath or disapproval. We live at times right now without praying as we should, even when we know it is the key to our power. We are weak and frail, but when Jesus comes again, we will talk with God like old friends. We will never again forget or neglect the privilege we have to connect with our Father.

Your access to God will be so real and evident that you will never again shrink away from Him.

Spiritual Sacrifices

Jesus sacrificed His own life and shed His own blood to bring us back to God. Why, then, would we ever need to sacrifice again? It is true that no more blood will ever be shed to bring us into a relationship with God, but we are still to offer sacrifices. So what type of sacrifices do we offer? There are no longer animals offered on the altar; instead, we are to offer prayers, praise, thanksgiving, love, and kindness (see 1 Peter 2:5).

We are God's royal priesthood forever. For all eternity we will offer spiritual sacrifices acceptable to God because of Jesus Christ. The Bible tells us the kinds of spiritual sacrifices we should offer:

- We offer ourselves as "living sacrifices" (Romans 12:1).
- We give sacrificial "offerings of faith" (Philippians 2:17).
- We give sacrifices of "praise and thanksgiving" (Psalm 107:21–22).

When Jesus returns, our spiritual sacrifices will forever and always be acceptable to God. Jesus' blood cleanses us and makes our sacrifices pleasing to God the Father. If you are a Christian, then God has made you a priest forever.

———

For all eternity we will offer spiritual sacrifices acceptable to God because of Jesus Christ.

———

PART FIVE

Redeemed Authority

CHAPTER 14

We Are Kings

Let's return to Jesus' teaching about His return in the Gospel of Luke:

> And there will be signs in the sun, in the moon, and in the stars;
> and on the earth distress of nations, with perplexity, the sea and
> the waves roaring; men's hearts failing them from fear and the ex-
> pectation of those things which are coming on the earth, for the
> powers of the heavens will be shaken. Then they will see the Son
> of Man coming in a cloud with power and great glory. Now when
> these things begin to happen, look up and lift up your heads, be-
> cause your redemption draws near (Luke 21:25–28 NKJV).

As I've already said, I believe we are living in the last days. In fact,
I believe we are living in the *last of the last days*. I also believe many of
us alive today will never die because we are the generation that will
be alive when Christ returns. Jesus said, "When you see these things
start happening, your redemption draws near" (see Luke 21:28).
It's an abbreviated period; in other words, it's not going to be another hundred or thousand years. Jesus said, "The generation that
sees these things will not pass away until all things are fulfilled"

(see Luke 21:32). One generation is going to see the beginning and the end of the last days. Look up! Jesus is coming soon.

Let me remind you of the different yet complementary ways the New Testament describes how Jesus redeems us:

- He buys us.
- He buys us back from Satan, who stole us and enslaved us.
- He buys us to be His own property, and we now belong exclusively to Him.
- He rescues us by paying a ransom for us.
- He liberates us by force like would be done in a commando raid.

Each of those is true for us today, but they all will be completely fulfilled when Jesus returns. And He will do it "in a moment, in the twinkling of an eye" (1 Corinthians 15:52 NKJV).

Adam as King

There's a huge trend right now for people to discover their genealogy or ancestry. I recently had a friend who got on one of the genealogy websites and was very excited to learn he has royalty in his lineage. I thought that was a pretty amazing discovery until I found out that almost every person of European descent has royalty somewhere in their lineage. The same is true for other continents. It is a mathematical probability. Did you realize if you go back 40 generations, then you would cumulatively have over two trillion great-grandparents? If you only went back to the time of the Protestant Reformation (an average of 18 generations), then you would have over 260,000 great-grandparents. The number grows exponentially with each subsequent generation. When numbers get that high, there is bound to be both royals and criminals somewhere in the list. I don't want to downplay my friend's genealogical research, but I do want to tell you that no matter who you are, you've got royal blood. Even more, if you are a believer, God says you're a king right now, and your royal lineage goes all the way back to Adam.

Adam and Eve had God's "whole package" in the paradise of the garden. They had perfect bodies and complete pleasure in that place called Eden, which means 'pleasure.' They also had *authority.* God created Adam and Eve with absolute authority (dominion) over the rest of the created order. God made us to reign over the earth. Genesis 1:27–28 says,

> So God created man in His own image; in the image of God He created him; male and female He created them. Then God blessed them, and God said to them, "Be fruitful and multiply; fill the earth and subdue it; have dominion over the fish of the sea, over the birds of the air, and over every living thing that moves on the earth" (NKJV).

God made us to reign over the earth.

Notice Genesis lists only two genders: male and female. There's a growing number of people today who believe there are many more. For example, the city of New York lists 31 distinct gender possibilities on the city's official documents.[14] This is another sign of the end times, which I mentioned in Chapter 5. In 2 Thessalonians 2, Paul says that there will be widespread apostasy or falling away from the truth. An example of this kind of falling away is when someone says, "I was a man, but now I'm a woman," or "I was a woman, and now I'm a man." This kind of thinking has even crept into some churches. It is affirming a state of being contrary to the way God created someone, and that is falling away.

This passage in Genesis 1 uses the Hebrew word *radah*, which means 'rule, subdue, or exercise dominion.' These are strong words that imply force or even to "tread down." God essentially told Adam and Eve, "You are the kings of the earth; under My authority, you are to rule and reign. I call you to subjugate the earth and take dominion over anything that would come against My will." He gave them total authority. Adam and Eve were to be the police, sheriff's department, mayor, governor, FBI, CIA, Homeland Security, Army, Navy, Air Force, Marines, and Coast Guard. They were the president, Supreme Court, and Congress. God gave Adam and Eve all physical authority and spiritual authority. They had 100 percent authority over the earth.

Kings in Israel

Kingship was always in the mind of God. I won't go into great historical detail about the kings of Israel and Judah, but I will give a general overview. In all, there were 42 kings and one queen who ruled instead of a king. God allowed Saul to be anointed as the first king. Saul ruled over the entire nation for 40 years. When he died, Israel was temporarily divided. Saul's son Ishbosheth ruled 11 tribes for two years, while Judah chose David. When Ishbosheth was assassinated, David ruled over all 12 tribes for 40 years. Then his son Solomon ruled the united country after him for 40 years.

Kingship was always in the mind of God.

When Solomon died, the people disagreed over who should rule, so the kingdom divided into the Southern Kingdom of Judah (the tribes of Benjamin and Judah) and the Northern Kingdom of Israel (the remaining 10 tribes). Each of the separate kingdoms had 19 rulers after dividing. The Bible says Israel had 18 evil rulers and makes no judgment on only one of them. Judah had seven good rulers, one mostly good ruler, 10 evil rulers, and one mostly bad ruler. Overall, the monarchy was not great for either Israel or Judah.

Was the monarchy a bad idea? Some Bible interpreters have thought so. There are those who believe Israel traded a theocracy (God's rule) for a monarchy (human rule). Of course, humans often choose their own way rather than God's, but the monarchy in itself was not rebellion against God. The mistake wasn't that Israel wanted a king, but it was *how* Israel asked for a king. I need to make this distinction, because even Christians will have those among us who want to throw off all human authority. I must say clearly that God did not have a problem with humans in authority, but He did have an issue with how Israel went about doing it.

For Israel, theocracy never meant God ruled directly without any humans involved. God always used human leaders, such as Moses,

Joshua, and the judges. The monarchy in itself was not an effort to throw off God's rule. The people did frequently rebel against God, but that is not an essential feature of human rule. God wanted to use kings for His purposes. Israel got into trouble when the kings disobeyed God and led the people to do the same.

Again, kingship was not against God's purposes for Israel. He always had a monarchy in mind. The Lord promised to Abraham,

> I will make you extremely fruitful. Your descendants will become many nations, and kings will be among them! (Genesis 17:6).

To Jacob, God made the same promise:

> Then God said, "I am El-Shaddai—God Almighty.' Be fruitful and multiply. You will become a great nation, even many nations. Kings will be among your descendants!" (Genesis 35:11).

Jacob prophesied to his sons:

> The scepter will not depart from Judah,
>   nor the ruler's staff from his descendants,
> until the coming of the one to whom it belongs,
>   the one whom all nations will honor (Genesis 49:10).

Moses laid out God's regulations for the kings (see Deuteronomy 17:14–20). God was moving His people toward kingship. When Samuel was born, his mother, Hannah, prophesied:

> Those who fight against the LORD will be shattered.
> He thunders against them from heaven;
>> the LORD judges throughout the earth.
> He gives power to his king;
>> he increases the strength of his anointed one (1 Samuel 2:10).

God's Messiah was always going to come from the line of King David. God did not suddenly hatch this plan as a concession to Israel's gripes. It was in His mind all along.

The people of Israel wanted a king so they could be like other nations who had them. However, God was never going to let that happen. Israel's kings would be different because they were expected to keep God's laws and lead the people to observe them as well. Kings of other nations may have ignorantly sinned against God, but Israel's rulers had no excuse. When they sinned, judgment was certain, and when they obeyed, blessings were assured. God was still Israel's ruler, no matter what. He did not give up His sovereign role simply because Israel put human kings on the throne.

So what did Israel do wrong? Their insistence on a king was a demand rather than a request. We cannot presume upon God or give Him ultimatums. He may give you want you want, but you won't like it. They also based their demand on comparing themselves with the other nations. Comparison almost always leads to nothing good. They should have wanted a king to unite the people in following God's laws and giving Him glory. Instead, they were driven by jealousy and blind ambition. They did not consider God's will or timing in their request. I believe God would have elevated David to the kingship regardless, but the people made demands of God about

30 years too soon. If we don't pursue God's will in God's way, the results are always disastrous. God wants to rule over human affairs, and He will use humans to do it, but He alone has the right to set the timing and standards for how we should live.

Jesus Christ, King of Kings

God did give the people of Israel what they wanted. He wasn't against kingship, but He was opposed to the way Israel pursued it. Consequently, God allowed them to have many rulers who did not follow His laws or give Him honor. Occasionally, there were good rulers, but the majority were disobedient and evil, and they led the people to rebel against God. Despite all this, God was still working on His rescue plan to give Israel and the world a new King.

> But you, O Bethlehem Ephrathah,
>> are only a small village among all the people of Judah.
> Yet a ruler of Israel,
>> whose origins are in the distant past,
>> will come from you on my behalf (Micah 5:2).

>> ———

> For a child is born to us,
>> a son is given to us.
> The government will rest on his shoulders.
>> And he will be called:
> Wonderful Counselor, Mighty God,
>> Everlasting Father, Prince of Peace.

His government and its peace
>   will never end.
He will rule with fairness and justice from the throne of his
>   ancestor David for all eternity.
The passionate commitment of the LORD of Heaven's Armies
>   will make this happen! (Isaiah 9:6–7).

The people of Israel repeatedly disobeyed the Lord, and as a result, He allowed the city of Jerusalem, along with its palace and Temple, to be destroyed by the Babylonians. Many of the people were taken as prisoners back to Babylon. After 70 years, a remnant returned in three waves to rebuild the Temple and the city, but God did not restore the kingship. For over 500 years after the Exile, the land of Israel was subjected to occupation and rule by foreign armies. The people hoped and prayed the Lord would send a liberator to free them from captivity. They anticipated a conquering warrior-king to defeat and drive out the foreign occupiers. They did not get what they expected.

Jesus was not what the people of Israel had in mind, especially not the religious leaders. The last person they thought God would send was the son of a humble carpenter from Nazareth.

"Nazareth!" exclaimed Nathanael. "Can anything good come from Nazareth?"
"Come and see for yourself," Philip replied (John 1:46).

Sometimes people were dismissive of Jesus, like Nathaniel before he became a disciple. At other times they saw Jesus as a very dangerous threat. Not long after He was born, some wise men from eastern lands came to Jerusalem looking for Jesus, "the newborn king." They wanted to worship Him. When King Herod heard about their intentions, he was "deeply disturbed," along with everyone else in Jerusalem (see Matthew 2:2–3). He told the wise men to find the king and report back his location. They found Jesus but never reported His location; instead, they left the area by another route. Herod responded by ordering the deaths of all male children two years old and younger in and around Bethlehem. When Jesus became an adult, the religious leaders saw Him as a threat. They rejected the idea that Jesus could be God's promised Messiah and King. Instead, they plotted to have Him executed.

During Jesus' trial, the Roman governor Pilate asked Jesus if He was the king of the Jews. "Jesus replied, 'You have said it'" (Mark 15:2). Then Jesus explained what kind of kingdom He was ruling:

> Jesus answered, "My Kingdom is not an earthly kingdom. If it were, my followers would fight to keep me from being handed over to the Jewish leaders. But my Kingdom is not of this world" (John 18:36).

Pilate did not understand the kind of king Jesus is, but neither did anyone else, including Jesus' own followers. Establishing an earthly kingdom was not on Jesus' agenda. One day, His Kingdom will envelope both heaven and earth, but only after the Tribulation. As for now, Jesus' Kingdom is spiritual:

> Jesus replied, "I tell you the truth, unless you are born again, you cannot see the Kingdom of God" (John 3:3).

In Luke 17:20–37, Jesus taught about His Second Coming. He began by talking directly with the Pharisees:

> One day the Pharisees asked Jesus, "When will the Kingdom of God come?"
>
> Jesus replied, "The Kingdom of God can't be detected by visible signs. You won't be able to say, 'Here it is!' or 'It's over there!' For the Kingdom of God is already among you" (Luke 17:20–21).

"God's Kingdom isn't coming like you expected, and the King won't look like how you imagined," Jesus was telling the Pharisees. The Messiah won't be a revolutionary warrior who will drive out the Romans. Jesus was telling the Pharisees that He *was* the Kingdom embodied. He is the King they need, though not the one they expect. The Messiah is standing right in front of them, but they are missing Him entirely. How will they know who He is?

> So Jesus said, "When you have lifted up the Son of Man on the cross, then you will understand that I AM he. I do nothing on my own but say only what the Father taught me" (John 8:28).

Some of the religious leaders were blinded by their own expectations. Others were deceived by sin and pride. Many of them would never recognize Jesus as King, but one day they will. In fact, all of us will know He is King one day.

> Therefore, God elevated him to the place of highest honor
>   and gave him the name above all other names,

that at the name of Jesus every knee should bow,
in heaven and on earth and under the earth,
and every tongue declare that Jesus Christ is Lord,
to the glory of God the Father (Philippians 2:9–11).

Isn't that an amazing revelation? One day, even the staunchest unbeliever will declare Jesus' kingship.

If I were to try to tell you everything you need to know about Jesus the King, I could not contain it in this book. He is the King of God the Father's Kingdom. It is not of *this* world, but one day it will be. Jesus will reveal Himself as the King of the whole universe, including the world in which we now live. The day is coming, but it is not yet here. However, when He reveals who He is in His fullness to all humanity, no one will be able to deny Him.

One day, even the staunchest unbeliever will declare Jesus' kingship.

Jesus is coming again soon. He came humble and lowly the first time, but from now on, we will see Him with power and authority. He is King of the universe. The Bible calls Jesus "King of all kings and Lord of all lords" three times:

At just the right time Christ will be revealed from heaven by the blessed and only almighty God, the King of all kings and Lord of all lords. He alone can never die, and he lives in light so brilliant that no human can approach him. No human eye has ever seen him, nor ever will. All honor and power to him forever! Amen (1 Timothy 6:15–16).

―――

Together they will go to war against the Lamb, but the Lamb will defeat them because he is Lord of all lords and King of all kings. And his called and chosen and faithful ones will be with him (Revelation 17:14).

―――

On his robe at his thigh was written this title: King of all kings and Lord of all lords (Revelation 19:16).

Jesus Christ is the Supreme Ruler and Authority of the universe. No one will ever be able to oppose Him again. He is the King right now, but one day soon He will bring everything under subjection to Him.

I have even better news––*we will rule with Jesus*! Look at what the apostle Paul told the Ephesian believers:

For he raised us from the dead along with Christ and seated us with him in the heavenly realms because we are united with Christ Jesus (Ephesians 2:6).

We have authority over sin, death, hell, and the devil, but we do not know the fullness of our authority yet. When Jesus returns in the Rapture, He will complete the work in us. We are kings because He is the King of all kings.

Jesus came and told his disciples, "I have been given all authority in heaven and on earth" (Matthew 28:18).

He is the faithful witness to these things, the first to rise from the dead, and the ruler of all the kings of the world (Revelation 1:5).

Our Identity as Kings When Jesus Returns

In the Church today, believers tend to shy away from God's specific call to dominion. I understand their hesitance because the concept has gotten misused. It does not imply violent destruction. If God has called us to rule, then He intends for us to rule responsibly. For example, we don't have permission to destroy nature just because we want to do it. God is inviting us to value His creation in the same way He values it. That is called "stewardship." A good ruler doesn't destroy the people. A righteous ruler serves, manages, and stewards the people and the nation.

Even now, those of us who are believers have been redeemed by Christ to take up the mantle God originally placed on Adam and Eve. We know God's will, so we should not be confused. We have the choice of whether we will obey it. The Bible clearly tells us, and the Holy Spirit fully empowers us, to have dominion over the earth even today. Through Jesus' death and resurrection, He defeated Satan. Jesus disarmed him and stripped him of all authority over the earth and over us. Even so, we do not always live according to the truth that is available to us.

Yes, God created you to rule the earth. That is who you are! So many secular theories have tried to undermine our place as rulers in this world. Evolutionary theory, secular psychology, social science, atheism, and political theories such as Marxism approach humans as though we are no better than accidents or animals who must be controlled by something other than God's commands. That is not the biblical story. I will address the difficulties related to evolutionary theory later in this book, but for now I want you to know we did not come from an accident, nor will we end in an accident. That is a lie the devil whispers to us. He wants you to think you have no purpose. But God speaks with a clear voice: "I created you in My image. I created you to rule."

The apostle John opens Revelation with this vision:

> John, to the seven churches which are in Asia:
>
> Grace to you and peace from Him who is and who was and who is to come, and from the seven Spirits who are before His throne, and from Jesus Christ, the faithful witness, the firstborn from the dead, and the ruler over the kings of the earth.
>
> To Him who loved us and washed us from our sins in His own blood, and has made us kings and priests to His God and Father, to Him *be* glory and dominion forever and ever. Amen (Revelation 1:4–6 NKJV).

We serve as priests. We rule as kings. John says God "made us kings," which is past tense. He washed our sins from us in His own blood, redeemed us, bought us back, and brought us back to whom He made us to be. It may seem odd for women to hear God made them sons and kings. As I said earlier, it's also a little unsettling when men hear we are the bride of Christ. We'll just have to get used to it. I will gladly be Jesus' bride. God has made us kings and priests, a priestly kingdom.

Yes, as a Christian, you are a king under the authority of King Jesus. That's who you really are. You may be thinking, *Wait a minute. I'm not a king. I work in childcare. I do landscaping. I work on contracts.* I want you to know you only do those things temporarily. Eternally, you are a ruler! Satan got us to hand over dominion of the earth, and we lost it because of disobedience. But Jesus redeemed it. He restores us to our true identity. We are priestly kings.

The apostle Peter echoes John's vision:

> But you *are* a chosen generation, a royal priesthood, a holy nation, His own special people, that you may proclaim the praises of Him who called you out of darkness into His marvelous light; who once *were* not a people but *are* now the people of God, who had not obtained mercy but now have obtained mercy (1 Peter 2:9–10 NKJV).

Peter is saying before you took hold of God's mercy, you were not redeemed. Now, however, you have reached out for God's mercy, and He has restored you to who you really are—a royal priest.

Although that is who God created you to be, I can understand why you may be struggling with this concept. Right now, many people mock God, Jesus, the Church, and the Bible. Christians around the globe still suffer severe persecution, and it is increasing daily. However, on the day Jesus returns, we will get our full authority back, and all the rules will change. I urge you to be patient. Jesus is coming, and it will all change in an instant. The apostle Paul says,

> If we endure,
> We shall also reign with *Him*.

If we deny *Him,*

He also will deny us (2 Timothy 2:12 NKJV).

This is God's promise to us.

One of the constant themes of the Bible is that of our authority. As I said, the Bible's first chapter tells us God vested in humanity authority over the entire earth (see Genesis 1:26). However, that is not all. In the Bible's last chapter, we learn we will "reign forever and ever" (Revelation 22:5 NKJV). Even so, as far as we know, Adam and Eve never exercised their authority to the extent God intended. The only thing we know Adam did was name the animals (see Genesis 2:19–20). That's as far as he got. Otherwise, there is no other record in Genesis that even hints to Adam and Eve using the authority God granted them. The devil is evil and in opposition to God, and the Lord would never grant him any authority. The only authority Satan has on earth is unused and misused human authority. He has no authority on his own. Everything the devil does in this world happens because there is a vacuum in human authority. When we don't exercise our God-given authority in a God-ordained way, we give the devil the opportunity to rule. Where he finds an opening, he will take it. Sin isn't just acting against God's will; it is acting in concert with the devil. As a result, our sin gives him authority in our lives to do as he wishes.

When we don't exercise our God-given authority in a God-ordained way, we give the devil the opportunity to rule.

Why didn't Adam and Eve use their God-given authority? It was because they chose the sin of disobedience rather than God's purpose and destiny for them. When they sinned, they handed the title deed to the earth over to the devil. And Satan quickly scratched his signature on it.

In fact, Jesus Himself refers to the devil as the "ruler of this world" (John 12:31 NKJV). Luke writes,

> Then the devil, taking Him up on a high mountain, showed Him all the kingdoms of the world in a moment of time. And the devil said to Him, "All this authority I will give You, and their glory; for *this* has been delivered to me, and I give it to whomever I wish. Therefore, if You will worship before me, all will be Yours" (Luke 4:5–7 NKJV).

When Satan says, "*This* has been delivered to me," the word translated *deliver* means 'to hand over.' Who handed it over? It wasn't God. Humans did it. You see, sin is not just rebelling against God; it's also agreeing with the devil and giving him authority. It should change how we think and act if we will recognize that our sin, in a sense, is enthroning the devil. You are the devil's worst nightmare because he knows the authority God wants you to have. The enemy knows if you realize it, then you will defeat him at every turn. Of course, all of us are imperfect, and we live by grace. Nevertheless, when we decide to pursue sin, we give the devil our marriages, our families, our lives, and our morality. We give him authority in those areas, and he encamps there with all the hosts of hell. Unused human authority is where the devil dances.

You are the devil's worst nightmare because he knows the authority God wants you to have.

James writes, "Therefore submit to God. Resist the devil and he will flee from you" (James 4:7 NKJV). Resist the devil. Fight him. Do it with all your might. The implications of sin are too great. The devil rules illegitimately in the vacuum of human rule!

The only way you can be free from the devil's rule is by willingly living under God's authority and rule. As you place yourself under God's authority, you will have authority. In the Kingdom of God, you will only have as much authority as you are willing to put yourself under. Through submission, fasting, and prayer, you will find an increase in your authority.

If you have chosen to rebel against God, then you will not be able to cast the devil off his own property. What I mean by this statement is that *rebellion is the devil's turf*. If you're in rebellion, then you will have no authority. James tells us to *submit* to God and *then* resist the devil, and he will flee from us. Why will the devil flee from us when we submit? Because He knows we are under God's authority, which then gives us authority.

How long have you been a believer? Before you answer, let me tell you that as far as authority is concerned, the amount of time does not matter. Your willingness to submit is what is important. If you have been a believer for only a few days, then you already have authority over the devil and all his demons. However, I need to reiterate that you must be under God's authority to be able to use the authority He's given you.

Jesus said, "All authority has been given to Me in heaven and on earth" (Matthew 28:18 NKJV). In Luke 4:5–7, the devil told Jesus if He would bow down to him, then he would give Jesus all the world's kingdoms. Jesus essentially said, "No, I'm going to go ahead and die for it." You see, Jesus would not take any shortcuts. He would not accept anything the devil had to offer, because He knew the devil from the beginning. Jesus knew anything the devil would propose would be corrupt. Jesus was offered a shortcut that would have been easy for most of us to accept, but He turned it down. He refused for our sake. Our salvation was more important than anything the devil could offer.

Jesus died on the cross for our sins, and then God made Him alive again. Through His death and resurrection, Jesus paid the penalty for us so we could be forgiven. He also took back the title deed of the earth that we had handed over to the devil. Jesus signed it with His own blood. When He said, "All authority has been given to me in heaven and on earth," Jesus meant He has all the authority in the whole universe. Conversely, that means the devil has zero authority—zero dominion—over your life. Jesus says, "I give you the authority to trample on serpents and scorpions, and over all the power of the enemy, and nothing shall by any means hurt you" (Luke 10:19 NKJV). Satan cannot harass you, come against your marriage, destroy your family, threaten your destiny, or come after any other precious thing in your life. When the devil attempts to come against you, then you must rise up as a king and priest and take authority over him. Jesus got it back for you!

We reign and rule because we are kings. That is who we are. I did not come up with the idea that God will make us kings to boost our self-esteem. Jesus Christ established us as royalty the minute He rose from the dead. Until the Rapture, we are to reign over our sinful passions, bringing our minds, wills, and affections into submission to Jesus by the power of the Holy Spirit through His Word.

When Jesus comes again, we will completely receive our authority back. Then we will rule over the earth just as God intended for Adam and Eve in the beginning. What was the nature of Adam's rule, and how does it apply to us after the Rapture? There are two aspects to our role as kings in the future: *authority and dominion.*

Authority

We are given authority in Christ when we accept Him as our Lord and Savior. However, there is also a future aspect to our reign with the Lord, a reign that will involve us judging even the angels (see 1 Corinthians 6:3). I cannot give a clear description of how or why we will judge the angels, but Paul wants us to know the extent of our authority. We should wait eagerly for this day in the future, and we should be growing in our authority under Christ even now. In the next chapter I will give a fuller description of the timeline and how we will reign with Christ in the Millennium.

Dominion

For us to have *dominion,* we must have *a domain,* which is an area over which we are in charge. We can know that sin no longer has dominion over us because we have been adopted as God's sons (see Romans 6:14; Galatians 4:1–7). Jesus Christ has given us the power by the Holy Spirit to conquer sin and pursue holiness. When Jesus comes again, we will no longer be influenced by sin, and it will never again be present in any dimension where we exist. In fact, we will have no need for the Law at all, because we will be present with the Lawgiver. We will be able to live according to the law of liberty as we serve our Creator for all eternity (see 1 Peter 2:16; James 1:25).

When Jesus returns, He will give us dominion, and He will also give us a domain. I personally believe He will give us authority over defined geographical areas. For example, He may choose me to rule over parts of Texas since that is where I live, though only He will get to decide. I will discuss more of this concept in the next chapter. Nevertheless, we can be sure that Jesus will be King, and we will reign as kings alongside Him.

When Jesus returns, He will give us dominion, and He will also give us a domain.

CHAPTER 15

What Will Happen and When?

John penned the book of Revelation, but Jesus is explicitly credited as the author because the words John wrote came directly from Jesus. In fact, Jesus dictated the letters to the seven churches in Revelation chapters 2 and 3 word for word to John. At the end of Jesus' letter to the church in Thyatira, He says,

> Now to you I say, and to the rest in Thyatira, as many as do not have this doctrine, who have not known the depths of Satan, as they say, I will put on you no other burden. But hold fast what you have till I come. And he who overcomes, and keeps My works until the end, to him I will give power over the nations—
>
> "He shall rule them with a rod of iron;
>
> They shall be dashed to pieces like the potter's vessels"—as I also have received from My Father (Revelation 2:24–27 NKJV).

When Jesus tells them they will be given "power," it is a translation of the Greek word *exousia*, which means 'authority to rule.' Jesus is telling the believers in Thyatira to be patient. If they will endure to the end, then He will give them power over the nations of the world that exist when the end comes. Those believers will rule with Him. We are also those believers by extension.

A Timeline of Events

I want to give you a timeline that includes *five major events* that will soon commence, beginning with Jesus' return. I will begin with the Rapture of the Church and end with our final eternal state. This is God's agenda:

1. The Resurrection of the Dead in Christ and the Rapture

I have coupled the resurrection of the righteous dead and the Rapture as a singular event. Those who are resurrected are people who are in Christ. The reason I place them together as a singular event is that they will happen so closely together that only God will know them as distinct events. God will raise the righteous dead first, but Jesus will gather those believers who are still living a split second later.

This two-part move of God is the next major even that will happen. I believe, and I think the evidence is clear, that it could happen any moment, even while I am writing these words. It is imminent. I'm not setting a date or time, because I don't know exactly when it will happen. I just see the signs, and they all point to the return of Christ in the very near future.

I am aware there are believers who question the Rapture of the Church. Some will even note that the word "rapture" is not in the Bible. Of course, it's not. Rapture is an English word, but the concept is clearly present. Paul writes,

> For this we say to you by the word of the Lord, that we who are alive *and* remain until the coming of the Lord will by no means precede those who are asleep. For the Lord Himself will descend from heaven with a shout, with the voice of an archangel, and with the trumpet of God. And the dead in Christ will rise first. Then we who are alive and remain shall be caught up together with them in the clouds to meet the Lord in the air. And thus we shall always be with the Lord. Therefore comfort one another with these words (1 Thessalonians 4:15–18 NKJV).

The phrase translated "caught up" is derived from the Greek verb form *harpagēsometha*, which is a form of the word *harpazō*. It means 'caught up or taken away.' Jerome, the translator of the Vulgate (the Latin version of the Bible), took that Greek term and used *rapere*, the infinitive form of the Latin verb *rapiō*, which also means 'to catch up or take away.' The English word rapture is derived from that Latin verb. Various English versions of the Bible have taken their meaning from both Greek and Latin and translated this phrase as "caught up." From there, English Bible scholars have recognized the English meaning of *rapiō* as the word "rapture."

This concept is not foreign to the Bible, because it is exactly what Paul is saying. He is comforting the believers in Thessalonica by telling them that all believers will be taken with Jesus when He returns.

They don't have to worry about their dead sisters and brothers in Christ. In fact, Jesus will raise them from the dead first. But only a brief fraction of a second later, He will gather all believers who are still alive. We will have a grand reunion together with the Lord in the air. When Jesus returns, God will set all His final moves in motion.

**When Jesus returns, God will set all
His final moves in motion.**

---

2. The Marriage Supper of the Lamb Followed by the Glorious Return of Jesus Together with Believers

The second thing that will occur after Jesus' return is the Marriage Supper of the Lamb and the glorious return of Jesus together with believers. Jesus will first return raising the dead in Christ and gathering the living believers in the Rapture. Then He will take all of us together to His Father's house. Jesus said, "In My Father's house are many mansions; if *it were* not *so*, I would have told you. I go to prepare a place for you" (John 14:2 NKJV). Using the Bible's measurements, the Father's house is a 1,380-mile cube, meaning it is equally long, wide, and tall (see Revelation 21:16).

First the Rapture occurs, and then a seven-year period begins. Daniel chapter 9 speaks of a 490-year period specifically for the Jewish people, of which 483 years have already passed, and only seven years remain. The worst time on earth in human history is called "the time of Jacob's trouble" (see Jeremiah 30:7 NKJV) or "the wrath of the

Lamb" (see Revelation 6:16 NKJV). As the wrath of the Lamb and the Tribulation happen on the earth, the Marriage Supper of the Lamb will be taking place in heaven. These two simultaneous events will last for seven years, which is symbolic of a Jewish wedding that takes seven days. Jesus will have raptured or resurrected all the believers of all the ages, and then He will marry them as His glorious bride. In those seven years, all believers will become Jesus' wife.

The apostle John writes about the end of the Marriage Supper of the Lamb:

> And I heard, as it were, the voice of a great multitude, as the sound of many waters and as the sound of mighty thunderings, saying, "Alleluia! For the Lord God Omnipotent reigns! Let us be glad and rejoice and give Him glory, for the marriage of the Lamb has come, and His wife has made herself ready." And to her it was granted to be arrayed in fine linen, clean and bright, for the fine linen is the righteous acts of the saints (Revelation 19:6–8 NKJV).

Hold the concept of "fine linen" in your mind because I will return to it.

Then in verses 11–16, John says,

> Now I saw heaven opened, and behold, a white horse. And He who sat on him *was* called Faithful and True, and in righteousness He judges and makes war. His eyes *were* like a flame of fire, and on His head *were* many crowns. He had a name written that no one knew except Himself. He *was* clothed with a robe dipped in blood, and His name is called The Word of God. And the armies

in heaven, clothed in fine linen, white and clean, followed Him on white horses. Now out of His mouth goes a sharp sword, that with it He should strike the nations. And He Himself will rule them with a rod of iron. He Himself treads the winepress of the fierceness and wrath of Almighty God. And He has on *His* robe and on His thigh a name written:

KING OF KINGS AND
LORD OF LORDS (NKJV).

Who makes up these "armies of heaven" clothed in fine linen? That is all believers, including you and me. We will be riding along with Jesus in His glorious return when the Marriage Supper of the Lamb comes to a close. This is a different kind of return. The Rapture will be a private event between Jesus and His Church. The people who remain on earth will know something has happened, but they will not see it in the same way believers will. They will know a lot of people are missing, but they won't fully understand why.

At His glorious return, every eye will see Jesus. This event will happen at the end of the Tribulation. The Church will return with Jesus, and He will set up a 1,000-year rule in which He and the Church will reign on earth.

What will happen on earth right before Jesus' glorious return? John writes this:

And I saw the beast, the kings of the earth, and their armies, gathered together to make war against Him who sat on the horse and against His army. Then the beast was captured, and with him the false prophet who worked signs in his presence, by which he deceived those who received the mark of the beast and those who worshiped his image. These two were cast alive into the lake of fire burning with brimstone. And the rest were killed with the sword which proceeded from the mouth of Him who sat on the horse. And all the birds were filled with their flesh (Revelation 19:19–21 NKJV).

John is describing Armageddon. This is the battle when all the armies of the world are gathered in the Valley of Megiddo near Jerusalem, and the fighting will extend into the city itself. In fact, many armies are preparing to gather even as I write this. If the US and a few other nations did not stand in the way, the United Nations would impose a two-state solution on Israel tomorrow, which would force the Israelis to concede East Jerusalem to the Palestinians. The United States is the only country with the power to stop it. Otherwise, the few other countries who would oppose it do not have the power to do anything more than something symbolic.

Take a few minutes to survey the scene of this last moment in human history. The prophet Zechariah provides this vivid description:

> Behold, the day of the LORD is coming,
> And your spoil will be divided in your midst.
> For I will gather all the nations to battle against Jerusalem;
> The city shall be taken,
> The houses rifled,
> And the women ravished.
> Half of the city shall go into captivity,
> But the remnant of the people shall not be cut off from the city.

LOOK UP!

Then the Lᴏʀᴅ will go forth
And fight against those nations,
As He fights in the day of battle.
And in that day His feet will stand on the Mount of Olives,
Which faces Jerusalem on the east.
And the Mount of Olives shall be split in two,
From east to west,
Making a very large valley;
Half of the mountain shall move toward the north
And half of it toward the south.
Then you shall flee *through* My mountain valley,
For the mountain valley shall reach to Azal.
Yes, you shall flee
As you fled from the earthquake
In the days of Uzziah king of Judah.

Thus the Lᴏʀᴅ my God will come,
And all the saints with You.

It shall come to pass in that day
That there will be no light;
The lights will diminish.
It shall be one day
Which is known to the Lᴏʀᴅ—
Neither day nor night.
But at evening time it shall happen
That it will be light.

And in that day it shall be

That living waters shall flow from Jerusalem,

Half of them toward eastern sea

And half of them toward the western sea;

In both summer and winter it shall occur.

And the LORD shall be King over all the earth.

In that day it shall be—

"The LORD *is* one,"

And His name one.

All the land shall be turned into a plain from Geba to Rimmon south of Jerusalem. *Jerusalem* shall be raised up and inhabited in her place from Benjamin's Gate to the place of the First Gate and the Corner Gate, and *from* the Tower of Hananel to the king's winepresses.

The people shall dwell in it;

And no longer shall there be utter destruction,

But Jerusalem shall be safely inhabited.

And this shall be the plague with which the LORD will strike all the people who fought against Jerusalem:

Their flesh shall dissolve while they stand on their feet,

Their eyes shall dissolve in their sockets,

And their tongues shall dissolve in their mouths.

It shall come to pass in that day

That a great panic from the LORD will be among them.

Everyone will seize the hand of his neighbor,

And raise his hand against his neighbor's hand;

Judah also will fight at Jerusalem.

And the wealth of all the surrounding nations

Shall be gathered together:

Gold, silver, and apparel in great abundance.

Such also shall be the plague

On the horse *and* the mule,

On the camel and the donkey,

And on all the cattle that will be in those camps.

So *shall* this plague *be*.

And it shall come to pass *that* everyone who is left of all the nations which came against Jerusalem shall go up from year to year to worship the King, the LORD of hosts, and to keep the Feast of Tabernacles. And it shall be *that* whichever of the families of the earth do not come up to Jerusalem to worship the King, the LORD of hosts, on them there will be no rain. If the family of Egypt will not come up and enter in, they *shall have* no *rain*; they shall receive the plague with which the LORD strikes the nations who do not come up to keep the Feast of Tabernacles. This shall be the punishment of Egypt and the punishment of all the nations that do not come up to keep the Feast of Tabernacles.

In that day "HOLINESS TO THE LORD" shall be *engraved* on the bells of the horses. The pots in the LORD's house shall be like the bowls before the altar. Yes, every pot in Jerusalem and Judah shall be holiness to the LORD of hosts. Everyone who sacrifices shall come and take them and cook in them. In that day there shall no longer be a Canaanite in the house of the LORD of hosts (Zechariah 14 NKJV).

The world has marched against Jerusalem with a demonic vengeance. Then Jesus comes riding in with His armies at His side. He casts the false prophet and the Antichrist alive into hell. Jesus will then kill all the other armies of the world that have come to destroy Jerusalem and fight against Him.

And where will we be? We will be flying with Jesus from heaven on our horses as He throws the false prophet and the Antichrist into hell. I can hardly wait!

We will be flying with Jesus from heaven on our horses as He throws the false prophet and the Antichrist into hell. I can hardly wait!

3. The Millennial Rule and the Total Authority of the Saints

The apostle John had a vision of what will happen after Jesus' glorious return and the Battle of Armageddon:

Then I saw an angel coming down from heaven, having the key to the bottomless pit and a great chain in his hand. He laid hold of the dragon, that serpent of old, who is *the* Devil and Satan, and bound him for a thousand years; and he cast him into the bottomless pit, and shut him up, and set a seal on him, so that he should deceive the nations no more till the thousand years were finished. But after these things he must be released for a little while.

And I saw thrones, and they sat on them, and judgment was committed to them. Then *I saw* the souls of those who had been beheaded for their witness to Jesus and for the word of God, who had not worshiped the beast or his image, and had not received *his* mark on their foreheads or on their hands. And they lived and reigned with Christ for a thousand years. But the rest of the dead did not live again until the thousand years were finished. This *is* the first resurrection. Blessed and holy *is* he who has part in the first resurrection. Over such the second death has no power, but they shall be priests of God and of Christ, and shall reign with Him a thousand years.

Now when the thousand years have expired, Satan will be released from his prison and will go out to deceive the nations which are in the four corners of the earth, Gog and Magog, to gather them together to battle, whose number *is* as the sand of the sea. They went up on the breadth of the earth and surrounded the camp of the saints and the beloved city. And fire came down from God out of heaven and devoured them. The devil, who deceived them, was cast into the lake of fire and brimstone where the beast and the false prophet *are*. And they will be tormented day and night forever and ever (Revelation 20:1–10 NKJV).

After the Antichrist and false prophet are thrown into the lake of fire, what happens to Satan? John tells us. Satan is symbolized in this passage as "the dragon, that serpent of old" (v. 2). The same devil who tempted Adam and Eve is still active near the end of the Bible. Jesus will give authority to an angel to lock Satan in chains and throw him into the bottomless pit. He will be sealed in. Neither Satan's power nor his words will be able to escape.

John mentions those who were beheaded or killed during the Tribulation for following Christ. Many of those who are saved during the Tribulation will be martyred, and they will become part of the believers who will rule with Christ. These believing martyrs will be resurrected and rewarded, and they will reign with Jesus as kings for 1,000 years, just as we will. All of us will be "priests of God." John also refers to us as "the saints."

After Jesus returns, the Antichrist and the False Prophet are thrown into the lake of fire, and Satan is thrown into the bottomless pit, then what happens? During that time, believers will rule with Jesus over the earth and the people in it. There will be millions or perhaps billions of people who survive the Tribulation. Jesus told us what would happen to these people in Matthew chapter 25:

"When the Son of Man comes in His glory, and all the holy angels with Him, then He will sit on the throne of His glory. All the nations will be gathered before Him, and He will separate them one from another, as a shepherd divides his sheep from the goats. And He will set the sheep on His right hand, but the goats on the left. Then the King will say to those on His right hand, 'Come, you blessed of My Father, inherit the kingdom prepared for you from the foundation of the world: for I was hungry and you gave Me food; I was thirsty and you gave Me drink; I was a stranger and you took Me in; I was naked and you clothed Me; I was sick and you visited Me; I was in prison and you came to Me.'

"Then the righteous will answer Him, saying, 'Lord, when did we see You hungry and feed You, or thirsty and give You drink? When did we see You a stranger and take You in, or naked and clothe You? Or when did we see You sick, or in prison, and come to You?' And the King will answer and say to them, 'Assuredly, I say to you, inasmuch as you did it to one of the least of these My brethren, you did it to Me.'

"Then He will also say to those on the left hand, 'Depart from Me, you cursed, into the everlasting fire prepared for the devil and his angels: for I was hungry and you gave Me no food; I was thirsty and you gave Me no drink; I was a stranger and you did not take Me in, naked and you did not clothe Me, sick and in prison and you did not visit Me.'

"Then they also will answer Him, saying, 'Lord, when did we see You hungry or thirsty or a stranger or naked or sick or in prison, and did not minister to You?' Then He will answer them, saying, 'Assuredly, I say to you, inasmuch as you did not do it to one of the least of these, you did not do it to Me.' And these will go away into everlasting punishment, but the righteous into eternal life" (Matthew 25:31–46).

According to Jesus, all of the gentile nations (people groups) that survived the Tribulation at His Second Coming will be separated into two divisions: the sheep nations and the goat nations. The separation will be based on how they treated the Jewish people. Notice in verse 40 how Jesus responded to the sheep nations when they acted astonished at the praise He was giving to them:

And the King will answer and say to them, 'Assuredly, I say to you, inasmuch as you did it to one of the least of these **My brethren**, you did it to Me (bold mine).

The reference to "My brethren" in that passage refers to the Jewish people. During the Tribulation the world will be hell on earth and the devil, working through the Antichrist, will be on a rampage—especially against the Jews in the last three and a half years. Antisemitism will be at an all-time high, and the Jewish people will be severely persecuted. By the way, in the story of the sheep and goat nations, Jesus never says the goat nations did anything bad to the Jews or to Israel. Their sin was in not showing compassion or doing anything for the Jewish people in their time of distress. That is an important lesson for all of us today.

But the sheep nations were different. They clothed, fed, and cared for the Jews in their hour of need, and their reward was eternal life. And this is interesting because they are never resurrected or changed into eternal beings. The only basis Jesus mentioned as the source of their salvation is in how they treated the Jews. And they then enter into the Millennium in their mortal bodies. The goat nations are sent to hell for eternity. Therefore, every mortal alive at the beginning of the Millenium is a sheep nation survivor of the Tribulation.

We know, according to Revelation 20, that by the end of the Millennium, the earth is full of nations in rebellion to God. When Satan is loosed at the end of the 1,000 years, he will lead them in a last-ditch attempt to kill us and Jesus (Revelation 20:9). God will destroy them, and Satan will be sent to hell forever.

But we need to know two things about these nations who are in rebellion to God:

1. They are descendants of the sheep nations who entered the Millennium in their natural bodies. It is the only possible

explanation for their existence since at the beginning of the Millennium the only mortals on earth are the sheep nations.

2. The sheep nations and their descendants are the ones we rule over for 1,000 years. Every person who is the wife of Jesus will be assigned geographical authority over people and territory on the earth during the Millennium. And I believe the basis of the level of authority we are given is on how we lived our lives in this present age.

We must understand, our actions on earth will continue to have an effect on our eternal existence. Many people think that once the Rapture happens, there will be a total reset, and all the believers will go to live forever in heaven. However, that is not what the Bible indicates. I want you to know that everything will be wonderful for believers. We will be "present with the Lord" (2 Corinthians 5:8), but that is not yet heaven. You will be blessed, forgiven, and given a new body and nature. You will no longer have a sin nature. Nevertheless, life will continue. Look at the parable Jesus tells in Luke 19:

Now as they heard these things, He spoke another parable, because He was near Jerusalem and because they thought the kingdom of God would appear immediately. Therefore He said: "A certain nobleman went into a far country to receive for himself a kingdom and to return. So he called ten of his servants, delivered to them ten minas, and said to them, 'Do business till I come.' But his citizens hated him, and sent a delegation after him, saying, 'We will not have this *man* to reign over us.'

And so it was that when he returned, having received the kingdom, he then commanded these servants, to whom he had given the money, to be called to him, that he might know how much every man had gained by trading. Then came the first, saying, 'Master, your mina has earned ten minas.' And he said to him, 'Well *done*, good servant; because you were faithful in a very little, have authority over ten cities.' And the second came, saying, 'Master, your mina has earned five minas.' Likewise he said to him, 'You also be over five cities.'

Then another came, saying, 'Master, here is your mina, which I have kept put away in a handkerchief. For I feared you, because you are an austere man. You collect what you did not deposit, and reap what you did not sow.' And he said to him, 'Out of your own mouth I will judge you, *you* wicked servant. You knew that I was an austere man, collecting what I did not deposit and reaping what I did not sow. Why then did you not put my money in the bank, that at my coming I might have collected it with interest?'

And he said to those who stood by, 'Take the mina from him, and give *it* to him who has ten minas.' (But they said to him, 'Master, he has ten minas.') 'For I say to you, that to everyone who has will be given; and from him who does not have, even what he has will be taken away from him. But bring here those enemies of mine, who did not want me to reign over them, and slay *them* before me'" (vv. 11–27 NKJV).

Our actions on earth will continue to have an effect on our eternal existence.

Jesus was teaching about what will happen when He returns. His disciples thought since Jesus was on His way to Jerusalem that His plan was to establish a political kingdom there. In their minds, Jesus was on His way to overthrow the Roman government and all their traitorous Jewish enablers. That was not in His plan, though. Instead, Jesus essentially told them,

> No, I'm about to go away on a journey and give *you* the kingdom, entrusting the world to you while I'm gone. I'll give you gifts, talents, favor, opportunity, and influence. And I want you to win souls and build My Church. Do good on the earth and restrain evil. Do business like I would if I were there until I return because when I return, I will call you to give an account. If you've been faithful stewards, then I'll let you rule over a geographic territory for 1,000 years.

That is what Jesus will do. He will come to us and say, "I'm giving you this geographic territory." I believe He will give us specific domains. As it is right now, we are not able to rule the way God intended; it's not the way things will be done in heaven. The purpose of the Millennial Reign is that for 1,000 years the world will be under Jesus' total control and authority. People will act the way they should. We will have a new nature so sin cannot lead us astray. There will be absolute, godly, and righteous authority ruling throughout the entire world. Those of us who are believers will be "God's Will Enforcement Officers," directly under the authority of Jesus Himself. The way we steward our lives on the earth will determine our sphere of authority, or our domain, during the Millennium.

Maybe you are looking at what you see in the world right now just as I am. We see evil and immorality all around us. We pray for God to intervene, and sometimes He does. Other times, He gives us the grace to endure it. The only true answer to the world's problems is the authority of Jesus Christ. Nothing else will give us peace, healing, and freedom. Here is the good news: it's coming! It is going to happen. Christ will rule and reign, and we will be by His side.

4. The Great White Throne Judgment

The next thing that will happen is the Great White Throne Judgment. This is not a good judgment for those in rebellion against God. The judgment of Christians has already occurred. When believers are judged, the righteousness of Jesus covers our sins and presents us blameless before God the Father. God will give us perfect bodies and reward us for deeds done while we were on earth. The Great White Throne Judgment, however, is for those who are evil and unsaved. These people will spend eternity in hell. John provides this vision:

> Then I saw a great white throne and Him who sat on it, from whose face the earth and the heaven fled away. And there was found no place for them. And I saw the dead, small and great, standing before God, and books were opened. And another book was opened, which is *the Book* of Life. And the dead were judged according to their works, by the things which were written in the books. The sea gave up the dead who were in it, and Death and

Hades delivered up the dead who were in them. And they were judged, each one according to his works. Then Death and Hades were cast into the lake of fire. This is the second death. And anyone not found written in the Book of Life was cast into the lake of fire (Revelation 20:11–15 NKJV).

At this point, God is finished with this earth as we know it. The final event that will happen is God's creation of a new heaven and a new earth.

5. The Creation of the New Heaven and New Earth

John says this about the time when God will make all things new:

Now I saw a new heaven and a new earth, for the first heaven and the first earth had passed away. Also there was no more sea. Then I, John, saw the holy city, New Jerusalem, coming down out of heaven from God, prepared as a bride adorned for her husband. And I heard a loud voice from heaven saying, "Behold, the tabernacle of God *is* with men, and He will dwell with them, and they shall be His people. God Himself will be with them *and be* their God. And God will wipe away every tear from their eyes; there shall be no more death, nor sorrow, nor crying. There shall be no more pain, for the former things have passed away."

Then He who sat on the throne said, "Behold, I make all things new." And He said to me, "Write, for these words are true and faithful."

And He said to me, "It is done! I am the Alpha and the Omega, the Beginning and the End. I will give of the fountain of the water of life freely to him who thirsts. He who overcomes shall inherit all things, and I will be his God and he shall be My son" (Revelation 21:1–7 NKJV).

As humans, we have lived on this planet for a long time, yet for the most part, we have forgotten who we are. God created us as the kings of the earth. He made us to be His priests. He called us to be a royal priesthood. But sin has corrupted our hearts and clouded our minds.

Do you know that in this life you have spiritual authority? It's true. As believers, we can rule right now. God has given us a Holy Spirit-empowered spirit of authority. From time to time, we exercise it, but we often forget we have that power. When Jesus gives us life again beyond this world, we will have total authority, and we won't forget. We will reign with Him as kings. He always intended to give us dominion, and as the wife of Jesus Christ, we will finally recognize it and live according to it.

Here is my next question: If you know you have authority, do you use it? Are you ruling today under Jesus and in the power of the Holy Spirit? If not, God is still waiting on you to take your rightful place. It's time to rule. He doesn't want you to be ruled over because He didn't design you that way. Step up and start ruling with spiritual authority.

If you know you have authority, do you use it?

What are you doing with your "mina"? What are you doing with the talents, abilities, influence, and gifts God gave to you? He will save you, to be sure. But God really wants to reward and bless you. You will stand before Him in judgment, but He won't punish you. God won't reject or refuse you. Regardless of what you have done, if you put your faith in Jesus Christ, you will be totally redeemed. However, there are rewards for those who have used their lives to further the gospel and the Kingdom. So I ask again: how are you using your mina? I encourage you to be a good steward and use what God has given you.

You are a ruler! You are a king! God knows the "real" you because He made you. He knows you are a kingly priest and a member of a royal priesthood. The devil is working overtime to keep you from knowing and embracing that fact. He wants to strip you of your identity so you will willingly hand over your authority to him. Don't fall for it. The devil intends to abuse you, use you, and hold you in bondage. God wants to lift you to your rightful place as a priest and king unto Him.

PART SIX

Redeemed Home

CHAPTER 16

Our Real Home

I have lived in my current home for more than 6 years. During that time, Karen and I have made several changes and improvements. We want a nice place to live, but we also want it to be a welcoming place for our children and grandchildren. We love our home.

You may be in your "forever" home, meaning you are at the stage of life in which you believe you have made your last home purchase. Or you might be looking for a home. You may rent a home or apartment and do everything you can to make it "yours." You might miss a home you once had. There are hundreds of possible scenarios we could consider when we think about our homes. It's not wrong to want a lovely place to live, but we need to keep things in perspective. Regardless of how much this earth might feel like home – it isn't!

In Luke 21:28, Jesus tells His followers their "redemption draws near." This statement is after He tells them about the coming signs of His return. You see, first Jesus tells His followers about the signs, and then He tells them how to have the right perspective. When these things begin to happen, now is the time to focus on God like never before. The world is not our permanent home. As lovely as our individual homes may be, they pale in comparison to what God is preparing for us.

If you know anything about biblical prophecy, then you know it's happening. The signs are evident and measurable. We can never say we haven't been warned, because these things are happening before our eyes. The Bible—the best-selling book in the world—has been telling people for many centuries what to expect. No one will have a legitimate excuse. Jesus is saying that when we see these things begin to happen, then our focus should be on God and eternal things. Don't get dragged down, discouraged, or distracted by earthly things. Focus on the things of God and look up because your redemption draws near. This is not our permanent home; we have another one not built by human hands (see 2 Corinthians 5:1).

We can never say we haven't been warned, because these things are happening before our eyes.

Adam and Eve had everything and lost it when they sinned, but Jesus redeemed it when He died to pay for all our sins. When we became Christians, we received a down payment of the redemption that's been promised to us, and when Jesus returns, we'll get everything back in full.

To review, there are *nine things* Adam and Eve lost when they fell because of their disobedience:

1. *Perfect bodies*
2. *Perfect pleasure*
3. *Perfect minds*
4. *Perfect identity*
5. *Total authority*
6. *Perfect home*
7. *Perfect intimacy*
8. *Perfect innocence*
9. *God-directed knowledge*

In this chapter, I want to tell you about *your home*. When Jesus comes again, we will get to return home. Adam and Eve were kicked out of the house about 6,000 years ago because they sinned. They had experienced home; they knew what it was like. They knew its beauty and perfection. They especially knew that God was close and intimate with them in the Garden of Eden.

When we became Christians, we received a down payment of the redemption that's been promised to us, and when Jesus returns, we'll get everything back in full.

You have never been home, and neither have I. When you leave work or school or wherever else you go every day, you return to a place you call "home," but I must tell you—that's not your home. If you are a believer, then your home is in heaven with God the Father,

Son, and Holy Spirit. God really wanted to live with people, and He created the perfect place for us to live in His presence. How can we know God really wants to live with us? Because when He made Adam and Eve, He lived and walked with them every day. And when Jesus comes back, He's going to take us home with Him.

This is what happened to Adam and Eve:

> Then the LORD God said, "Behold, the man has become like one of Us, to know good and evil. And now, lest he put out his hand and take also of the tree of life, and eat, and live forever"—therefore the LORD God sent him out of the garden of Eden to till the ground from which he was taken. So He drove out the man; and He placed cherubim at the east of the garden of Eden, and a flaming sword which turned every way, to guard the way to the tree of life (Genesis 3:22–24 NKJV).

God created us to live in paradise with Him, but when people sinned, He had to make them leave. Sin cannot dwell in God's presence. The only way we can be in God's presence again is for our sin to be removed. That is what Jesus did for us through His sacrifice on the cross. His blood covers our sin, and we can be in God's presence once again. Jesus died, rose again, and ascended to His Father, but He has been working ever since. He tells us where He is today, what He is doing, and that He is going to come back to take us with Him:

> Let not your heart be troubled; you believe in God, believe also in Me. In My Father's house are many mansions; if *it were* not so, I

would have told you. I go to prepare a place for you. And if I go and prepare a place for you, I will come again and receive you to Myself; that where I am, *there* you may be also. And where I go you know, and the way you know (John 14:1–4 NKJV).

Jesus told His followers He was leaving. He also told them He wants to show them where He is going. It will help us understand exactly what Jesus is saying if we recognize He is using Jewish wedding language, which I discussed briefly already. A first-century Jew would understand that Jesus is talking about marrying us. He is saying, "I'm going to my Father's house to prepare a place for you. One day, I'll return for you and take you to be with Me forever." When the Rapture happens, we will go home. For the first time in our lives, we will step into a new place and recognize we are finally home in the Father's house, the New Jerusalem. Jesus is preparing mansions for all of us there.

___

When the Rapture happens, we will go home.

___

In the next chapter, I want to tell you about your new home. I will tell you these three key facts about the New Jerusalem:

1. It is a real, physical place.
2. It is where we will marry Jesus.
3. It is home.

CHAPTER 17

The Father's House

I like to fly planes. I have my pilot's license, and I enjoy going to new places. However, I never want to go if I don't know what to expect on the other end of the trip. What is the weather like? What are the conditions of the approach and runway? What else do I need to know before I take off? Knowing these things not only increases the safety for me and my passengers, but it also lets me know what to expect on the other side. I like to know as much as I can.

I think part of the reason people don't get more excited about the Father's house is that they don't know what to expect on the other end of the trip. They have heard popular stories, followed family traditions, or even read books and watched movies. I want to correct some of the things you have thought or heard. Even more, I want you to know about the wonderful things God has in store for us at the end of the journey. It should comfort and encourage you.

I am going to share *three key facts about your new home.* I want to tell you about your destination before you get there. This is your Father's house—your real home. You will be glad you came.

1. It is a real, physical place.

Heaven is a real, physical place—the ultimate paradise. We will be able to touch and feel it. Our senses will be heightened in our new bodies, and we will experience heaven with all our senses. This real, physical place will be beyond description and far outside our current ability to comprehend. The apostle John records this description:

> Then one of the seven angels who had the seven bowls filled with the seven last plagues came to me and talked with me, saying, "Come, I will show you the bride, the Lamb's wife." And he carried me away in the Spirit to a great and high mountain, and showed me the great city, the holy Jerusalem, descending out of heaven from God, having the glory of God. Her light *was* like a most precious stone, like a jasper stone, clear as crystal. Also she had a great and high wall with twelve gates, and twelve angels at the gates, and names written on them, which are *the names* of the twelve tribes of the children of Israel: three gates on the east, three gates on the north, three gates on the south, and three gates on the west.
>
> Now the wall of the city had twelve foundations, and on them were the names of the twelve apostles of the Lamb. And he who talked with me had a gold reed to measure the city, its gates, and its wall. The city is laid out as a square; its length is as great as its breadth. And he measured the city with the reed: twelve thousand furlongs. Its length, breadth, and height are equal. Then he measured its wall: one hundred *and* forty-four cubits, *according* to the measure of a man, that is, of an angel. The construction of its wall was *of* jasper; and the city *was* pure gold, like clear glass. The foundations of the wall of the

city *were* adorned with all kinds of precious stones: the first foundation *was* jasper, the second sapphire, the third chalcedony, the fourth emerald, the fifth sardonyx, the sixth sardius, the seventh chrysolite, the eighth beryl, the ninth topaz, the tenth chrysoprase, the eleventh jacinth, and the twelfth amethyst. The twelve gates *were* twelve pearls: each individual gate was of one pearl. And the street of the city *was* pure gold, like transparent glass.

But I saw no temple in it, for the Lord God Almighty and the Lamb are its temple. The city had no need of the sun or of the moon to shine in it, for the glory of God illuminated it. The Lamb *is* its light. And the nations of those who are saved shall walk in its light, and the kings of the earth bring their glory and honor into it. Its gates shall not be shut at all by day (there shall be no night there). And they shall bring the glory and the honor of the nations into it. But there shall by no means enter it anything that defiles, or causes an abomination or a lie, but only those who are written in the Lamb's Book of Life.

And he showed me a pure river of water of life, clear as crystal, proceeding from the throne of God and of the Lamb. In the middle of its street, and on either side of the river, *was* the tree of life, which bore twelve fruits, each *tree* yielding its fruit every month. The leaves of the tree *were* for the healing of the nations (Revelation 21:9–22:2 NKJV).

When John writes about the "bride" and the "wife," he means believers. We are the bride of Christ, and we will become His wife. Our new city will be almost 1,400 miles long, wide, and tall, like a cube. An architect could design a lot of mansions to fit in that amount of space. There will be twelve gates, three on each side, and they will be made of pearl. On each gate will be inscribed the name of one of Israel's patriarchs.

The city will also contain twelve foundations with the names of the twelve disciples written on them. There are two possible ways to explain these foundations. One is that there will be twelve foundations underneath the wall that is 1,380 miles high. Another possibility is there are twelve stories with a foundation at each level. I don't know which interpretation is correct. If there were twelve stories in that structure, each one would be over 100 miles above the next.

If the city is twelve levels and you lived on one of them, you might live on the Peter level near the Judah gate. Or you might live on the Andrew level by the Ruben gate. No matter where you live in this city, it will be beautiful, beyond human description, and eternal. You will move in but never have to move out. Currently, the average American moves every four years, even though most people hate moving. In the heavenly city, you will never have to move again.

In today's real estate market, builders have certain set plans to build houses in new subdivisions. If you are shopping for a home in one of these areas, you have limited choices of models. Sometimes these are called "cookie cutter" or "spec" homes. I do not believe this is the way Jesus is preparing our mansions. God didn't use a cookie cutter to make people, and He's not going to use one to make our mansions either. You won't have to worry that your house will look exactly like your neighbors' house. It is going to be a house that looks like you, designed for you. I believe you are going to walk into your house in heaven, and your jaw will drop. You will look around and think, *This is me!* It won't be your "dream home"; it will be your "beyond your wildest dreams home." Every detail of your new house will fit your personality exactly. This mansion is only part of the reward for giving yourself to Jesus and living for Him. Every believer will have one.

Here on earth, many people struggle with the financial cost of a house, but in heaven there's no struggle. There will be no payments, no upkeep, no insurance, no taxes, no need for a security system or pest control, and no utilities. Everything in your house will be composed of precious stones, gold, and pearls. It will be stunningly gorgeous with colors and textures no one on earth has ever seen before. Your power source is Jesus Himself because "the Lamb *is* its light (Revelation 21:23 NKJV).

How much would you have to love someone to buy them a house, pay all the bills, and expect nothing in return? Most of us would only do it for our spouses. Jesus will do it for us because we are His Bride. It took God six days to create the earth, but Jesus has been in heaven for more than 2,000 years preparing a place for you. Imagine how amazing it must be. He explicitly told the disciples, "I'm leaving and going to My Father's house. There are many mansions there. I'm going to prepare a place for you. As surely as I leave, I'll come back and get you so you can be with Me forever."

I don't know how nice your house is here on earth, though I hope it is very nice. But I can tell you it's going to be like a rubbish heap compared to what the Lord is preparing for you. Jesus said to lift up our heads and look up. In other words, don't become so focused on earthly things that you forget about your Lord and the place He is preparing for you. Enjoy the blessings of earth, but don't marry them. Save the wedding for Jesus. He is building your home in the Father's house, and it is a real place.

In the middle of our eternal home is the Tree of Life. John writes,

> In the middle of its street, and on either side of the river, *was* the tree of life, which bore twelve fruits, each *tree* yielding its fruit every month. The leaves of the tree *were* for the healing of the nations (Revelation 22:2 NKJV).

Remember, humanity was kicked out of our home in the Garden of Eden because Adam and Eve chose to eat from the wrong tree (see Genesis chapter 3). They could have chosen the right tree. They could have chosen eternal life. The good news is God still has that tree, and He has planted it in the new Eden, our eternal home. We will eat of the Tree of Life, and death will be no more!

2. It is where we marry Jesus.

The second thing I want to tell you about the Father's house is this is where we will marry Jesus. John writes, "Then one of the seven angels who had the seven bowls filled with the seven last plagues came to me and talked with me, saying, 'Come, I will show you the bride, the Lamb's wife'" (Revelation 21:9 NKJV). We are now Jesus' bride, but we will become His wife.

In Revelation 19, John describes the Marriage Supper of the Lamb. There are many parallels between what he lays out and a traditional Jewish wedding. There are many practices in Jewish life and history that symbolize significant events for Christians. For example, for the Passover Feast, a lamb was traditionally killed, and its blood was placed over the doorposts of each house. This ritual was done to commemorate the passing over of the death angel. Christians see this event as a picture of the sacrifice of Jesus' blood on the cross for our sins. In a similar way, a Jewish wedding is a picture of our relationship with Jesus and how we are going to marry Him. As I described earlier, a traditional Jewish wedding began as the groom left his house and traveled to the bride's house. He then paid a bride price or dowry to her family. Then the bride and groom were legally betrothed, sealed by drinking wine from the same cup. After this ceremony, the groom would leave the bride at her house and return to his father's house to prepare a place for her. While he was preparing, the couple was separated for about a year, but they were "betrothed" in marriage.

When the time of preparation drew to a close, the groom still needed to wait for his father's permission to bring the bride home. When his father consented, he would usually return to the bride at night. She knew the groom was coming at some point in the near future, but she did not know the exact hour to expect him. To announce his arrival, the groom would shout for her. The bride would leave her family home and return with the groom to his house. Once there, a celebration began that would last for the next seven days.

Can you see how this is a picture of our marriage to Jesus? The events of the wedding have already begun. This is a picture of our marriage to Jesus! More than 2,000 years ago, the Son of God left His Father's house and came to our home. He paid the most generous price for us. Over a cup of wine at the Last Supper, Jesus said He would not drink wine again until He drinks it together with us in His Father's Kingdom. Over that same cup, He declared the eternal covenant we have with Him in His blood (the final covenant). At that moment, all of us who are believers were legally betrothed to Jesus. We are now His betrothed bride. Jesus then returned to His Father's house to prepare a dwelling place for us. He will not return until the Father is ready. Jesus told us that only the Father knows the hour of His return. He is waiting for the instruction from His Father to come to us and take us to our new home.

Jesus told His followers that when He comes, two people will be engaged in the same activity. One will be taken while the other is left. We don't know exactly when He's coming because it will be a surprise (see Matthew 24:36–44). However, it will not be a total surprise. We are watching and waiting for Him, knowing the signs of the times in which we live.

The apostle Paul says the Lord will descend from heaven with a shout (see 1 Thessalonians 4:16). Remember, the groom shouted as he approached his betrothed wife's home. He was there to finally bring her back with him. The shout gave her a brief moment to prepare. Paul says this is how the Lord will come:

> For the Lord Himself will descend from heaven with a shout, with the voice of an archangel, and with the trumpet of God. And the dead in Christ will rise first. Then we who are alive and remain shall be caught up together with them in the clouds to meet the Lord in the air. And thus we shall always be with the Lord. Therefore comfort one another with these words (1 Thessalonians 4:16–18 NKJV).

We will be in heaven marrying Jesus for a period of seven years. I wish I could give you more details about the actual Marriage

Supper, but the Bible doesn't provide very many. However, I can say with confidence that it will be the greatest party any of us have ever attended.

Jesus is the best groom in the world. I can assure you He will also be the best husband in all the universe. Many people don't feel completely loved, even in marriage. In fact, some people feel very unloved. You may feel your needs aren't being met. You may not be treated very well. The good news is that from the day Jesus comes, you will never have another unloved second for the rest of eternity. He will love you and care for you forever. That's how much Jesus loves and cares for us. He wants to be with us and have a relationship with us. Love like that is beyond our comprehension.

Jesus is the best groom in the world. I can assure you He will also be the best husband in all the universe.

I have told you about being kings and priests, but I have also told you that you are the betrothed bride of Jesus. You will soon become His beloved wife. This is contrary to the teaching of evolutionism. I told you how evolutionary theory gets our origins wrong. Where did we come from? The Bible gives the true answer: we were created in God's image. Evolutionary theory also gets our end wrong, but the Bible gets it right: we are the betrothed bride of Christ, and our end is going to be glorious. In the next chapter, I will tell you how evolutionary theory runs counter to the Bible's view of your final destiny, but for now I want you to know they are not compatible views.

3. It is home!

The third important fact about the Father's House, the New Jerusalem, is that it is home. Jesus will return one day, and He will take home those who have made Him Lord of their lives. I will restate what I said at the beginning of this book: if you have not made this choice, it is time for you to believe in Jesus and follow Him. This world is not our permanent home. We are just passing through. Heaven is our home!

If you're a believer, then this is the time to focus your attention on God and prepare for heaven. Jesus is going to come, and your final redemption will happen on that day. You are going to go home to the Father's house. There we will marry Jesus and experience something we can't even put into words.

***

If you're a believer, then this is the time to focus your attention on God and prepare for heaven.

***

Our sin natures will be gone, and Satan and all his demons will finally be consigned to hell forever. We will all eat from the Tree of Life. In the meantime, Satan is still at work, and we have the choice of death or life. The apostle John wrote,

Do not love the world or the things in the world. If anyone loves the world, the love of the Father is not in him. For all that *is* in the world—the lust of the flesh, the lust of the eyes, and the pride of life—is not of the Father but is of the world. And the world is passing away, and the lust of it; but he who does the will of God abides forever (1 John 2:15–17 NKJV).

Don't set your affections on the lusts and pleasures of this life. Focus on your relationship with God.

Jesus said regarding the end times,

Remember Lot's wife. Whoever seeks to save his life will lose it, and whoever loses his life will preserve it. I tell you, in that night there will be two *people* in one bed: the one will be taken and the other will be left. Two *women* will be grinding together: the one will be taken and the other left. Two *men* will be in the field: the one will be taken and the other left (Luke 17:32–36 NKJV).

The Rapture is for those who love God and have not fallen in love with the world, as Lot's wife did. Now, there's nothing wrong with enjoying the pleasures of earth. However, there is something very wrong with exchanging our dependence on God for wealth, ego satisfaction, and the physical pleasures of this world. Our choices have eternal consequences. Jesus can return at any moment. Look up! Our responsibility is to be ready to meet Him when He comes.

CHAPTER 18

Evolution Is Not Our Destiny

We are sons of God, created in His image, declared a priestly kingdom, and empowered as prophets. Jesus has already chosen us as His spotless and wrinkle-free betrothed bride (see Ephesians 5:27). We will soon become His wife. These claims are opposite of the teachings of evolution. Evolution is really a sinister assault of Satan to attack us on the level of our identity and destiny. I want to write to you about the significant differences between what the Bible teaches and evolutionary theory. Why do I feel I need to do this? Because there are some, even in the church, who believe in evolution, which is the idea that through the survival of the species we evolved from single-celled organisms into primates (apes) and finally into humans. Some believers have been taught by teachers and professors that this is a fact. These educators will say it is a "theory" but also ridicule any contrary evidence into oblivion. So while it's called a "theory," in practice, it's delivered as a "fact." If you do believe in this theory, I ask you to please consider what I am saying.

The belief that we evolved from a single-celled organism into apes runs counter to the biblical narrative. It is also contrary to biblical ontology because it is not the nature of our being as God created us. The Bible's grand story tells us we were created in the image of God, Christ died for us individually and collectively, and when we die, we have an eternal destiny based on our free will response to God. On the other hand, evolution says we were created in the image of the last organism from which we evolved, sin is a social construct from which we need no redemption, and when we die, we simply cease to exist. In summary, evolutionary theory strips us of our God-given identity.

Three Significant Problems with Evolutionary Theory

If you are a Christian and believe in creationism, what I am about to say will help you articulate your own beliefs and equip you to share them with someone else. I'm going to address *three significant problems with evolutionary theory*.

1. The Complexity Problem

If you explore Charles Darwin's teachings about evolution, you will discover his understanding of a process known as natural selection. In Darwin's *The Origin of Species*, he claims this blind, mindless force of natural selection exists from the very beginning of all life, although he is unable to explain the origin of life itself. His theory of natural selection begins with a single-celled organism that then becomes multiple-celled life. One cell is added to another and another until, eventually, humans come into existence.

This theory of natural selection cannot explain *the complexity of life,* and that is the first problem I am going to address. The human eye, for example, is one of the most, if not *the* most, complex organs in the body. "It is absurd to believe the human eye is the product of natural selection." Those are not my words—those are Charles Darwin's words! Here's a direct quote found in chapter six of *The Origin of Species*:

> To suppose that the eye with all its inimitable contrivances for adjusting the focus to different distances, for admitting different amounts of light, and for the correction of spherical and chromatic aberration, could have been formed by natural selection, seems, I freely confess, absurd in the highest degree.[15]

It may look as though Darwin was admitting the possibility of an Intelligent Designer of the universe. However, that is precisely what he was arguing against. He believed that given enough time, anything could happen. How can a buffalo descend from a butterfly? It takes a long time. That is Darwin's answer for the complexity problem. He does admit the human eye itself is hard to explain by natural selection and the evolutionary processes, but he still held onto the idea that given small mutations over eons of time, even the human eye is possible.

If the complexity of the human eye was a problem for early evolutionists such as Darwin, then DNA delivers a knock-out blow.

Darwin could not even conceive of life at the DNA level since it was still undiscovered in his lifetime. DNA is composed of four chemicals. The order in which they are arranged instructs a cell's actions. Every cell in your body carries a DNA code that is roughly six-billion letters long. If the DNA from a single human cell were stretched out from end to end, it would extend to six feet in a microscopically thin strand. It's so tiny that nearly 200 copies of the human genome can fit on the head of a pen. And if you stretched out the DNA strands from every cell in your entire body and lined them up, it would be almost twice the diameter of the solar system. For the layperson, it is difficult to wrap our minds around the dimensions and complexity of the human genome. It is incredibly tiny and amazingly huge at the same time.

DNA tells the story of where you came from biologically and genetically. Our daughter, Julie, gave us AncestryDNA as a gift for Christmas a couple of years ago. I discovered I'm 40 percent Irish/Welsh/Scottish, 30 percent Western European, 20 percent Scandinavian, 10 percent Russian, *and 0 percent ape*! It really is interesting.

Dr. Francis Collins, the Director of the Human Genome Project and a committed believer, led the group that mapped human DNA. He said, "One can think of DNA as an instructional script, a software program, sitting in the nucleus of the cell."[16] In some ways, DNA is like a complex computer program, made up of a series of ones and zeros. The order of these two numerals makes the program function according to its design. In a similar way, the four chemicals in DNA are represented by four letters: A, T, G, and C. Like ones and zeros, the arrangement of these chemicals determines everything genetic about a living organism. If 99.9 percent of your DNA corresponds to every other person, just a fractional difference in the arrangement of those chemicals is what make you the unique person you are. The structure of your DNA is a unique six-billion-lettered script that informs everything about you from a physical perspective.

Why is DNA so important for believers to understand? It's one more important piece of evidence for the existence of God. He is the Intelligent Designer, which means He knows everything about you and what you need in your life. Perry Marshall, an information specialist, commented on the implications of DNA: "There has never existed a computer program that wasn't designed ... [whether it is] a code, or a program, or a message given through a language, there is always an intelligent mind behind it."[17] As far as you and I are concerned, God is that intelligent mind.

Anthony Flew was one of the world's leading atheists for many years. He participated in many debates with Christians, including C. S. Lewis. He would take a position in favor of evolution and in opposition to creationism and intelligent design. Flew remained an atheist and an avid proponent of evolution until the discovery of DNA. In 2004 he changed his position, saying he had come to believe in an intelligent Creator of the universe. This about-face shocked his academic colleagues and fellow atheists. He did not become a Christian, as far as we know, but God became a possibility for him. In 2007 Flew laid out the reasons why he had changed his mind in *There Is a God: How the World's Most Notorious Atheist Changed His Mind*:

> The latest work I have seen shows that the present physical universe gives too little time for these theories of abiogenesis to get the

job done. The philosophical question that has not been answered in origin-of-life studies is this: How can a universe of mindless matter produce beings with intrinsic ends, self-replication capabilities, and 'coded chemistry'? Here we are not dealing with biology, but an entirely different category of problem.[18]

Abiogenesis is the part of evolutionary theory that tries to explain how inanimate matter became living organisms. It essentially means that something living came from something that never lived. This is the first significant problem with evolutionary theory. How could something as complex as human life have come from inanimate matter? How can we reconcile human existence with Darwinian theory? Modern science finds increasingly new evidence showing just how complex life really is. This issue alone was enough to open the possibility for Anthony Flew to believe in God. Despite the evidence, though, many people still hang on to evolution—not because of its merits, but because they refuse to believe God created us. It isn't a matter of information; it is a matter of rebellion.

How could something as complex as human life have come from inanimate matter?

2. The Scientific Problem

Second, there is a scientific problem with the theory of evolution. Some people will blithely say, "The Bible is not scientific, but evolution is." The reason Darwinian evolution is taught in our public schools and creationism is shunned is because of the common belief that evolution is science and the Bible is religion. So is evolution science and the Bible non-scientific?

Theodore N. Tahmisian, a physiologist with the Atomic Energy Commission, said,

> Scientists who go about teaching that evolution is a fact of life are great con men, and the story they are telling may be the greatest hoax ever. In explaining evolution, we do not have one iota of fact. A tangled mishmash of guessing games and figure juggling. If evolution occurred at all, it was probably in a very different manner than the way it is now taught.[19]

Edwin Conklin, Professor and Chairman of the Biology Department at Princeton University, said, "The probability of life originating from accident is comparable to the probability of the unabridged dictionary resulting from an explosion in a printing shop."[20] Sir Fred Hoyle, an astrophysicist, said, "The chance that higher life forms have emerged in this way is comparable with the chance that a tornado sweeping through a junkyard might assemble a Boeing 747 from the materials therein."[21]

You may have heard, *Well, this is science, but the Bible is just religion.* Is that entirely true? The Bible does address our deepest spiritual needs, but that is not all it does. Astrophysicist Hugh Ross became a Christian because he recognized the scientific accuracy of the Bible. Ross said he did a survey of every major religion's holy book he could find over the course of two years. He found all of them factually undependable except the Bible. Ross says about the Bible,

> Its predictive power persuaded me to think it must have been inspired by One who knows and guides the past, present, and future. I had essentially proven to myself that the Bible is more reliable than the laws of physics I focused on in my university courses. The only reasonable conclusion I could see was that the Bible must be the inspired Word of God.[22]

This is coming from an astrophysicist! You see, I also believe the Bible is scientifically correct, and Darwin's theory is pseudoscience. Evolution fails biology and chemistry because it can't be proven nor replicated. It fails paleontology because fossil records refute it. The truth is, evolution isn't science at all. After 150 years of research into the theory of evolution, it is still only theory—conjecture with no proven results.

The Bible establishes scientific facts about the universe and creation. Hugh Ross came to God through the scientific accuracy of the Bible. He also found the order of creation in Genesis 1 to be scientifically correct, and that if things had happened in any other order, life could not have existed. The Bible is a reliable book. I don't question the Bible; I question people who question the Bible. Though they may be sincere in their questions, I personally find that their facts don't measure up.

**The Bible establishes scientific facts
about the universe and creation.**

---

3. The Human Problem

The third problem related to evolutionary theory is the human problem. It strips us of our dignity, identity, and eternal destiny. Natural selection is not your destiny. Evolution is not your end. The psalmist writes,

> For You formed my inward parts;
> You covered me in my mother's womb.
> I will praise You, for I am fearfully *and* wonderfully made;
> Marvelous are Your works,
> And *that* my soul knows very well.
> My frame was not hidden from You,
> When I was made in secret,
> *And* skillfully wrought in the lowest parts of the earth.
> Your eyes saw my substance, being yet unformed.
> And in Your book they all were written,
> The days fashioned for me,
> When *as yet there were* none of them.
> How precious also are Your thoughts to me, O God!
> How great is the sum of them!
> *If* I should count them, they would be more in number than the sand;
> When I awake, I am still with You (Psalm 139:13–18 NKJV).

America has been raising an entire generation to believe they are no better than animals. There is nothing special or sacred about our lives. Evolutionists tell us matter-of-factly that we are the products of a mindless accident. Darwin made no distinction between types of life. In the grand picture of evolution, if what he says is true, we are no more important than rats or cockroaches.

But I'm telling you that you've been made in the image of God, from your mother's womb. You are a son of God, a prophet, priest, and king unto God, and the wife of Jesus. You are divinely made. You are beloved. You are special. You have more value than you will ever understand. What the devil wants to do is strip us down and beat us up until we have no self-esteem. He wants to tell us we're animals so we will act like animals. But Jesus wants us to believe we are sons of the living God and act like it! As I said earlier, evolution can provide no satisfactory answers to human ontology or eschatology. It cannot tell you who you are or where you came from, and it certainly can't tell you where you're going.

Jesus wants us to believe we are sons of the living God and act like it!

PART SEVEN

Redeemed Intimacy

CHAPTER 19

Relationship Regained

When Adam and Eve chose to disobey God and sin, they lost their relationship with Him. When Jesus returns and takes us with Him to heaven, He will completely restore our relationship with the Father. God made the first two humans perfect, but sin robbed them of their perfection. If you have been saved, Jesus has redeemed you, yet you only have a portion or a down payment of the full redemption you will receive on the day He returns.

The most important thing Adam and Eve lost when they sinned was their perfect, intimate relationship with God. They lived with God in the Garden of Eden and saw Him face-to-face every day. Our relationship with God has been restored, but we still don't have the fullness of that relationship. The apostle Paul says, "For now we see in a mirror, dimly, but then face to face. Now I know in part, but then I shall know just as I also am known" (1 Corinthians 13:12 NKJV). There are two important aspects to this verse. First, we will get to see Jesus face-to-face on the day He comes back. When you have a face-to-face relationship with someone, you get to see what their face looks like when you are present with them. You read their facial expressions and learn their body language. You know what they are thinking and how they are feeling. You will know when they are pleased or disappointed. You will pick up on their moods and expressions.

The most important thing Adam and Eve lost when they sinned was their perfect, intimate relationship with God.

Satan tries to take advantage of us and harasses us because he knows we can't see Jesus' face. We know from the Bible that Jesus loves us, we are His accepted and beloved friends, and He has removed our sins from us by the power of His blood. Then the devil tries to come in and say, "God doesn't really love you. In fact, He's quite angry with you. You've sinned too much to be loved by Him." The devil will try to manipulate us because we can't see Jesus' face. If we could see Jesus' face, then we would know how much He loves us. The day is coming when you will see His face and see it forevermore.

Right now, we see Jesus like the image in a cloudy mirror. I realize some of the people reading this book may have seen Jesus in a vision or a dream, but even then, it was like looking into a dim mirror. But when Jesus comes to get us in the Rapture, we will see Him face-to-face and know with complete certainty that He loves us.

Second, this verse tells us we will no longer be ignorant about Jesus. Ignorance doesn't mean we are stupid; it simply means we don't know. Paul says, "I shall know just as I also am known." We are going to know Jesus as intimately and perfectly as God knows us today. If you are a believer, I know you know Jesus. You've been saved, and you've been experiencing a down payment on your relationship with Him. Nevertheless, you can only know Jesus in part. But in Ephesians 1:13–14, Paul says,

> In Him you also *trusted*, after you heard the word of truth, the gospel of your salvation; in whom also, having believed, you were sealed with the Holy Spirit of promise, who is the guarantee of our inheritance until the redemption of the purchased possession, to the praise of His glory (NKJV).

Yes, the Holy Spirit is our guarantee. In other words, He's our earnest money. If you are buying a new house, you will have to give a small amount of money to the seller in earnest. This lets the current owner know you are serious about the final purchase. It also prevents someone else from buying it. It's like a down payment, but it means there is a solid commitment. The Holy Spirit has laid down the money and made a solid commitment to you that you will receive everything God has promised.

When God created Adam and Eve, He breathed His Spirit into them, giving them life. When they sinned, they lost that Spirit, and they lost life. They still had air in their lungs, but their spirits were dead because the Spirit of God departed from them. Eventually their bodies would follow in that death march. That is what it means to be lost and apart from God. We inherited dead spirits from Adam and Eve, and eventually we have dead bodies. But on the day, you received Jesus as your Lord and Savior, the Holy Spirit entered and breathed new life into you, the same way God did when He made

Adam. He makes your spirit alive again, and He will ultimately give life to your body. That's why it's called being "born again"—you're re-born in the Spirit. That's a down payment from the Holy Spirit.

The Holy Spirit has laid down the money and made a solid commitment to you that you will receive everything God has promised.

God is earnest; He means business with you. When you got saved, He gave you His Holy Spirit as a guarantee and pledge. However, that's only a down payment of what you will receive on the day Jesus returns. When He comes back, you will know Him as well as He knows you right now. Not only will you see Him face-to-face, but you will also have infinite, perfect knowledge of the Son of God.

When I preach on eternity and the end times, I often receive this question: *Will we know each other in heaven?* When you have the wrong concept of heaven, you may not want to go there. One of the most important purposes of this book is to help you under-stand how wonderful heaven is going to be. Some people think that we will be like ghosts who have been given lobotomies, and all we will do is float around with no ability to know anything or recognize any friends or family members. But the truth is that in heaven you'll know everybody. Sadly, it is here on earth right now that we don't know each other. We keep our guard up, hide our insecurities and hang-ups, and cover our relationship issues. We don't know whom we can trust. But in heaven, we can trust everybody. No sin nature can remain in heaven. We'll finally be able to know each other intimately. At last, we will be in perfect relationships for all of eternity. In heaven, there will be no egos, pride, competition, jealousy, or envy. All dysfunctions will end. Our past hurts and bad memories will be gone. We will be able to love fully without fear for all eternity.

The most important thing in heaven is that we will know Jesus and have perfect and total intimacy with Him. The apostle John writes,

> Then I, John, saw the holy city, New Jerusalem, coming down out of heaven from God, prepared as a bride adorned for her husband. And I heard a loud voice from heaven saying, "Behold, the tabernacle of God *is* with men, and He will dwell with them, and they shall be His people. God Himself will be with them *and be* their God. And God will wipe away every tear from their eyes; there shall be no more death, nor sorrow, nor crying. There shall be no more pain, for the former things have passed away."
>
> Then He who sat on the throne said, "Behold, I make all things new." And He said to me, "Write, for these words are true and faithful."
>
> And He said to me, "It is done! I am the Alpha and the Omega, the Beginning and the End. I will give of the fountain of the water of life freely to him who thirsts. He who overcomes shall inherit all things, and I will be his God and he shall be My son" (Revelation 21:2–7 NKJV).

That is redemption. I want you to know that day is coming very soon; in fact, it could happen any moment. We will get every single thing back that we lost, the most important of which will be a face-to-face relationship with God for all eternity. That's the biggest prize of all.

PART EIGHT

Redeemed Innocence

CHAPTER 20

Innocence Reborn

Every year new words gain popularity in the English language. They get used, misused, and overused until everyone gets tired of them. Some words have political connotations. Some have other meanings. A few make it into a standard dictionary. One of the words I'm already weary of hearing is *gaslighting*, not because the word isn't meaningful but because it gets misused so frequently. It showed up in common speech about a decade ago but has recently become quite popular on social media. The word originated from a 1944 film based on a 1938 play named *Gaslight*. The movie tells the story of an unscrupulous man who marries with the intention of stealing all his wife's wealth. He takes several actions to make her question her own reality and sanity. He hopes to have her declared mentally unfit so he can gain control of her property. One tactic he employs is lowering and increasing the fuel to the house's gaslights. The wife notices the lights flickering and dimming, but the husband denies it is happening so she will question her own experience. The plot is a bit more complicated, but in the end, she discovers his malicious activities, and he is taken away by the police.

Gaslighting is a real problem in relationships. However, common use has come to mean anyone who disagrees with you is "gaslighting" you. It's made the term mostly meaningless because of this popular usage, but it's still an important concept.

The Father of Lies

I bring up the word *gaslight* for one important reason: *The devil is a notorious gaslighter.* He wants to make you doubt reality. Your life was marked by sin and failure, but then you heard about what Jesus Christ did for you on the cross to remove your sins and give you victory. You turned away from sin and toward Him. You asked Jesus to be your Lord and Savior. He removed your sin and shame and covered you with His righteousness. All good so far.

The devil is a notorious gaslighter.

But then something dreadful happened. You started hearing voices. No, I'm not trying to gaslight you. You aren't crazy. Real voices were speaking to you, telling you that God does not love you, He can't be trusted, and you are worthless. Not only did you hear those voices, but you also started to believe them. You may not have heard audible voices, but you still thought and felt everything I'm describing here. I am telling you those thoughts and feelings aren't your imagination. Then who was speaking to you? Jesus said,

[The devil] was a murderer from the beginning. He has always hated the truth, because there is no truth in him. When he lies, it is consistent with his character; for he is a liar and the father of lies (John 8:44).

The apostle John calls Satan "the one deceiving the whole world" (Revelation 12:9). Paul says, "Satan disguises himself as an angel of light" (2 Corinthians 11:14). To stay with our theme, he is an angel of gaslight!

The devil and his demons have *two primary lies they tell unbelievers and two lies they tell believers.* To **unbelievers**, they say,

1. "God doesn't care about sin. In fact, there might not even be a God. Live your life and do as you please."
2. "You are too bad for God to ever love and forgive you. You are doomed. Just accept it."

But to **believers**, the devil and his demons say:

1. "You've been saved, so it doesn't matter how much you sin. You can do what you want. Don't worry because God will forgive you."
2. "You just thought you were saved. Do you really think God can forgive all the bad things you've done? Who are you fooling?"

Do you see the similarities between these two sets of lies? The devil is deceptive and sinister, but he can never be creative or original. His essential motive is to get you to believe that God is not the answer to your problem with sin. Satan first accused God before he ever accused any humans (see Genesis 3:1). Satan's first and last lie is always about God. He wants you to believe God cannot solve your problem. If you were an unbeliever, the devil would be trying to tell you God either doesn't exist or doesn't have the power or grace to fix your predicament. If you are a believer, then the enemy wants you to think that you can ignore God or that the power of your sin is greater than God's grace. In any situation, the devil lies about God. I am telling you, Jesus Christ is your only solution, so the devil is doing his best to get you away from the Lord.

Hear Paul's double warnings.

- **For unbelievers:**

The god of this age has blinded the minds of unbelievers, so that they cannot see the light of the gospel that displays the glory of Christ, who is the image of God (2 Corinthians 4:4 NIV).

- **For believers:**

But I am afraid that just as Eve was deceived by the serpent's cunning, your minds may somehow be led astray from your sincere and pure devotion to Christ (2 Corinthians 11:3 NIV).

10 Truths About Satan's Lies

When Satan lied to Adam and Eve, they believed him. When Satan tried to lie to Jesus, our Lord used the Word of God to counteract the enemy's deceptions. Before we move on to the topic of shame and innocence, I want to share with you some important truths from the Bible that tell us how to approach Satan's lies.

1.   Our battle is spiritual.

For we are not fighting against flesh-and-blood enemies, but against evil rulers and authorities of the unseen world, against mighty powers in this dark world, and against evil spirits in the heavenly places (Ephesians 6:12).

2.   The devil is a liar, and he wants to destroy us.

Stay alert! Watch out for your great enemy, the devil. He prowls around like a roaring lion, looking for someone to devour. Stand firm against him, and be strong in your faith. Remember that your family of believers all over the world is going through the same kind of suffering you are (1 Peter 5:8–9).

———

Don't be afraid of what you are about to suffer. The devil will throw some of you into prison to test you. You will suffer for ten days. But if you remain faithful even when facing death, I will give you the crown of life (Revelation 2:10).

3.   God cannot lie, and Jesus Christ is the basis of truth.

This letter is from Paul, a slave of God and an apostle of Jesus Christ. I have been sent to proclaim faith to those God has chosen and to teach them to know the truth that shows them how to live godly lives. This truth gives them confidence that they have eternal life, which God—who does not lie—promised them before the world began (Titus 1:1–2).

———

God is not a man, so he does not lie.

He is not human, so he does not change his mind.

Has he ever spoken and failed to act?

Has he ever promised and not carried it through?

(Numbers 23:19).

———

Jesus told him, "I am the way, the truth, and the life. No one can come to the Father except through me" (John 14:6).

4.   Jesus is the only source for a rich and satisfying life.

The thief's purpose is to steal and kill and destroy. My purpose is to give them a rich and satisfying life (John 10:10).

5.   Jesus is stronger than the devil's lies.

But when people keep on sinning, it shows that they belong to the devil, who has been sinning since the beginning. But the Son of God came to destroy the works of the devil (1 John 3:8).

———

And you know that God anointed Jesus of Nazareth with the Holy Spirit and with power. Then Jesus went around doing good and healing all who were oppressed by the devil, for God was with him (Acts 10:38).

6.   Sin does not have to be our ongoing practice.

The temptations in your life are no different from what others experience. And God is faithful. He will not allow the temptation to be more than you can stand. When you are tempted, he will show you a way out so that you can endure (1 Corinthians 10:13).

———

So stop telling lies. Let us tell our neighbors the truth, for we are all parts of the same body. And "don't sin by letting anger control you." Don't let the sun go down while you are still angry, for anger gives a foothold to the devil (Ephesians 4:25–27).

7. We do not have to continue carrying shame and guilt for our sins.

But if we confess our sins to him, he is faithful and just to forgive us our sins and to cleanse us from all wickedness (1 John 1:9).

———

Such love has no fear, because perfect love expels all fear. If we are afraid, it is for fear of punishment, and this shows that we have not fully experienced his perfect love (1 John 4:18).

8. We should learn how the devil operates.

So that Satan will not outsmart us. For we are familiar with his evil schemes (2 Corinthians 2:11).

———

So I am writing to you not because you don't know the truth but because you know the difference between truth and lies (1 John 2:21).

9. The devil will use other people to spread his lies.

Beware of false prophets who come disguised as harmless sheep but are really vicious wolves. You can identify them by their fruit, that is, by the way they act. Can you pick grapes from thornbushes, or figs from thistles? A good tree produces good fruit, and a bad tree produces bad fruit (Matthew 7:15–17).

———

But evil people and impostors will flourish. They will deceive others and will themselves be deceived (2 Timothy 3:13).

———

For false messiahs and false prophets will rise up and perform great signs and wonders so as to deceive, if possible, even God's chosen ones (Matthew 24:24).

10. **God can equip us to stop the devil's attempts to work in our lives.**

Put on all of God's armor so that you will be able to stand firm against all strategies of the devil (Ephesians 6:11).

I have incredibly good news for you: *Satan will ultimately lose!* He will finally be thrown into the lake of fire (see Revelation 20:10). The apostle Paul reminds us:

The God of peace will soon crush Satan under your feet. May the grace of our Lord Jesus be with you (Romans 16:20).

———

I have incredibly good news for you:
Satan will ultimately lose!

———

The Day Innocence Died and Shame Was Born

Satan has been busy trying to deceive the human family, but it was not always that way. Shame did not always exist. Innocence always existed, but not shame. Shame was not born until Adam and Eve listened to the devil and bit into the fruit God had told them not to eat. For the first time in their lives, they realized they were naked. Often when we think about sex in our culture, we think about things we call "shameful acts." Our media is overrun with stories of shameful, sinful, and even criminal behavior relating to sexuality. There was none of that in the Garden of Eden, at least not until Adam and Eve disobeyed God's explicit command.

> At that moment their eyes were opened, **and they suddenly felt shame** at their nakedness. So they sewed fig leaves together to cover themselves.
>
> When the cool evening breezes were blowing, the man and his wife heard the LORD God walking about in the garden. So they hid from the LORD God among the trees. Then the LORD God called to the man, "Where are you?"
>
> He replied, "I heard you walking in the garden, so I hid. I was afraid because I was naked."
>
> "Who told you that you were naked?" the LORD God asked. "Have you eaten from the tree whose fruit I commanded you not to eat?" (Genesis 3:7–11, bold mine).

I don't know about you, but when guests come over to my house, I make sure I have clothes on. But Adam and Eve's concern about their nakedness wasn't just based on social expectations. Once they sinned, they felt naked about more than their bodies, and no wonder. Because of sin, they now stood guilty before their Creator God. But it was also about their bodies. Now that they sinned, humans began to use their bodies in sinful ways. Sexuality was never dirty or perverse when God created Adam and Eve. Sin made it possible to turn something beautiful into something despicable. Adam and Eve had never felt threatened by anything in their lives, but now everything became a threat. The way they felt about each other changed, and now Satan has made it his full-time job to get them to keep on sinning and even misusing each other.

Adam was a beloved son of God, faithful husband, diligent prophet, intimate priest, and powerful king, but suddenly he doesn't identify himself in any of those ways anymore. He realizes he is weak, sinful, and damaged. The world around him is terrifying and threatening. For the first time, humans recognized they were under God's righteous judgment (see Genesis 3:17; John 3:19; Romans 6:23). When God found them concealing themselves after they sinned, the Lord wasn't playing a game of hide-and-seek with the humans. He's God, and He knew where they were. They were now sinners, and God rejects sin. Even more, the enemy was ready to tell them just how bad they had blown it (see Revelation 12:10). *Innocence died that day, and shame was born.*

Naked and Ashamed

A common dream many people have is finding themselves naked or in their underwear in a public place, such as school or work. We think of that kind of experience as a nightmare. The truth is, we live that dream while we are awake because we are ashamed of our weaknesses, faults, and failures. It was not always that way, though.

Genesis 2:25 says Adam and Eve were "both naked, but they felt no shame." Only a few verses later, they felt intense shame (see Genesis 3:10). Adam says they are hiding because they are naked, which seems to make no sense, especially because sin is the real reason why they are hiding. Adam was created naked. He didn't suddenly get naked—he's always been naked. Then God asks a question: "Who told you that you were naked?" (Genesis 3:11). God knows Satan, the great gaslighter, whispered it to them. Satan told them they were broken, and even the most beautiful and intimate parts of their lives were now defective.

We might wonder why God didn't ask them about the fruit of disobedience they just ate. Is there anyone concerned about their nakedness? Anyone *at all*? No, because nakedness isn't the real issue. For Adam and Eve, nakedness was life as usual. They were free and unbothered by anything. When sin entered the picture, innocence died, God's glory departed, and shame took their place. People began to think of sexuality as a problem to fix rather than a blessing to enjoy. But human fixes without God are never true repairs. Shame over their sinfulness led them to think two ways about their sexuality:

1. Libertinism

"We are already broken, so we can do anything we want with anyone we want."

2. Legalism

"Sex is so shameful that I can never enjoy it. Even when I follow God's plan for sex, I am not allowed to take any pleasure in it."

Both of these are lies the devil tells us, but most humans believe them.

The main Hebrew word translated as shame is *bosh*. The primary meaning of the word is 'to fall into disgrace, usually by failure.' The failure could be yours or someone else's, but the emotion is the same. In English, *shame* is usually described as "a feeling of guilt from having done something wrong." Is that what Adam is feeling? Did you realize neither Adam nor Eve ever admitted their sin, at least not in what the Bible records? They don't repent. When David finally came to terms with his sin over adultery with Bathsheba and the murder of her husband, he told the prophet Nathan, "I have sinned against the LORD" (2 Samuel 12:13). But not Adam or Eve. They are only concerned about themselves. Adam is bothered because *he is naked*, not because he has sinned against God. Something has dramatically changed in Adam's life, but it's not that he suddenly became "more" naked than naked. Something shifted in his heart and mind. He's worried about something external—his lack of clothing—but something internal just went very wrong.

Adam only had two jobs, and they were very simple tasks: delight in his wife and steward the garden, all while focusing his energies on God. Sin changed his plans. His focus is no longer God, the garden, or his wife. The new agenda is fear and shame. Adam stopped nurturing his wife and the garden and began serving himself. He was called to be a prophet, priest, and king, but he exchanged it all for his own desires. He forgot that this world is God's world, and he claimed the earth as his own property. When Adam's agenda and awareness shifted, he suddenly became aware of his nakedness. Shame and guilt are often confused, but they are not the same. Guilt says, "I feel responsible for something wrong I did. I must repent and repair the situation or relationship." Shame might include unresolved feelings of guilt, but it also includes the feeling we get when others mistreat us. Shame says, "I am worthless and inadequate. I hate myself, and there's nothing I can do about it except hide or lash out. Even if it hurts me, I will take matters into my own hands." Shame is the experience of knowing my agenda is no longer God's agenda. I have become the king of my own world and the god of my own destiny, even if my final destiny is my own destruction.

Shame and guilt are often confused, but they are not the same.

Why does Adam realize he is now naked? It's not because he walked over to one of Eden's ponds and saw his own reflection. It's not because he suddenly discovered he had no clothes. It is because he realizes his desires are no longer God's desires, and he no longer finds joy in the things that cause God delight. He is hiding from the person he has become. If he can cover and hide, then maybe he will forget he has replaced God with himself. As far as we know, Adam didn't lash out, but his son Cain sure did, murdering his brother Abel. Father and son are both the centers of their own universes. He could repent and throw himself on the mercy of God, but Adam won't do that, and neither will Cain. It's become a family tradition. I don't know what God would have done if Adam had truly changed his heart and mind, but I'm sure it would be very different from what happened. Shame and pride are two sides of the same issue. Adam was too ashamed and too prideful to repent.

Breaking the Chains of Shame

Most of us would instinctively cover ourselves if someone accidentally entered a dressing room where we were changing our clothes. Is the reflex to hide wrong? No, it's not. We need a place to hide from both physical and spiritual nakedness, but we need to hide in the right place. The only place we can run to that will offer us real shelter from spiritual nakedness is Jesus Christ—He is our refuge (see Hebrews 6:18–20). There is no other truly safe harbor. No one else can save us (see Acts 4:12).

In 1973, psychiatrist Karl Menninger wrote a book titled *Whatever Became of Sin?* He believed that in the future sin would no longer be part of the human language or experience. He said sin would be replaced with other terms, such as illness, disorder, dysfunction, or syndrome. Any wrongdoing could be excused or explained away by biochemistry, the environment, personal experience, or trauma. Menninger believed society would no longer punish crime because every activity would be justified as some sort of medical or psychological issue. I hate to tell you, but I think Karl Menninger could see the future. I must also tell you that if you get the diagnosis wrong, then you'll never find the cure. If sin is the root of our shame, fear, and pride, then no amount of therapy or medication can deal with a problem that has sin as its origin.

Shame tells us we are deficient, but the Bible tells us Jesus' grace is sufficient (see 2 Corinthians 12:9). Shame tells us we are guilty, but Jesus' blood removes our guilt (see Romans 5:9–11). How do we approach Jesus? The apostle John says when we confess our sins and come to Jesus in faith, He makes us children of God (see John 1:12).

There is only one cure for sin: repentance. The Hebrew word usually translated repent is *shub* or *shuv*, which means 'turn back or return.'

The best illustration I have heard to describe the use of *shuv* happened not many years ago in Israel. A Christian tour group was walking down a side street when they saw a toddler moving toward the road. There weren't many cars, but any parent gets concerned when a toddler gets out of reach. Just then a mother stepped from behind a gate and yelled after the child, "Shuv!" The toddler turned to looked but ignored the mother's command. Just then the mother increased her volume and intensity and shouted again, "Shuv-eh!" The child turned around immediately and went back into the safety of the courtyard walls.

How do you approach Jesus? *Shuv-eh!* Stop whatever you are doing and turn around immediately. Turn back. Return. Repent. If you have never accepted Jesus as your Lord and Savior, then repent. If you have had your sins cleansed by the blood of Jesus, then you still must confess your sins and repent on a regular basis. You have been saved, but you are still awaiting the full measure of God's blessings you will receive when Jesus returns. When you sin, and you will sin, turn away from any transgression and toward the Lord. If you are not a believer, the same is true—you cannot escape your sin on your own. Turn around right now and turn to the Lord.

> This includes you who were once far away from God. You were his enemies, separated from him by your evil thoughts and actions. Yet now he has reconciled you to himself through the death of Christ in his physical body. As a result, he has brought you into his own presence, and you are holy and blameless as you stand before him without a single fault (Colossians 1:21–22).

If you struggle with any leftover feelings of shame, then hear this reminder from the apostle Paul:

So now there is no condemnation for those who belong to Christ Jesus. And because you belong to him, the power of the life-giving Spirit has freed you from the power of sin that leads to death (Romans 8:1–2).

Repentance, not hiding, is the answer to shame. Hiding away in your home or away from your home won't help. You might try to hide in business or busyness, but the answer is not there. Shame can find you behind your computer, on your telephone, or in front of your television. Social media isn't a refuge. You may try to put on a different face, but underneath the facade, the shame lingers. There's only one answer: turn away and turn to the Lord.

Repentance, not hiding, is the answer to shame.

I don't know if Adam and Eve ever stopped hiding from their shame and regret over their disobedience and loss of innocence. I do know they were ashamed because of their nakedness. They may have never repented. If they didn't turn to the Lord, then they lived long and sad lives after they were expelled from the garden.

Instantly Innocent, Forever Unashamed

Did you realize the last verse in the Bible before Adam and Eve sinned says, "They were both naked, the man and his wife, and were not ashamed" (Genesis 2:25 NKJV)? Then the very first thought Adam had after they sinned was, *We're naked!*

> At that moment their eyes were opened, and they suddenly felt shame at their nakedness. So they sewed fig leaves together to cover themselves (Genesis 3:7).

Sin changes something deep within us. We want to hide it away. Our guilt strips us bare. Why does the book of Genesis mention their nakedness? Before the humans sinned, they were focused on God and doing His work and not on themselves. They only knew innocence. Then they ate from the Tree of the Knowledge of Good and Evil, and we know what happened. Shame came from the knowledge of evil. Before Adam and Eve sinned, there was no evil to even know about. They were pure and innocent in their relationships with each other and with God. They didn't notice they were naked any more than a dog knows it's naked.

Everything changed when they ate from the tree. They turned their eyes from God to themselves. Now they know guilt, fear, pride, and shame. Now they feel naked and exposed. They want to hide their spiritual and physical nakedness. Innocence completely disappears. Ever since Adam and Eve sinned, nakedness became associated with shame.

Consider the first of two Scripture passages from the book of Revelation:

> You say, "I am rich. I have everything I want. I don't need a thing!" And you don't realize that you are wretched and miserable and poor and blind and naked. So I advise you to buy gold from me—gold that has

been purified by fire. Then you will be rich. Also buy white garments from me so you will not be shamed by your nakedness, and ointment for your eyes so you will be able to see" (Revelation 3:17–18).

Jesus doesn't have very many good things to say to the church in Laodicea. Even so, the believers there seem to be unaware of their own problems. They are like the emperor in Hans Christian Andersen's fairytale *The Emperor's New Clothes*—they are naked and don't even know it. The believers in Laodicea think everything is fine because they have wealth and prosperity. However, Jesus tells them they are actually naked. The Laodiceans can't even see because they are almost blind. They are a physically wealthy yet spiritually poor church. They are in danger of their lampstand being removed.

A second passage in Revelation is a caution for believers and a warning for unbelievers:

Look, I will come as unexpectedly as a thief! Blessed are all who are watching for me, who keep their clothing ready so they will not have to walk around naked and ashamed (Revelation 16:15).

Jesus warns believers and unbelievers alike about being clothed when He returns. One traditional interpretation of the background of this verse is that priests in the Jewish Temple stood watch during various times. If they were to fall asleep on watch, their clothing was burned, and they had to return home naked. I don't know if this is a true account, but the warning is serious. Adam and Eve were ashamed when God came looking for them because of their nakedness. That shame is similar to the experience of those who are unprepared for the Rapture. Believers should be clothed in the righteousness of Jesus, and they should also put on the whole armor of God. As royal priests, we must be dressed and ready. Both passages in Revelation associate nakedness with shame. The people in Laodicea are covering their shame with riches. Those who are not clothed and ready when Christ returns will experience a similar kind of shame.

Believers should be clothed in the righteousness of Jesus, and they should also put on the whole armor of God.

Jesus came to restore us to God. When we come in childlike faith, we become innocent like Adam and Eve were before they knew sin.

"I tell you the truth, anyone who doesn't receive the Kingdom of God like a child will never enter it." Then he took the children in his arms and placed his hands on their heads and blessed them (Mark 10:15–16).

Jesus is telling us to recover the humility and wonder of children. Children are dependent on those who care for them. Before they learn the ways of adults, children do not try to mask or hide their thoughts and feelings. It is this natural humility Jesus calls His followers to recover. Humility is not contrived, nor is it worn as a mask to deceive. It is this natural humility that we are to recover. The world wants us to do whatever we can to stay on top or to hide it when we can't. Jesus offers us childlike innocence and humility. He is the one who really cares for us. Those are the attitudes that really count in heaven.

We continue to struggle with pride and shame. They cause us to hide because we don't want to face our sin, or they make us puff ourselves up to appear that we are more than we are. When the Rapture happens, all the hiding and pretending will end. When Jesus returns, *five things will happen simultaneously* that relate to our shame and innocence.

1. Sin will cease, so there will be no reason for us to feel shame or guilt because of sin.
2. We will see Jesus face-to-face, so we will know He is not angry or disappointed with us.
3. We will be clothed in Jesus' righteousness, so we will not feel ashamed or exposed.
4. We will not be able to compare our sin or innocence with anyone else's, because everyone will know that only the grace of God has saved them.
5. We will never again focus on ourselves, but only on what delights God. That will be our work, and we will never grow tired of doing it.

If you are a believer, I urge you to stay close to the Lord. Look up! Jesus is coming, so prepare yourself. Continually examine your heart and remove anything that would draw you away from the Lord. When we see Jesus, He will restore all things. Innocence will return, and shame will be gone.

PART NINE

What About Knowledge?

CHAPTER 21

What About Knowledge?

One of the reasons I wrote this book is so you would get excited about where you are going and understand many of the events that will happen. I also want to answer a few questions you may still have.

I have told you Jesus' return will redeem our bodies, minds, pleasure, identity, authority, home, intimacy, and innocence. You may look at this list and think I have missed something. For example, why didn't I list knowledge as one of the things people lost in the fall and will get back when Jesus returns?

The answer is that Adam and Eve didn't have knowledge, at least not in the conventional sense. What they did know was God and His instructions to them. As far as other kinds of knowledge are concerned, they were intelligent but not knowledgeable people. As far as the Bible records, the only thing God specifically instructed them to do was "Be fruitful and multiply; fill the earth and subdue it; have dominion" (Genesis 1:28 NKJV) and "Don't eat from the tree of the knowledge of good and evil" (see Genesis 2:17). If God told them anything else, Genesis does not record it.

Why would God create Adam and Eve and not give them knowledge? As I have said, He gave them something better—Himself. The Lord wanted to teach them through relationship. He is omniscient, which means He knows everything. God lived with them in the Garden of Eden as their Mentor. He loves being a Father. In a sense, He divinely disables all of us so we will need Him. Even though God gave them many other things, He didn't give Adam and Eve knowledge, because He gave them Himself. Can you imagine having God standing next to you any time you had a question? That is how it was for the first two humans.

Maybe you have one of those devices in your home that is part of your home's smart technology. I'm not a fan, and I'm not naming the companies that control them. Someone or something is listening on the other end of it—maybe hostile foreign powers. Who knows? I'm probably not a good spokesperson for them. But you might say to the device, "Hey, [whatever name it is], How far is it to the sun?" Then it replies, "It is 93 million miles to the sun. Would you like to search the internet for 'sun'?" These devices are listening *all the time*! I think it's a little invasive and eerie.

Can you imagine having God standing next to you any time you had a question?

But here is one thing I know about those machines: They cannot tell you about your destiny. They don't know you, even if they are gathering data about you. They can't answer spiritual questions, even though they have access to billions of web pages. Now, I suppose they can be handy devices to have around because you can ask them questions, and they can control almost any electronic device in your home. But just imagine being able to walk up to God and ask Him face-to-face, "Why was I created? What's the meaning of the sun, moon, and stars? What's the meaning of my life? Tell me about marriage. Help me understand science and the universe."

If you wanted to know anything, God has the answer, but that is not the way He works in this world. God could have downloaded any amount of information He wanted into Adam and Eve. In fact, He could do it for you right now. But God is not a downloader; He's a Father. He doesn't want to make you instantly perfect as long as you live in this world. What God wants is to father you into perfection.

When we get to heaven, God will make us perfect in every way. We will finally get to rest from our sin nature and the other limitations of this world. God created us to be dependent upon Him. Your spiritual intimacy will always correspond to your spiritual dependency. You can only be intimate with God to the degree that you're dependent on Him. Independence is the recipe for the loss of intimacy.

What God wants is to father you into perfection.

As humans, we have a real problem with dependence. Throughout the Bible, one of the major images used to describe our relationship to God is that of sheep to their shepherd. King David, once a shepherd himself, beautifully describes this relationship:

The Lord *is* my shepherd;

I shall not want.

He makes me to lie down in green pastures;

He leads me beside the still waters (Psalm 23:1–2 NKJV).

And Jesus said, "I am the good shepherd. The good shepherd gives His life for the sheep" (John 10:11 NKJV).

When God looks at us, He sees sheep. He's the Shepherd. Sheep are cute, but they are also pathetically weak. They can't navigate on their own; you'll never hear of a "homing sheep." They can't bear burdens; you'll never hear of a "pack sheep." And they can't defend themselves; you've certainly never heard of an "attack sheep." They're completely dependent upon the shepherd. In comparison to him, they are unintelligent, weak, and defenseless. That is an apt description of us. The prophet Isaiah said,

But He *was* wounded for our transgressions,

He was bruised for our iniquities;

The chastisement for our peace *was* upon Him,

And by His stripes we are healed.

All we like sheep have gone astray;

We have turned, every one, to his own way;

And the Lord has laid on Him the iniquity of us all (Isaiah 53:5–6 NKJV).

We really need to understand an important dynamic that took place in the Garden of Eden, because the same thing is happening in our lives right now. God the Father created these wonderful, perfect beings, but they were incomplete because He wanted them to depend on Him. Instead of giving them knowledge, He gave them Himself. More than any father on this earth, God loves being a Father to us and answering all our questions.

There are two sides to the cross. On our side, we look up and say, "Thank You, Jesus, for the price You paid so we could be forgiven and come back into Your presence." Then there's another side to the cross—God's side—and He is saying, "It was worth everything that was paid to get you back into My presence." This heartsick Daddy sent His one and only Son so He could be back in your presence. He loves being with us more than we could possibly understand.

Adam and Eve were incredibly naive. When Satan came into the Garden of Eden in the form of a serpent, he did what he does to all of us—he offered them an exchange. He wanted them to take something as a trade for Someone. The couple exchanged God the Father and their intimate relationship with Him for a piece of fruit that offered them instant knowledge. God had wanted to mentor them in a loving relationship over eons of time. But the devil told them they didn't need God. If they would only eat that fruit, then they would be just like God and know everything He knows.

When Adam and Eve traded God for the fruit, they fell from that relationship and died. The devil is a liar; he always overpromises and underdelivers. He will guarantee us things he does not own or have the authority to give. He has been trying the same scheme on all of us. He wants to lure us away from our Father and give us some*thing* for Some*one*.

The apostle John wrote,

> Do not love the world or the things in the world. If anyone loves the world, the love of the Father is not in him. For all that *is* in the

world—the lust of the flesh, the lust of the eyes, and the pride of life—is not of the Father but is of the world. And the world is passing away, and the lust of it; but he who does the will of God abides forever (1 John 2:15–17 NKJV).

When John says not to love the world, he does not mean the physical earth itself. God created the earth and called it "good." It is a wonderful thing. If you enjoy God's creation, it does not mean you are "worldly." When John writes about the "world," he means it is a system that Satan is using to try to replace God. When the apostle tells us not to love the world, which includes "the lust of the flesh, the lust of the eyes, and the pride of life," he means those things that are used in an attempt to replace God as Father.

Mammon, the Counterfeit of Provision

For everything God the Father offers us, the devil tries to give us a counterfeit substitute. One example is mammon versus provision. In the Lord's Prayer, Jesus told His followers to go to God the Father every day and say, "Give us this day our daily bread" (Matthew 6:11 NKJV; see also Luke 11:3). God, your Father, wants to provide for you. When you think of the word *provision*, also remember it is *for the vision*. When God provides, He doesn't simply give us money and things to do whatever we want with them; He gives us direction for our lives. He doesn't just throw money at us; He gives us Himself. When we get provision, we get God, peace, direction, and vision. God may give us money and things to accomplish His purpose but not because He wants to fill our pockets.

The devil, however, offers us mammon. For the Syrians, Mammon was a deity, the god of wealth. Mammon has a demonic quality because it tries to offer everything that God does but without concern for God. Jesus says, "You cannot serve God and mammon" (see Matthew 6:24 NKJV). Mammon will tell you, "I'll make you secure." Notice how many advertisements promise security and independence. I am not telling you to avoid investing or to be unconcerned for your future, because those are simply good stewardship tools. However, I am saying that only God can provide for you and secure your future.

God says He will make us free. Mammon says, "Money will make you free." God says He'll give you an identity. Mammon says, "Go show this money around. It'll give you an identity and make you look important." Mammon comes to us and says, "You don't have to serve God; you don't even have to be moral. You have no allegiance to a higher moral being. All you need is money." This is the mantra of the world. Many people are unknowingly serving a demonic idol. Remember the warnings Paul gave Timothy about the end times. The apostle told him one of the signs of the end is that people would become "lovers of money" (see 2 Timothy 3:1–5 NKJV). People will even say they love God, but they will not trust Him to provide for them. The devil wants to lure you away from a relationship with your Father. God wants to provide for you as your Daddy. The devil wants you to chase money. But when you get true provision, you will receive both money and God. You will have enough.

**I am saying that only God can provide
for you and secure your future.**

Lust, the Counterfeit of Love

The devil will offer you lust as a substitute for love. John warned that people would pursue the lust of their eyes and their flesh. Look again at what Paul says people will be like in the last days. The apostle tells Timothy people will be "lovers of pleasure rather than lovers of God" (2 Timothy 3:4 NKJV).

I want to begin what I am about to tell you by saying God is a forgiving God. The reason I know this is because He forgave me. When I was growing up, I was very immoral, and I had no shame about it. I was not a believer. In fact, the week before Karen and I got married, she told me she wouldn't marry me because of how immoral I was. I admit it, I was. I would roll out of bed every morning with pleasure as my main pursuit. Unfortunately, I was remarkably successful at finding it, and I now regret it. I went to college fraternity parties where things happened that should never happen. But it was what I wanted and what I was pursuing. After having an evening of every kind of indulgent pleasure you can imagine, I remember going to bed feeling empty and lonely. Night after night I felt that way. But the next morning, I would be at it again.

The night after my bachelor party was when Karen told me she wouldn't marry me. She found out some of the shameful things I had done. I got up the next morning and stared at myself in the mirror at my friend's house. I thought to myself, *This road does not lead where I thought it was going to lead.* I had heard of Jesus, so I prayed to Him: "Jesus, I give my life to You, and I'll serve You for the rest of my life and never turn back." It took a crisis to get me there, but God is exceptionally good with crises.

He came into my life at that point, and I felt true love on the inside of me for the first time. I still feel His love for me more than 49 years later. The devil will tell you, "I'll give you silos and treasure chests of pleasure." God says, "I will give you love, an eternal abiding love. And you'll never feel lonely or empty again." Don't exchange love for lust. It is a fool's bargain.

Don't exchange love for lust. It is a fool's bargain.

Pride, the Counterfeit for Promotion

A third substitute the devil will offer us is pride for promotion. In the world, people seek to advance by following pride, but God the Father promotes us. In 2 Timothy 3:2, Paul says people will be "boasters, proud" before Jesus comes again. The devil will say, "Talk about yourself, try to promote yourself, and exalt yourself, because it's all about you." But James says, "Humble yourselves in the sight of the Lord, and He will lift you up" (James 4:10 NKJV).

You do not have to promote yourself. God the Father will promote you if you humble yourself. We have a perfect Father who will provide for us, love us, promote us, and teach us if we will depend on Him. Our sin nature despises dependency. Before the Fall, God the Father divinely disabled Adam and Eve, and He was there to mentor them. They traded a relationship with Him for a counterfeit. It's the same thing the devil is trying to do to all of us today.

You Father wants to raise you to the point that you become a mature believer. He wants to have an intimate relationship with you. The Lord wants to hear you say, "I embrace my weakness, and I love being dependent upon You. You're the best Daddy in the world, and I'm going to talk to You about the things that are happening in my life every day. I trust You above anything or anyone else."

CHAPTER 22

What About Temptation?

Adam and Eve sinned in the Garden of Eden. The Bible is unmistakably clear about that. But people often wonder:

- Why didn't God stop them?
- If God knew they would be tempted and ultimately sin, then isn't God really responsible for their temptation and sin? That seems unfair.
- Isn't God responsible for their failure by allowing the Tree of the Knowledge of Good and Evil to grow in the garden? That also seems unfair.

Please know that God did not set Adam and Eve up for temptation and failure. It was not a trap. But I will answer this series of questions or concerns by asking another question: *What kind of God is God?* By posing that question, I am asking you to consider God's character. Given who He is, what would or could He do and still maintain His character? We know many things about God, but what are some of the questions we need to ask about His character related to this event?

What kind of God would live alone and not create any other beings to relate to?

The God of the Bible is *relational*. He created us for relationship, and He even sent His own Son to die so He could restore that relationship. The apostle Paul summarizes God's desire for a relationship with us:

> Now all things *are* of God, who has reconciled us to Himself through Jesus Christ, and has given us the ministry of reconciliation, that is, that God was in Christ reconciling the world to Himself, not imputing their trespasses to them, and has committed to us the word of reconciliation.
>
> Now then, we are ambassadors for Christ, as though God were pleading through us: we implore *you* on Christ's behalf, be reconciled to God (2 Corinthians 5:18–20 NKJV).

The God of the Bible is *relational*.

God sent Christ to restore our relationship with Him. Now, as believers, He calls us to tell everyone else about what He has done to be in a relationship with them. We are His ambassadors, His ministers of reconciliation.

What kind of God would make a creature He could relate to but then have a very uncaring and distant relationship?

Throughout history, there have been people who believed in a deity but thought of their god as very distant or unconcerned about his creation. That belief is called *deism.* Deists see God as a sort of watchmaker who created the world, put it in motion, and then left it to fend for itself. He is very dispassionate and uninvolved in the details of humanity. Some of America's founding fathers were influenced by this thought, including Thomas Jefferson and Benjamin Franklin. There are many deists still in the world today; they will acknowledge a divine being, but it is not a personal God.

Our God is *personal.* Jesus told His followers that God knows every hair on their heads (see Matthew 10:30). He is more interested in them than the birds or the grass, though He also takes care of those mundane parts of His creation (see Matthew 6:25–34). If He will even care for birds and grass, how much more does He care for us? Our God is neither uncaring nor dispassionate; He is a doting Father and very much unlike the god of deism.

What kind of God would create humans with a desire to relate to them yet not give them a free will?

God is not an authoritarian tyrant—He is a *benevolent King.* He gave us a free will, which means we are also free to reject Him or stand against Him. His greatest desire is for us to freely choose to love Him. Free will is not really free will unless we can use it against the person who gave it to us. If there wasn't a Tree of the Knowledge of Good and Evil in the Garden of Eden, then Eden would have been a sham. If God created Adam and Eve in a world where there was no possibility to oppose His will, then they could not use their wills against Him. There had to be a tree they couldn't eat from and a choice they could make against God. Otherwise, they didn't really have a free will.

God is not an authoritarian tyrant—He is a *benevolent King*.

Because of His character, God has to be able to say, "I did give you a free will and the opportunity to use it against Me." If God had created a world without that tree, He would have been a huckster perpetuating a hoax. He would have told us we had a free will, when in fact we did not. He would have said we loved Him when we couldn't have done anything other than love Him. God wants us to freely love Him. The tree had to be there.

What kind of God would create people with free wills and then put billions of Trees of the Knowledge of Good and Evil in the Garden of Eden?

God graciously made many trees and told the couple they could eat from any of them *except one*. He did not create a whole forest of Trees of the Knowledge of Good and Evil. If He had, then Adam and Eve would have thought, *Ah! Watch out! There's another one. He's trying to trap us!* The Lord is not a cruel or capricious God who tries to set you up for failure. God does not tempt or trick us. *God is good, and His character is always good.* He always wants our obedience, but He wants us to choose to obey.

What kind of God would create us with a free will we could use against Him with only one choice to rebel, but then would pay the penalty for our rebellion Himself to redeem us, bring us back into relationship with Him, and restore everything we lost?

Our God would! He is the only kind of God who could and would do that. That is His character.

Look Up!
Redemption Is Near

In my book *Tipping Point*, I make the same claim over and over again: not only do I believe we are in the end times, but I also believe we are in the *end of the end times*. Jesus is coming back very soon. I don't know the day or the hour, but I do know that all the signs are here. If you are a Christian, Jesus is about to redeem everything about you. He is going to restore your body, remake your mind, give you the pleasure He always wanted you to have, reestablish your identity, empower you with authority, place you in your new, beautiful home, live forever in a perfect and intimate relationship with you, and take away all shame. Everything we lost is about to be regained. It can never be taken from us again for all eternity.

Don't be caught off guard. The prophecies of the Bible are being fulfilled moment by moment every day. If you have not read *Tipping Point*, I really want to encourage you to get a copy, sit down and read it, and pray for the Holy Spirit to reveal the truth about what God is saying about the end times. We have reached a critical and unstoppable point. Jesus is coming soon, and there is no going back.

Everything we lost is about to be regained. It can never be taken from us again for all eternity.

As I said, the signs are here. Israel is God's super sign. It is in the crosshairs of many nations and groups that want to do the Jewish people harm. God said it would happen. Astronomical signs in the sky have arrived even as I have been writing this book. God said it would happen. Truth, decency, and morality are daily under assault as believers are forced into a defensive posture. God said it would happen. Sexual immorality is reaching new lows at blazing speed. God said it would happen. Innovations and advances in science and technology are happening faster than ever before. God said it would happen. Time is running out.

Yes, Jesus is coming again. He is coming soon. God said it would happen. Now, the only question is will you be ready? Will you go with Him? Will you be His bride?

I am going. I am sure of it. I want you to go with me. Look up!

Do you know Jesus? Remember what I said to Jesus at my friend's house? "Jesus, please come into my life, and I'll serve You and never turn back." Have you ever prayed anything like that? Please don't go another minute without having the certainty that you know Jesus Christ and have given your life to Him. It will change your eternity from this point forward. When Jesus comes, you will go with Him and be with Him for the rest of eternity.

I want to close with a word of hope, even if things seem hopeless. I am writing this book on the front side of the Rapture, but what if you pick up this book and Jesus has already returned to gather the believers on earth? I don't want to leave you without hope. There is still hope. I have written a book titled *Where Are the Missing People? The Sudden Disappearance of Millions and What Happens Next.* I wrote the book as a guide for those who may be left behind when Jesus returns. If we are still waiting for the return of Christ, I urge you to get a copy of this book to give to someone who is not a believer. I also encourage you to leave one around for when the Rapture does happen. This book may be the only guide someone will have once the Church is taken to be with the Lord. In the appendix to this book, I am going to summarize *Where Are the Missing People?* just in case someone cannot get a copy of it after Jesus comes again.

Appendix

Where Are the Missing People?

You may be reading this book after millions disappeared from the earth, and it seems to have happened in an instant. Without any warning, a huge portion of the earth's population is gone. Chaos ensued. But you're still here reading this.

You have many questions: *What happened? Where did they go? Why did they disappear? And why am I still here?* I am going to tell you the truth about what happened and what to expect in the near future.

Someone may have given you this book long ago, and you just now remembered it. You might be in the home of a missing relative or friend. You found this book somewhere prominent, like a coffee table or shelf. You may have found your way into a building looking for supplies—or answers. Regardless, you've found this book. Take it with you, read it all the way through, and then share it with others.

Where Did They Go?

People vanished in an instant, in the blink of an eye. As I am writing this, I do not know the exact timing of when it will happen, but by the time you're reading this, there's been plenty of speculation. You can ignore all the theories you are hearing. This book will tell you what happened.

> But let me reveal to you a wonderful secret. We will not all die, but we will all be transformed! It will happen in a moment, in the blink of an eye, when the last trumpet is blown. For when the trumpet sounds, those who have died will be raised to live forever. And we who are living will also be transformed (1 Corinthians 15:51–52).

The Bible explained almost 2,000 years ago what was going to happen. Many passages of Scripture describe the mass disappearance. Jesus, the Son of God, spoke to His followers and disciples about it. Other spiritual teachers, such as the apostle Paul, wrote about it. Since then, many books have been written about this event. Over the centuries, many preachers have given sermons about it. The event is commonly known as "the Rapture." The people who have disappeared have one thing in common: they were all followers of Jesus Christ. Though the event itself may have left you surprised, frightened, or confused, many of those who vanished had been anticipating the Rapture for years.

One text of Scripture describes the Rapture explicitly. The apostle Paul wrote,

> And now, dear brothers and sisters, we want you to know what will happen to the believers who have died so you will not grieve like

people who have no hope. For since we believe that Jesus died and was raised to life again, we also believe that when Jesus returns, God will bring back with him the believers who have died.

We tell you this directly from the Lord: We who are still living when the Lord returns will not meet him ahead of those who have died. For the Lord himself will come down from heaven with a commanding shout, with the voice of the archangel, and with the trumpet call of God. First, the believers who have died will rise from their graves. Then, together with them, we who are still alive and remain on the earth will be caught up in the clouds to meet the Lord in the air. Then we will be with the Lord forever. So encourage each other with these words (1 Thessalonians 4:13–18).

Does this sound familiar to you? Many believers in Christ simply disappeared. Again, I am writing before the Rapture, so I don't know the details you now know. Christians knew the Rapture was coming, but they did not know precisely when or how the event would happen. Now they know. Nevertheless, Jesus took these humans away from earth to heaven.

Another prominent Bible passage about what happened comes from Jesus Christ Himself. He compared the last days of the modern world to the days of Noah before God sent a great flood to destroy the earth. He also compared it to the last days of Lot, a man who lived in the wicked cities of Sodom and Gomorrah. God destroyed these cities with fire for their sinfulness. This is how Jesus described what was going to happen:

In those days, the people enjoyed banquets and parties and weddings right up to the time Noah entered his boat and the flood came and destroyed them all.

And the world will be as it was in the days of Lot. People went about their daily business—eating and drinking, buying and selling, farming and building—until the morning Lot left Sodom. Then fire and burning sulfur rained down from heaven and destroyed them all. Yes, it will be 'business as usual' right up to the day when the Son of Man is revealed. On that day a person out on the deck of a roof must not go down into the house to pack. A person out in the field must not return home. Remember what happened to Lot's wife! If you cling to your life, you will lose it, and if you let your life go, you will save it. That night two people will be asleep in one bed; one will be taken, the other left. Two women will be grinding flour together at the mill; one will be taken, the other left (Luke 17:27–35).

Jesus said people would be going about their daily business when the Rapture happens. Life would feel normal, but that will end. The Bible says the Rapture would happen someday, and that is exactly what has happened. Every Christian believer who was alive at that instant was "caught up in the air" to meet the Lord. They are no longer here—they are rejoicing in the presence of God in heaven.

In a Moment

Consider this Bible passage from the apostle Paul one more time:

But let me reveal to you a wonderful secret. We will not all die, but we will all be transformed! It will happen in a moment, in the blink of an eye, when the last trumpet is blown. For when the trumpet sounds, those who have died will be raised to live forever. And we who are living will also be transformed (1 Corinthians 15:51–52).

The Rapture happened "in a moment." However, it didn't gather just the believers who were alive, but also the countless Christians who had died before this event. God resurrected them and reunited their spirits with their now glorified bodies. The missing have been raptured, just as the Bible predicted in the first century.

Who Was Taken?

Jesus gathered up the millions of believers in the Rapture. But who is a *believer*? They were the followers of Jesus Christ. Regardless of how you might refer to them, they all had one thing in common: they had accepted Jesus Christ as their Lord and Savior and committed to living their lives according to the teachings of the Bible.

Accepting this gift is sometimes referred to as being "born again." The Bible teaches that sin has divided us from God. Our decisions that go against God separate us from Him. Though we are alive physically, we are spiritually dead because of sin. This keeps us from a relationship with God and leads to death.

Only Jesus can free us from a life dominated by sin and death. The only way to escape our sinful nature is rebirth—being "born again" spiritually. This new birth is into the family of God. If we are not born again, then we will live in spiritual death and in rebellion against God. Jesus came to save us from that reality.

Everlasting Life

One of the most famous verses in the entire Bible is John 3:16:

> For God so loved the world that He gave His only begotten Son, that whoever believes in Him should not perish but have everlasting life (NKJV).

Jesus came to save us by dying on the cross to pay for our sins. It is a debt we could never pay. Because of Jesus' perfect, sinless life, God accepted His Son's death to pay for the sins of humanity.

If we believe God sent Jesus into the world to pay for our sins, then we can be born again of the Holy Spirit and saved from sin and hell. To accept this gift, we must recognize the lordship of Jesus and that He alone is the Savior of the world. Then we need to confess that with our mouths.

> If you openly declare that Jesus is Lord and believe in your heart that God raised him from the dead, you will be saved. For it is by believing in your heart that you are made right with God, and it is by openly declaring your faith that you are saved (Romans 10:9–10).

Salvation occurs when you both believe and confess, which is what God requires and nothing else. People who took those steps before the Rapture are now with the Lord. They were "caught up in the air" by Him, which is why they suddenly disappeared.

A Free Gift

The apostle Paul said salvation is a free gift, which we can neither earn nor deserve. We can only accept or reject it.

> Once you were dead because of your disobedience and your many sins. You used to live in sin, just like the rest of the world...
>
> But God is so rich in mercy, and he loved us so much, that even though we were dead because of our sins, he gave us life when he raised Christ from the dead. (It is only by God's grace that you have been saved!) For he raised us from the dead along with Christ and seated us with him in the heavenly realms because we are united with Christ Jesus. So God can point to us in all future ages as examples of the incredible wealth of his grace and kindness toward us, as shown in all he has done for us who are united with Christ Jesus.
>
> God saved you by his grace when you believed. And you can't take credit for this; it is a gift from God. Salvation is not a reward for the good things we have done, so none of us can boast about it. For we are God's masterpiece. He has created us anew in Christ Jesus, so we can do the good things he planned for us long ago (Ephesians 2:1–2, 4–10).

Being saved or born again isn't simply believing something you didn't believe before. Now that the truth of the Rapture has convinced you of the existence of God and the salvation He offers through Jesus Christ, you may be ready to reevaluate what you believed before. However, it is more than changing your mind. You must decide to no longer live only for yourself. You don't want to give in to sin anymore. You're ready to surrender your life to Jesus Christ and follow Him as your Lord.

But Is It Too Late for You?

It's not too late! The Rapture has already happened, but you can still make the choice to accept Jesus as your Lord and Savior. He'll give you the strength to endure the dark days you are experiencing now and the even more severe time that is coming. Without Him, you're on your own. This is the most important decision you will ever make—not just in this life right now on earth, but for all of eternity.

Whether you have read this book carefully or just taken a quick look at the contents, you have discovered that most of the book is written to encourage people before the Rapture. I told them about all the wonderful things Jesus was going to do when He came again to remove Christians from the earth. I said He would redeem many things about them. But then the Rapture came, they disappeared, and you are still here. What about you? Of all the promises those people received about what Jesus would do for them at the Rapture, how many of them apply to you? The answer is *all of them*. You may have missed Jesus' return, but don't lose heart. He can do all those wonderful things for you too, and He will if you accept Him as your Lord and Savior.

That is why I included this section in this book. The importance of your decision could be the reason someone kept this book and left it, hoping that someone like you might find it after the Rapture. They knew you would have questions and feel confused. They knew you would need help navigating the world after the believers disappeared.

A Prayer of Salvation

Are you ready to make Jesus your Lord? If so, you can be born again by praying the following prayer. These words aren't magical or a special formula, but if they represent your heart and beliefs, then God will honor your confession. He will eternally change you and secure your salvation. If you are ready, then pray this aloud to the Lord:

Lord Jesus, I have sinned and rebelled against You, a holy God, and there is no excuse. I confess my sins to You now and repent of my rebellion. I ask for Your forgiveness, and I believe You died for my sins on the cross. I receive Your forgiveness now and believe that Your blood is more powerful than my worst sins. I am now totally forgiven by You, and I forgive myself. The past is behind me. I confess You as my Lord and Savior. I step down from the throne of my heart, and I pray that You will sit on that throne as my Lord and King. Come into my heart and give me the gift of eternal life. I know I don't deserve it, but I receive it by faith as a free gift. I believe I am forgiven, born again, and on my way to heaven. I will live the rest of my life for You. Fill me with Your Holy Spirit and lead me, speak to me, and give me the power to make right decisions and live for You. In Jesus' name, Amen.

If you sincerely prayed this prayer, then you are born again and have just been given the promise of eternal life.

What Does It Mean to Be a Christian?

For this reason we also, since the day we heard it, do not cease to pray for you, and to ask that you may be filled with the knowledge of His will in all wisdom and spiritual understanding; that you may walk worthy of the Lord, fully pleasing *Him*, being fruitful in every good work and increasing in the knowledge of God (Colossians 1:9–10 NKJV).

Now that you understand why the world's Christians were "taken up" in the Rapture and how important it is to commit yourself to Jesus, you may be thinking about other people in your life who claimed to be followers of Jesus. Are they still around? If they are still here, then this has been incredibly distressing to them. They are devastated. You may also know some people who are missing, and this surprises you. *They* were caught up in the air? These people may not have struck you as "the faithful," but the truth is that those who gave their lives to Christ never became perfect. They simply realized they needed God.

"Follow Me"

Now that you have given your life to Christ, what should you do next? As a new believer, try to find a Bible. No doubt the Rapture has resulted in many of the world's Bibles being left behind. In fact, since you are holding this book, it is very likely that there is also a Bible somewhere nearby. Go look for one. Then take it with you. Any person who owned a Bible before being raptured would absolutely want you to have it. Keep it and read it for yourself.

The best place to start is in the last half of the Bible, which is the New Testament, because it tells the story of Jesus Christ. I recommend starting in the Gospel of John. Also read sections from Psalms and Proverbs, located near the middle of the Bible in the Old Testament. These books are enlightening, filled with wisdom, and very comforting. Then examine the book of Revelation, which is the last book in the Bible. It is about the last days, and it describes many of the things happening now and the terrible events yet to come. It is important to understand these times.

As you read the Gospel of John, you'll find many uses of the word "follow." When Jesus taught His disciples and others, He gave them a command: *Follow Me*, which means "Do what I do."

> Then Jesus spoke to them again, saying, "I am the light of the world. He who follows Me shall not walk in darkness, but have the light of life" (John 8:12 NKJV).

I am going to tell you about several important activities that follow Jesus' example.

Baptism

After Jesus was resurrected from the dead, during one of the last times His followers saw Him before He went to heaven, He gave them a commandment. This is known as the Great Commission:

Jesus came and told his disciples, "I have been given all authority in heaven and on earth. Therefore, go and make disciples of all the nations, baptizing them in the name of the Father and the Son and the Holy Spirit. Teach these new disciples to obey all the commands I have given you. And be sure of this: I am with you always, even to the end of the age" (Matthew 28:18–20).

After we accept Jesus as Lord and Savior, He commands us to be baptized. He was publicly baptized Himself very early in His ministry. Jesus did it as an act of obedience to God, and as His followers, we should follow His example and command. Water baptism means we are publicly identifying ourselves with Christ as His followers and declaring our love and loyalty for Him.

As a new believer, find someone to baptize you if you can. Your baptism can happen anywhere there is enough water to cover you. All you need is someone to temporarily lower you under the water and say something like: "Because of your profession of faith in the Lord Jesus, I baptize you in the Name of the Father and the Son and the Holy Spirit." If you can't find anyone to baptize you, then lower yourself into water and say those words to yourself. The most important thing is that you are making a profession of faith in Jesus. Baptism illustrates the new life you have accepted through Jesus Christ. God will honor you for your obedience in taking this important step in your faith.

Communion

Another sacred sign of your relationship with Christ is communion, which is also called "the Lord's Supper" or "the Eucharist." Communion is the ongoing sign that follows the example of Jesus. He first introduced this to His followers right before His crucifixion. Jesus commanded them to continue doing it in remembrance of Him.

> He took some bread and gave thanks to God for it. Then he broke it in pieces and gave it to the disciples, saying, "This is my body, which is given for you. Do this in remembrance of me."
>
> After supper he took another cup of wine and said, "This cup is the new covenant between God and his people—an agreement confirmed with my blood, which is poured out as a sacrifice for you" (Luke 22:19–20).

A generation later, the apostle Paul described the significance of communion this way:

> On the night when he was betrayed, the Lord Jesus took some bread and gave thanks to God for it. Then he broke it in pieces and said, "This is my body, which is given for you. Do this in remembrance of me." In the same way, he took the cup of wine after supper, saying, "This cup is the new covenant between God and his people—an agreement confirmed with my blood. Do this in remembrance of me as often as you drink it." For every time you eat this bread and drink this cup, you are announcing the Lord's death until he comes again (1 Corinthians 11:23–26).

Paul said we are proclaiming the Lord's death, which means we are celebrating the freedom Jesus gained for us by dying for us on the cross. Taking the wine and bread of communion alone or together with other Christians helps us remember Jesus died for us and the benefits we now have because of His death and resurrection.

Before the Rapture, some churches served communion every time they gathered together. Others used to do it once a month or every few months. Some churches used actual wine, while others used grape juice. Both symbolize Christ's blood.

You are in a unique time in the history of the world. To be clear, this book was published before the Rapture, which means I could not be certain about all the things you will experience. Many churches may be meeting secretly for fear of persecution. If you are able to join them, please do. You will find communion and other Christian practices to be powerful, spiritual experiences. If you can't find other believers, then take some wine or juice and some bread or crackers and take communion on your own. God will bless you for your obedience in remembering Jesus' death.

Baptism in the Holy Spirit

I want to tell you about a type of baptism that differs from immersion in water.

> Once when he was eating with them, he commanded them, "Do not leave Jerusalem until the Father sends you the gift he promised, as I told you before. John baptized with water, but in just a few days you will be baptized with the Holy Spirit."

"But you will receive power when the Holy Spirit comes upon you" (Acts 1:4–5, 8).

Jesus often referred to the Holy Spirit as "the Helper," which is a translation of the Greek word *parakletos,* meaning 'comforter.' The Spirit is someone who walks alongside us to help us.

In the Gospel of John, Jesus described the Holy Spirit's work:

> But the Helper, the Holy Spirit, whom the Father will send in My name, He will teach you all things, and bring to your remembrance all things that I said to you (John 14:26 NKJV).

> ----

> When the Spirit of truth comes, he will guide you into all truth. He will not speak on his own but will tell you what he has heard. He will tell you about the future. He will bring me glory by telling you whatever he receives from me (John 16:13–14).

The New Testament describes something called the baptism in the Holy Spirit. Jesus told His disciples in Acts 1 to wait in Jerusalem until the Holy Spirit empowered them to be His witnesses on earth. At the Feast of Pentecost 10 days later, it happened. The Holy Spirit descended on a group of believers all at once, transforming their lives. The book of Acts describes it like this:

> On the day of Pentecost all the believers were meeting together in one place. Suddenly, there was a sound from heaven like the roaring of a mighty windstorm, and it filled the house where they were sitting. Then, what looked like flames or tongues of fire appeared

and settled on each of them. And everyone present was filled with the Holy Spirit and began speaking in other languages, as the Holy Spirit gave them this ability.

At that time there were devout Jews from every nation living in Jerusalem. When they heard the loud noise, everyone came running, and they were bewildered to hear their own languages being spoken by the believers (Acts 2:1–6).

Peter, one of Jesus' disciples, spoke to the crowd using an Old Testament passage from the book of Joel about the end times:

"In the last days," God says,
"I will pour out my Spirit upon all people.
Your sons and daughters will prophesy.
Your young men will see visions,
and your old men will dream dreams.
In those days I will pour out my Spirit
even on my servants—men and women alike—
and they will prophesy.
And I will cause wonders in the heavens above
and signs on the earth below—
blood and fire and clouds of smoke.
The sun will become dark,
and the moon will turn blood red
before that great and glorious day of the Lord arrives.
But everyone who calls on the name of the Lord
will be saved" (Acts 2:17–21).

That day, a large number of believers received the baptism in the Holy Spirit, which helped them know and serve God. They already trusted Jesus, but this was a separate and unique experience. It doesn't happen automatically because we are saved. Baptism in the Holy Spirit is about enjoying the powerful assistance of God every day. We must have continual partnership with the Holy Spirit.

The best way to receive the Holy Spirit is to ask a Spirit-filled believer to lay their hands on you and pray for you to be baptized in the Spirit. But if you can't do that, then you can receive Him by simply asking God and receiving the Spirit by faith. You can say a simple prayer like this:

Lord, I ask You to baptize me in Your Holy Spirit and fill me with the power to live for You. Holy Spirit, I need You in my life to be able to live victoriously for Jesus. Baptize me now and be my daily Helper to comfort, teach, and empower me to live for God. I receive You by faith as a free gift. In Jesus' name, Amen!

Christian Friendship

Because I am writing this before the Rapture, it is difficult for me to know how hard it will be to find other Christian believers. Even so, finding them and a figuring out a way to gather is extremely important. It will be a great challenge to get through the next few years on earth without them.

Choose your friends carefully. Here is a truth you should remember: *you will always become like the people closest to you.* In 1 Corinthians 15:33, the apostle Paul put it this way: "Bad company corrupts good character." When you are in close relationship with someone, the negative has greater power than the positive. You will likely have to rely on others, but you should be very careful with those relationships. It will be extremely easy to fall into relationships that harm your faith, especially friendships with those who are not actively living as Christians.

That is not to say you should abandon your spouse if both of you were left behind after the Rapture. You should remain married. You will need each other now more than ever before. But be very aware of the influence nonbelievers can have on you as a believer. Show everyone love but be cautious with your closest relationships.

I want to share one more Bible passage about your relationships with other believers:

> Let us think of ways to motivate one another to acts of love and good works. And let us not neglect our meeting together, as some people do, but encourage one another, especially now that the day of his return is drawing near (Hebrews 10:24–25).

These verses instruct us to meet regularly with other believers. We need to encourage each other to love God and serve others, especially "now that the day of his return is drawing near." You see, the Rapture is not the only time Jesus will return to earth. If you are reading this after the Rapture, then His return is nearer than ever. You are living in an evil world right now. You need a community of believers more than ever. Without it, you may find it very difficult to endure the temptation, deception, and persecution of these days. But with strong Christian relationships, you can keep the faith.

How Important Is Church in the Post-Rapture World?

You may have preexisting opinions about church because of your experience before the Rapture. You may even have attended a church. You will need to adjust your perspectives. Before the Rapture, there were many large churches. You may never see anything like that again. That's okay. The earliest gatherings of Christian believers took place in people's homes or outdoors. They would simply meet together, sing some songs of worship, read Scripture in the form of scrolls or letters, and pray together. That was church for them. That may be church for you as well.

After all the world's Christians were removed from the earth, it will take time for a new generation of Christians to rise up. Most of them will be like you—new believers who have encountered a book like this or a Bible or who have met someone who recently gave their lives to Christ. Slowly but surely, the Christian Church will rebuild. Gatherings of Christians will increase. Remember, almost every believer you meet will be a new Christian, just like you. You need each other, so seek out these new believers.

Jesus had encouraging words for small groups of believers:

> For where two or three gather together as my followers, I am there among them (Matthew 18:20).

Ask God to help you find others who share your commitment to Christ. He will answer that prayer because that is what He wants for you.

How Important Is the Bible?

You have probably already noticed how frequently I refer to the Bible in this book. That's because it is God's Word and the standard for all truth.

It is essential for you to read Scripture regularly. The Holy Spirit inspired the writers of the Bible, and He will help you understand it as you read. As Jesus told the disciples in John 16:13, "When the Spirit of truth comes, he will guide you into all truth."

In times like these, you need to know the Word. It will give you strength to endure the difficulties of this world. If you don't have a Bible, it should be fairly easy to find one. You may still be able to download a Bible on your phone, tablet, or computer. Be wise if you are using an electronic version of the Bible so you will not be tracked by those who will be persecuting believers.

There are *three crucial roles* the Bible plays in the life of a believer:

1. It renews our minds to think as we should.

The apostle Paul wrote,

> Don't copy the behavior and customs of this world, but let God transform you into a new person by changing the way you think. Then you will learn to know God's will for you, which is good and pleasing and perfect (Romans 12:2).

God equipped us with incredible bodies and brains, but sin has corrupted us. It hinders our relationship with God and warps how we relate to others. This sin nature spread from one human generation to the next, and the result is the chaos and evil you see in the world today. The Bible helps us counter our sin nature. It is so much more than mere words. As you read it, Scripture will fill your spirit with the light of God. Reading God's Word every day will transform your heart and mind.

> For the word of God is alive and powerful. It is sharper than the sharpest two-edged sword, cutting between soul and spirit, between joint and marrow. It exposes our innermost thoughts and desires (Hebrews 4:12).

2. It creates intimacy with God.

The apostle John opens his Gospel with these words:

> In the beginning the Word already existed.
> The Word was with God,
> and the Word was God.
> He existed in the beginning with God.
> God created everything through him,
> and nothing was created except through him.
> The Word gave life to everything that was created,
> and his life brought light to everyone (John 1:1–4).

This passage is one of the most important in the Bible because it reveals Jesus as "the Word." John tells us Jesus is God and the Creator of all things, the perfect living portrayal of the truth of God. Jesus is the embodiment of everything the Bible has to say. The Word is not some*thing*—it is Some*one*. The Bible is the revelation of Jesus.

The apostle Paul said,

All Scripture is inspired by God and is useful to teach us what is true and to make us realize what is wrong in our lives. It corrects us when we are wrong and teaches us to do what is right. God uses it to prepare and equip his people to do every good work (2 Timothy 3:16–17).

The words "inspired by God" from this passage literally mean 'breathed by God' in the original Greek text. The Bible is God-breathed, which means it comes directly from God! When you read the Bible, you will find you feel more alive than before and stronger mentally and spiritually. You will encounter God.

You will find that you need that connection with God more than ever in these dark days. Jesus once said this about His words: "The very words I have spoken to you are spirit and life" (John 6:63). Dedicate yourself to reading the Bible and rely on the Holy Spirit for guidance. You will enjoy a more vibrant, intimate, and personal relationship with the Lord. It is simply not possible to know Him intimately apart from His Word.

3. It empowers us for victory.

Our most serious enemies are spiritual enemies. The apostle Paul wrote,

A final word: Be strong in the Lord and in his mighty power. Put on all of God's armor so that you will be able to stand firm against all strategies of the devil. For we are not fighting against flesh-and-blood enemies, but against evil rulers and authorities of the unseen world, against mighty powers in this dark world, and against evil spirits in the heavenly places.

Therefore, put on every piece of God's armor so you will be able to resist the enemy in the time of evil. Then after the battle you will still be standing firm. Stand your ground, putting on the belt of truth and the body armor of God's righteousness. For shoes, put on the peace that comes from the Good News so that you will be fully prepared. In addition to all of these, hold up the shield of faith to stop the fiery arrows of the devil. Put on salvation as your helmet, and take the sword of the Spirit, which is the word of God (Ephesians 6:10–17).

Be aware of the presence of evil forces, controlled by Satan and sent to keep you from fulfilling God's will for your life. Evil is real, and our true adversaries are not "flesh and blood." We can defend ourselves against this unseen, demonic enemy by putting on the spiritual armor God has given us to defend ourselves.

Ultimately, Jesus has already defeated the devil by dying on the cross and rising again. He has given us victory. However, victory each day isn't automatic just because we are believers. We must rely on the authority God has given us to succeed and live as we should.

Paul lists mostly defensive weapons against the "fiery arrows" of the enemy, except for one: the sword of the Spirit, which represents the Word of God. The Bible is an offensive weapon because its truth strikes a deathblow against every force that comes against us. One Scripture spoken in faith can vanquish the powers of hell. The devil may attempt to overwhelm you with doubt, fear, condemnation, confusion, and lies. He will bring deception and temptation. As a result, you may face negative and destructive thoughts from time to time. These are the "fiery arrows" of the devil. Protect yourself with the armor of God and strike back against them with the Bible.

With God's Word, you can win any battle. Read it, believe it, and confess it.

What Will Happen Next?

Jesus delivers Good News. The word *gospel* comes from an old Anglo-Saxon word that means 'good news.' He paid the price for your sin and offers you the free gift of salvation, securing your place in God's Kingdom and promising an eternity in His presence in heaven. If you have given your life to Jesus, then you made the most important decision of your life.

I do, however, have some bad news. Now that the Rapture has occurred, the world has been thrust into violence, chaos, and confusion. Likely by the time you read this, the chaos has intensified. Things are getting worse and worse. This moment may already be difficult for you, but it is only going to get worse. According to the Bible, the time you are living in now is called "the Tribulation." Jesus spoke about it:

> For there will be greater anguish than at any time since the world began. And it will never be so great again. In fact, unless that time of calamity is shortened, not a single person will survive. But it will be shortened for the sake of God's chosen ones (Matthew 24:21–22).

"God's chosen ones" now includes you as a new believer. This time will be terrible, but God will limit its length for you and other Christians. The Bible says the Tribulation will last seven years. The most important thing for you right now is after the seven years people will no longer have an opportunity to repent and be saved. Hopefully, you have already made that choice to follow Jesus. The world will make it harder and harder for you to follow Jesus as the days go by. If you think things are bad now, the Bible says the last half of the Tribulation—the final three-and-a-half years—will be even worse than it is now. Don't wait! At the end of the seven-year Tribulation, you will be joined forever with Jesus. If you don't repent and ask Jesus to be Lord of your life—if you deny Christ—then you will go to hell for eternity.

What is the Tribulation?

The Rapture set in motion the last days of humanity predicted thousands of years ago in the Bible. When God removed His believers through the Rapture, He was protecting them from experiencing what the Bible calls His "wrath" (see 1 Thessalonians 5:9 NKJV), which represents God's holy anger directed at a world of sin and rebellion. During the Tribulation God will unleash His wrath on the earth as a form of judgment.

The Tribulation reflects the most dangerous and distressing time in human history. In fact, it is the final seven years of human history. Since the Rapture has already happened, you can assume that the Tribulation has begun. It is going to get worse. Society will deteriorate beyond even what you have experienced already.

What is the Antichrist?

If you still have access to global news, you may have heard about a peace treaty. The Bible says the Tribulation will begin after the Rapture with the confirmation of a peace treaty between Israel and an individual described in Scripture as "the Antichrist" and "the Beast." This person likely will not refer to himself this way. He will be human and have a name like anyone else. But he will emerge as a great global leader. He is probably very charismatic and charming. The Bible says the Antichrist will be a male.

Depending on when you read this book, you may already know exactly who this individual is. He may still be in the process of coming to power. Regardless, it will soon become clear that this is the most evil person to have ever walked the earth. Here are a few ways the Bible describes him:

- Despicable

  The next to come to power will be a despicable man who is not in line for royal succession. He will slip in when least expected and take over the kingdom by flattery and intrigue (Daniel 11:21).

- A Blasphemer

  The king will do as he pleases, exalting himself and claiming to be greater than every god, even blaspheming the God of gods. He will succeed, but only until the time of wrath is completed. For what has been determined will surely take place (Daniel 11:36).

- Destructive and Lawless

  For that day will not come until there is a great rebellion against God and the man of lawlessness is revealed—the one who brings destruction. He will exalt himself and defy everything that people call god and every object of worship. He will even sit in the temple of God, claiming that he himself is God (2 Thessalonians 2:3–4).

· **The Beast**

When they complete their testimony, the beast that comes up out of the bottomless pit will declare war against them, and he will conquer them and kill them (Revelation 11:7).

This person will knowingly and intentionally oppose God's law. The Antichrist may be a powerful, charming leader, yet he will also be extremely manipulative. Even worse, he will directly disobey the Word of God. The Antichrist will oppose God and His Son, Jesus Christ. He may promise and even bring temporary peace, but it will be counterfeit and based on a lie.

What Will Happen in the First Half of the Tribulation?

The first half of the Tribulation, following the Rapture and the peace treaty of the Antichrist, will be dominated by the ministry of two people the Bible refers to as the "two witnesses" or the "two prophets." They will accomplish God's work while the Antichrist rises to political and military power. The Bible doesn't identify them by name. Before the Rapture, some Bible scholars speculated that they could be the return of biblical figures like Elijah or Enoch. By this point, you may know who they are by name.

These two witnesses will have miraculous power from God and gain the world's attention. The Bible says God will spiritually empower them to preach His Word boldly. Here is what the book of Revelation says about them:

> These two prophets are the two olive trees and the two lampstands that stand before the Lord of all the earth. If anyone tries to harm them, fire flashes from their mouths and consumes their enemies. This is how anyone who tries to harm them must die. They have power to shut the sky so that no rain will fall for as long as they prophesy. And they have the power to turn the rivers and oceans into blood, and to strike the earth with every kind of plague as often as they wish (Revelation 11:4–6).

The godless Antichrist will eventually kill the two witnesses in a very public way, which will capture the world's attention. Unbelievers will celebrate.

> When they complete their testimony, the beast that comes up out of the bottomless pit will declare war against them, and he will conquer them and kill them. And their bodies will lie in the main street of Jerusalem, the city that is figuratively called "Sodom" and "Egypt," the city where their Lord was crucified. And for three and a half days, all peoples, tribes, languages, and nations will stare at their bodies. No one will be allowed to bury them. All the people who belong to this world will gloat over them and give presents to each other to celebrate the death of the two prophets who had tormented them (Revelation 11:7–10).

Then, while some rejoice over their death, the two witnesses will be resurrected right in front of the entire world, convincing many of the power of God. This miracle will also be accompanied by a devastating, deadly catastrophe:

> But after three and a half days, God breathed life into them, and they stood up! Terror struck all who were staring at them. Then a loud voice from heaven called to the two prophets, "Come up here!" And they rose to heaven in a cloud as their enemies watched.
>
> At the same time there was a terrible earthquake that destroyed a tenth of the city. Seven thousand people died in that earthquake, and everyone else was terrified and gave glory to the God of heaven (Revelation 11:11–13).

According to God's Word, the Antichrist will eventually place an image of himself in the Temple in Jerusalem and blasphemously demand that the world worship it. He will also try to force every single human to get some kind of mark on their hand or forehead. The Bible describes this identifier as "the mark of the beast," which will allow individuals to buy, sell, and take part in the world's economy. Without it, they will be shut out.

The mark will be the secret to the Antichrist's power. He will have military and political power, but financial power will be his true control. Once he controls buying and selling, that global financial power will give him ultimate authority over every society and country.

It is impossible to describe the details of this mark before the Rapture. We only know that the mark won't be optional. But it should be avoided at all costs! Do not worship the Antichrist and do not take his mark. If you do, you will be subject of God's wrath. Here is what the Bible says about it:

> Then a third angel followed them, shouting, "Anyone who worships the beast and his statue or who accepts his mark on the forehead or on the hand must drink the wine of God's anger. It has been poured full strength into God's cup of wrath. And they will be tormented with fire and burning sulfur in the presence of the holy angels and the Lamb. The smoke of their torment will rise forever and ever, and they will have no relief day or night, for they have worshiped the beast and his statue and have accepted the mark of his name."
>
> This means that God's holy people must endure persecution patiently, obeying his commands and maintaining their faith in Jesus (Revelation 14:9–12).

Accepting the mark is a form of accepting the godless ideology of the beast. It is alignment with the Antichrist against God. That is why this sin is unforgivable and will be met with God's wrath. You cannot be forgiven. Once you accept it, you will be giving yourself over to an eternity in hell.

Refusing the mark will result in another kind of temporary trouble. According to the Bible, all those who refuse it will be persecuted, and some will be killed. You may want to take the easy way out and accept the mark, but for the sake of your faith in Christ and your eternal soul, you must reject it.

What Will Happen in the Second Half of the Tribulation?

Already the Tribulation sounds very bad, but the most intense part of it will be the second half, which is the last three-and-a-half years known as "The Great Tribulation." You are living in a traumatic period of human history, even if the Rapture occurred only a few days ago or even years. These are the earth's darkest days. Take comfort that God is with you and will give you strength as you depend upon Him.

Nevertheless, be aware that the Antichrist is literally the devil incarnate. He is the evilest person in history. He hates God and God's Word, so naturally he hates believers who refuse to take the mark or worship him. This time will require extreme commitment and courage. It may cost your life. The Bible describes multiple plagues and judgments during the Tribulation. Some are natural catastrophes, but others are supernatural and demonic. Nation will rise against nation. Families will be torn apart from strife.

Meanwhile, the Antichrist will kill millions of people who refuse to worship him because they have decided to follow Jesus. The Antichrist will come to power during the first half of the Tribulation, after the Rapture. After the death of the two witnesses, he will have full reign over the world. This passage of Scripture describes the second half of the Tribulation:

> Then the beast was allowed to speak great blasphemies against God. And he was given authority to do whatever he wanted for forty-two months. And he spoke terrible words of blasphemy against God, slandering his name and his dwelling—that is, those who dwell in

heaven. And the beast was allowed to wage war against God's holy people and to conquer them. And he was given authority to rule over every tribe and people and language and nation. And all the people who belong to this world worshiped the beast. They are the ones whose names were not written in the Book of Life that belongs to the Lamb who was slaughtered before the world was made.

> Anyone with ears to hear
>> should listen and understand.
> Anyone who is destined for prison
>> will be taken to prison.
> Anyone destined to die by the sword
>> will die by the sword.

This means that God's holy people must endure persecution patiently and remain faithful (Revelation 13:5–10).

I am not telling you this to frighten you, but I need to warn you about what is coming. Prepare yourself to endure persecution and hardships and remain faithful. The world is being severely judged by God because of humanity's sins and rejection of Jesus, but it won't last forever. This period of severe judgment will only last for seven years. It is not the end of the story.

Is There Any Hope?

The seven-year Tribulation will be the most terrible years for the planet. That sounds like bad news, but the darkness will not last, because Jesus is returning. Yes, there is hope.

The Bible reveals the Second Coming of Jesus, which is different from the Rapture. Here is what the Jesus says about it:

> Look, I am coming soon, bringing my reward with me to repay all people according to their deeds. I am the Alpha and the Omega, the First and the Last, the Beginning and the End (Revelation 22:12–13).

The Second Coming will be public and dramatic. Jesus will come at the end of the Tribulation with power and glory and the sound of trumpets. Paul's letter to Titus describes it as "that wonderful day when the glory of our great God and Savior, Jesus Christ, will be revealed" (Titus 2:13).

Jesus described His Second Coming to His followers right after He informed them about the anguish of the Tribulation:

> Immediately after the anguish of those days,
>> the sun will be darkened,
>>> the moon will give no light,
>> the stars will fall from the sky,
>>> and the powers in the heavens will be shaken.
>
> And then at last, the sign that the Son of Man is coming will appear in the heavens, and there will be deep mourning among all the peoples of the earth. And they will see the Son of Man coming on the clouds of heaven with power and great glory. And he will send out his angels with the mighty blast of a trumpet, and they will gather his chosen ones from all over the world—from the farthest ends of the earth and heaven (Matthew 24:29–31).

Jesus will return along with His angels as Conqueror and Eternal King. He will destroy sin and death. All those who committed their lives to Him during the Tribulation, including you, will be gathered from all over the world. Those who are still living at that time will be raptured, just like so many others were a few years earlier.

The initial Rapture was a private event between Jesus and the Church. But the Second Coming will be an extremely public event. Every eye will see Jesus come out of the clouds in glory. Those who know Him will rejoice. But those who do not know Him—those who took the mark of the beast and worshipped the Antichrist—will have the opposite response. This is how the book of Revelation describes this event:

> The armies of heaven, dressed in the finest of pure white linen, followed him on white horses. From his mouth came a sharp sword to strike down the nations. He will rule them with an iron rod. He will release the fierce wrath of God, the Almighty, like juice flowing from a winepress (Revelation 19:14–15).

When Jesus returns in the Second Coming, He is coming as the Great Judge to release the fierce wrath of God upon unbelievers at the worst moment in the history of the world. He will defeat the Antichrist and the False Prophet, throwing them into the lake of fire. The description of this scenario in Scripture is explicit:

> Then I saw the beast and the kings of the world and their armies gathered together to fight against the one sitting on the horse and his army. And the beast was captured, and with him the false

prophet who did mighty miracles on behalf of the beast—miracles that deceived all who had accepted the mark of the beast and who worshiped his statue. Both the beast and his false prophet were thrown alive into the fiery lake of burning sulfur. Their entire army was killed by the sharp sword that came from the mouth of the one riding the white horse. And the vultures all gorged themselves on the dead bodies (Revelation 19:19–21).

This final event ends human history as we know it. If we did not meet before the Rapture, then this is when you will meet me. I look forward to seeing you. The Second Coming will be followed by the Millennial Reign, which is the final period of 1,000 years.

What is the Millennial Reign?

Sinful people have ruled throughout history, and the world has always been plagued with violence and war. But when Jesus returns, He will rule the earth for 1,000 years from Jerusalem. His followers will rule and reign with Him during this time. Under Jesus' rule, the earth will finally experience true peace.

Those who held onto their faith before the Rapture, Jesus caught up in the air to prevent them from going through the horrors of the Tribulation. When Jesus returns in the Second Coming, they will return with Him. Then what is next for you?

Holy Authority

The Bible says all believers will rule and reign with Christ during the thousand-year rule, so that also includes all new believers during the last days and the people taken up in the Rapture. You will be given authority at the end of the Tribulation, along with all those who may have been killed for their faith during the past seven years. Revelation describes this glorious moment:

> Then I saw thrones, and the people sitting on them had been given the authority to judge. And I saw the souls of those who had been beheaded for their testimony about Jesus and for proclaiming the word of God. They had not worshiped the beast or his statue, nor accepted his mark on their foreheads or their hands. They all came to life again, and they reigned with Christ for a thousand years (Revelation 20:4).

Who will they reign over? Before the Rapture, there are various opinions, but many scholars believe a significant number of people from nations who protected the Jewish people will survive the Tribulation. The world may be in ruins, but some people will live through it as mortals. If they do, then they will be subject to the thousand-year rule of Jesus. Some of those people will have descendants born who may be so wicked that God doesn't allow them to die. These will be the worst of the worst, and God will supernaturally keep them from death so they must experience the Thousand-Year Reign.

These disobedient people will discover firsthand what it is like to be subject to Jesus and the saints, who will rule with an "iron rod," a phrase that indicates severity. Prior to the Tribulation, the world was in an Age of Grace in which God withheld His punishment for sin and rebellion. That age will end with the Rapture and Tribulation. God gave the world its chance. Jesus will rule from His throne in Jerusalem and share authority with His followers. We will never sin again, so there will be no need for grace. Jesus will give us authority under Him to rule with power over an unbelieving world. His government will be perfect during the Millennium. Jesus will be the King of kings and the Lord of lords. We will rule with perfect truth and morality as God's Word is lifted up over all the earth.

Unbelievers will hate this time. These wicked people will be forced to abide by God's rules. The Bible says they will eventually rise up and try to kill the saints and Jesus at the end of the Millennium.

The book of Revelation says Satan will be bound for these years:

Then I saw an angel coming down from heaven with the key to the bottomless pit and a heavy chain in his hand. He seized the dragon—that old serpent, who is the devil, Satan—and bound him in chains for a thousand years. The angel threw him into the bottomless pit, which he then shut and locked so Satan could not deceive the nations anymore until the thousand years were finished (Revelation 20:1–3).

But after Jesus and the believers reign for a thousand years, Satan will be released from his prison. He will then attempt to lead a rebellion against the forces of God. He will go on a rampage in his final opportunity to defeat Jesus:

When the thousand years come to an end, Satan will be let out of his prison. He will go out to deceive the nations—called Gog and Magog—in every corner of the earth. He will gather them together for battle—a mighty army, as numberless as sand along the seashore. And I saw them as they went up on the broad plain of the earth and surrounded God's people and the beloved city. But fire from heaven came down on the attacking armies and consumed them.

Then the devil, who had deceived them, was thrown into the fiery lake of burning sulfur, joining the beast and the false prophet. There they will be tormented day and night forever and ever (Revelation 20:7–10).

Satan will rally the nations who hate Jesus and the believers, and he will lead them in battle against the righteous. The uprising will not succeed, though; God will put down the rebellion from His throne with fire and destruction. Then He will judge the dead according to their works. The old heaven and earth will pass away. In its place the Lord will create a new heaven and new earth filled with the light of Jesus.

At the end of the age, Jesus will transform the ruins of the Tribulation into a paradise like the Garden of Eden. It will be a literal, physical Kingdom of God where we will live forever with Jesus. The Bible describes it this way:

I saw no temple in the city, for the Lord God Almighty and the Lamb are its temple. And the city has no need of sun or moon, for the glory of God illuminates the city, and the Lamb is its light. The nations will walk in its light, and the kings of the world will enter the city in all their glory. Its gates will never be closed at the end of day because there is no night there. And all the nations will bring their glory and honor into the city. Nothing evil will be allowed to enter, nor anyone who practices shameful idolatry and dishonesty—but only those whose names are written in the Lamb's Book of Life (Revelation 21:22–27).

A Final Word of Encouragement

If you have gotten this far in this book, then the most important issue is whether you have given your life to Jesus or not. The Rapture is now in the past, and you are about to enter the worst season of world history (or you are already in it). The fact you are alive and have discovered this book shows God has a plan for you. He hasn't given up on you. If you gave your heart to Him, then He welcomes you into His Kingdom.

All the promises of redemption to those who were raptured belong to you as well. The only problem is your timing. You are in the final years of the Age of Grace, but you waited until the door had closed for the Rapture of the Church. Now you will have to experience the horrors of the reign of the Antichrist—the evilest man in world history—and the judgments of the Tribulation.

God is with you. He can help you endure. Jesus Christ promises strength to you. God will reward you if you persevere and obey until the very end. In the coming days, read the Bible, find other believers, and stand firm against evil. God sees and knows what you are experiencing. He is *with* you amid the sin and chaos. He is protecting you and giving you strength to continue following Jesus.

LOOK UP!

The Bible offers many of promises for those who persevere through trials:

- **God will reward you.**

But as for you, be strong and courageous, for your work will be rewarded (2 Chronicles 15:7).

- **You will rule with God.**

If we endure hardship,

    we will reign with him.

If we deny him,

    he will deny us (2 Timothy 2:12).

- **God will give you eternal love.**

The LORD will work out his plans for my life—

for your faithful love, O LORD, endures forever (Psalm 138:8).

- **God will give you power to stay strong.**

For I can do everything through Christ, who gives me strength (Philippians 4:13).

- **God will give you strength.**

We also pray that you will be strengthened with all his glorious power so you will have all the endurance and patience you need. May you be filled with joy, always thanking the Father. He has enabled you to share in the inheritance that belongs to his people, who live in the light (Colossians 1:11–12).

- **God will rescue and deliver you.**

Yes, and the Lord will deliver me from every evil attack and will bring me safely into his heavenly Kingdom. All glory to God forever and ever! Amen (2 Timothy 4:18).

- **God will give you endurance, strength of character, and hope of salvation.**

We can rejoice, too, when we run into problems and trials, for we know that they help us develop endurance. And endurance develops strength of character, and character strengthens our confident hope of salvation. And this hope will not lead to disappointment. For we know how dearly God loves us, because he has given us the Holy Spirit to fill our hearts with his love (Romans 5:3–5).

These are dark days, but brighter days are coming. Keep your thoughts on God and look the future with hope. The Holy Spirit will give you the patience and power to make it through these times. You will soon live in God's presence. He will redeem everything about you. The current chaos is only temporary. Depend on Him, and He will be faithful to you!

About the Author

Jimmy Evans is a long-time pastor, Bible teacher, and best-selling author. He is the Founder and President of XO Marriage, a ministry devoted to helping couples thrive in strong and fulfilling marriages. For 30 years, Jimmy ministered as Senior Pastor of Trinity Fellowship Church in Amarillo, Texas, where he now serves as Apostolic Elder. During his time as senior pastor the church grew from 900 to over 10,000 members. Jimmy loves mentoring pastors and helping local churches grow to reach their potential. He is a popular speaker at churches and leadership conferences across America. Jimmy has written more than 18 books including *Marriage on the Rock, The Four Laws of Love, 21 Day Inner Healing Journey*, and *Tipping Point*. Jimmy and Karen have been married for 49 years and have two married children and five grandchildren.

Notes

1   John Arendzen, "Docetae," The Catholic Encyclopedia, Vol. 5 (New York: NY, Robert Appleton Company, 1909), accessed June 10, 2022, http://www.newadvent.org/cathen/05070c.htm.

2   "What Is Cognitive Behavioral Therapy?" (American Psychological Association, July 2017), https://www.apa.org/ptsd-guideline/patients-and-families/cognitive-behavioral.

3   "Facts & Statistics," Anxiety and Depression Association of America, ADAA, accessed June 13, 2022, https://adaa.org/understanding-anxiety/facts-statistics.

4   T. C. Russ et al., "Association between Psychological Distress and Mortality: Individual Participant Pooled Analysis of 10 Prospective Cohort Studies," *BMJ* 345, no. jul31 4 (2012), https://doi.org/10.1136/bmj.e4933.

5   Ramsey Solutions, "Money Ruining Marriages in America: A Ramsey Solutions Study" (Ramsey Solutions, February 7, 2018), https://www.ramseysolutions.com/company/newsroom/releases/money-ruining-marriages-in-america.

6   Don Piper and Cecil Murphey, *90 Minutes in Heaven: A True Story of Death & Life* (Grand Rapids, MI: Revell, 2004), 37–38.

7   Brittany Yesudasan, "Your Identity in Christ: How God Sees You," Cru.org, accessed June 16, 2022, https://www.cru.org/us/en/train-and-grow/spiritual-growth/core-christian-beliefs/identity-in-christ.html.

8   See John Beeson, "Why the Bible Calls Women 'Sons of God'," Preach It, Teach It, accessed June 24, 2022, https://preachitteachit.org/articles/detail/why-the-bible-calls-women-sons-of-god.

9   Brenda Cobb Murphy, "How Does a Man Love Jesus as His Bridegroom?" Brenda Cobb Murphy | A Lover of Jesus, June 27,

2017, https://brendacobbmurphy.com/how-does-a-man-love-jesus-as-his bridegroom/# :~:text=Indeed%2C%20men%20are%20 the% 20 bride%20of%20Christ%20just,an%20invitation%20to%20 experience%20deep%20intimacy%20with%20God.

10 *Dead Poets Society,* Motion Picture (Buena Vista Pictures Distribution, 1989).

11 See Matthew 24:36–39, 42–44, 48–51; 25:6–13; Mark 13:32–33, 35–37; Luke 12:37–40, 45; 21:36; Acts 1:7; 1 Thessalonians 5:2–4, 6; 2 Peter 3:10; Revelation 2:5; 3:3; 16:15; 22:7, 12, 20.

12 For a complete account of ancient Jewish wedding customs and how they relate to the bride of Christ, see Jamie Lash, *The Ancient Jewish Wedding: and the Return of Messiah for His Bride* (Fort Lauderdale, FL: Jewish Jewels, 1997).

13 Mitchell First, "What Is the Meaning of Navi?" (JewishLink, January 7, 2016), https://jewishlink.news/ divrei-torah/11183-what-is-the-meaning-of-navi.

14 New York City Commission on Human Rights, "Gender Identity/ Expression," accessed June 22, 2022, https://www1.nyc.gov/assets/ cchr/downloads/pdf/publications/GenderID_Card2015.pdf.

15 Charles Darwin, *On the Origin of Species by Means of Natural Selection, or the Preservation of Favoured Races in the Struggle for Life* (London: John Murray, Albemarle Street, 1859), 186.

16 Francis S. Collins, *The Language of God: A Scientist Presents Evidence for Belief* (New York: Simon and Schuster, 2006), 102.

17 "Is God Real?," EveryStudent.com, accessed June 22, 2022, https:// www.everystudent.com/wires/is-god-real.html.

18 Anthony Flew, *There Is a God: How the World's Most Notorious Atheist Changed His Mind* (New York: HarperOne, 2008), 124.

19 *The Fresno Bee,* August 20, 1959, 1-B.

20 Edward Grant Conklin, quoted in Cliff Knechtle, *Give Me an Answer: That Satisfies My Heart and My Mind: Answers to Your Toughest Questions about Christianity* (Colorado Springs: IVP Books, 1986), 70.

21 Fred Hoyle, "Hoyle on Evolution," *Nature*, vol. 284, November 12, 1981.

22 Hugh Ross, "My Story: Dr. Hugh Ross," Cru.org, accessed June 22, 2022, https://www.cru.org/us/en/how-to-know-god/my-story-a-life-changed/hugh-ross.html.

The Tipping Point Prophecy Update

by Jimmy Evans

In this timely email newsletter, Jimmy Evans draws on decades of study, experience and biblical expertise as he explains the striking parallels between current world events and the prophecies of Scripture.

Subscribe to this newsletter for just $7/month. You'll get insightful emails every week, exclusive access to podcast episodes and much more.

ENDTIMES.COM